LEVEL **2**

문제로 마스터하는 중학영문법

문제로 마스터하는 중학영문법 LEVEL 2

지은이	NE능률 영어교육연구소
연구원	신유승 노지희 박서경 이강혁
영문 교열	Patrick Ferraro Nathaniel Galletta August Niederhaus MyAn Thi Le
디자인	안훈정 오솔길
맥편집	이정임

· 본 교재의 독창적인 내용에 대한 일체의 무단 전재·모방은 법률로 금지되어 있습니다.
· 파본은 구매처에서 교환 가능합니다.

NE능률이
미래를
창조합니다.

건강한 배움의 고객가치를 제공하겠다는 꿈을 실현하기 위해
40년이 넘는 시간 동안 열심히 달려왔습니다.

앞으로도 끊임없는 연구와 노력을 통해
당연한 것을 멈추지 않고

고객, 기업, 직원 모두가 함께 성장하는 NE능률이 되겠습니다.

NE능률

Start where you are.
Use what you have.
Do what you can.

당신이 있는 곳에서 시작하라.

당신이 가진 것을 사용하라.

당신이 할 수 있는 것을 하라.

- Arthur Ashe

Structure & Features

1 자세하게 나뉜 문법 POINT

문법 항목을 세분화하여 그에 따른 각각의
POINT를 제시하였습니다. 각 POINT를
차례대로 학습하면 큰 문법 항목을 보다
쉽게 이해할 수 있습니다.

2 개념 쏙쏙

각 Chapter에서 배울 문법 내용을
한눈에 보기 쉽게 정리하였습니다.

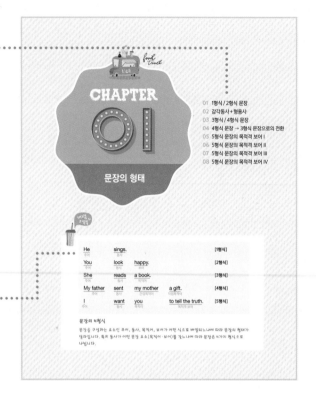

CHAPTER
01
문장의 형태

He	sings.			[1형식]
You	look	happy.		[2형식]
She	reads	a book.		[3형식]
My father	sent	my mother	a gift.	[4형식]
I	want	you	to tell the truth.	[5형식]

3 핵심만 담은 문법 설명

문법 설명에서 군더더기를 걷어내고, 중학교
과정에서 꼭 배워야 하는 핵심 문법 내용만을
체계적으로 제시하였습니다. <PLUS TIP>과
<내신만점 TIP>을 통해 알아두면 좋은 문법
사항과 기출 포인트를 익힐 수 있습니다.

4 문법 항목별로 주관식 위주의 문제 다수 수록

세분화된 문법 항목별로 많은 수의 주관식
문제를 수록하였습니다. 스스로 써 보는 문제를
많이 풀어 보면서 확실하게 문법에 대한 이해를
점검하고 작문 실력을 향상시킬 수 있으며,
나아가 중학 영문법을 마스터하게 될 것입니다.

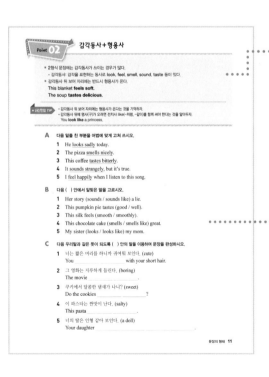

⑥ 서술형 따라잡기

다양한 유형의 서술형
문제들을 통해 응용력과
문제 해결력을 높이고,
실제 서술형 평가를 효과적
으로 준비할 수 있습니다.

⑤ 내신대비 TEST

통합적인 문제들을 제시하여 해당 Chapter의 학습 내용을 빠짐없이
확인할 수 있게 하였습니다. 최신 기출 유형 문제들이 포함되어 있어
어려워진 학교 시험에도 완벽하게 대비할 수 있습니다.

⑦ SELF NOTE

각 Chapter에서 배운 문법 사항을 스스로 정리하고,
<이것만은 꼭!>을 참고하여 확인 문제를 풀어보면서
문법 실력을 탄탄하게 다질 수 있습니다.

⑧ 총괄평가

3회분의 총괄평가를 별도 제공하였습니다.
총괄평가를 통해 내신 대비에 필요한 실전
감각을 기를 수 있습니다.

Contents

Contents

CHAPTER 01

문장의 형태

He 주어	sings. 동사			[1형식]
You 주어	look 동사	happy. 보어		[2형식]
She 주어	reads 동사	a book. 목적어		[3형식]
My father 주어	sent 동사	my mother 간접목적어	a gift. 직접목적어	[4형식]
I 주어	want 동사	you 목적어	to tell the truth. 목적격 보어	[5형식]

문장의 5형식

문장을 구성하는 요소인 주어, 동사, 목적어, 보어가 어떤 식으로 배열되느냐에 따라 문장의 형태가
달라집니다. 특히 동사가 어떤 문장 요소(목적어·보어)를 갖느냐에 따라 문장은 5가지 형식으로
나뉩니다.

1형식 / 2형식 문장

1형식 문장	주어＋동사	**The piano lesson starts** at ten in the morning. 　　　주어　　　　　동사　　　　　부사구
2형식 문장	주어＋동사＋보어	**That woman is my sister**. 　　주어　　동사　보어

■ 2형식 문장의 보어는 주어의 성질·상태·신분 등을 설명해 주는 역할을 하여 주격 보어라고도 한다.

A 다음 문장에서 주어, 동사, 보어(2형식일 경우)를 찾아 밑줄로 표시하시오.

1 Elizabeth lives in England.

2 Many children play on the playground.

3 These bags are too heavy.

4 I will be a famous singer someday.

5 The plant will die without water.

6 The leaves turn red in autumn.

B 다음 우리말과 같은 뜻이 되도록 ( ) 안의 말을 배열하여 문장을 완성하고, 몇 형식인지 쓰시오.

1 우리 누나는 이 식당에서 일한다. (sister, my, works)
_____ at this restaurant. 〈　　　〉형식

2 우리 아버지는 담배를 피우신다. (my, smokes, father)
_____. 〈　　　〉형식

3 강원도에는 눈이 많이 온다. (a lot, snows, it)
_____ in Gangwon-do. 〈　　　〉형식

4 내일은 내 남자친구의 생일이다. (is, birthday, boyfriend's, my)
Tomorrow _____. 〈　　　〉형식

5 그는 수영을 매우 빨리 할 수 있다. (swim, can, he)
_____ very fast. 〈　　　〉형식

6 그 영화는 매우 재미있었다. (was, interesting, very)
The movie _____. 〈　　　〉형식

7 Joe는 내년에 의사가 될 것이다. (a doctor, become, will)
Joe _____ next year. 〈　　　〉형식

감각동사＋형용사

- 2형식 문장에는 감각동사가 쓰이는 경우가 많다.
  - 감각동사: 감각을 표현하는 동사로 look, feel, smell, sound, taste 등이 있다.
- 감각동사 뒤 보어 자리에는 반드시 형용사가 온다.

This blanket **feels soft**.

The soup **tastes delicious**.

★ 내신만점 *TIP*
- 감각동사 뒤 보어 자리에는 형용사가 온다는 것을 기억하자.
- 감각동사 뒤에 명사(구)가 오려면 전치사 like(~처럼, ~같이)를 함께 써야 한다는 것을 알아두자.
  You **look like** a princess.

A 다음 밑줄 친 부분을 어법에 맞게 고쳐 쓰시오.

1 He looks <u>sadly</u> today.

2 The pizza <u>smells nicely</u>.

3 This coffee <u>tastes bitterly</u>.

4 It <u>sounds strangely</u>, but it's true.

5 I <u>feel happily</u> when I listen to this song.

B 다음 ( ) 안에서 알맞은 말을 고르시오.

1 Her story (sounds / sounds like) a lie.

2 This pumpkin pie tastes (good / well).

3 This silk feels (smooth / smoothly).

4 This chocolate cake (smells / smells like) great.

5 My sister (looks / looks like) my mom.

C 다음 우리말과 같은 뜻이 되도록 ( ) 안의 말을 이용하여 문장을 완성하시오.

1 너는 짧은 머리를 하니까 귀여워 보인다. (cute)
You _____ _____ with your short hair.

2 그 영화는 지루하게 들린다. (boring)
The movie _____ _____.

3 쿠키에서 달콤한 냄새가 나니? (sweet)
Do the cookies _____ _____?

4 이 파스타는 짠맛이 난다. (salty)
This pasta _____ _____.

5 너의 딸은 인형 같아 보인다. (a doll)
Your daughter _____ _____ _____ _____.

3형식 / 4형식 문장

3형식 문장	주어＋동사＋목적어	**He plays the guitar** in his school band. 주어 동사 　목적어
4형식 문장	주어＋동사＋간접목적어(～에게) ＋직접목적어(～을 / 를)	**My father bought me a new cell phone**. 　주어 　　　　동사 간접목적어 　직접목적어

■ 목적어가 두 개인 4형식 문장에 자주 쓰이는 동사는 give, lend, tell, teach, show, buy, make 등이며,
이 동사들은 모두 '～해 주다'라는 의미를 지니고 있어 '수여동사'라 부른다.

A 다음 우리말과 같은 뜻이 되도록 ( ) 안의 말을 배열하여 문장을 완성하고, 몇 형식인지 쓰시오.

1 누나는 우리에게 케이크를 만들어 주었다. (made, a, us, cake)
My sister _____. 〈 　〉형식

2 Sean은 매일 아침 영자 신문을 읽는다. (English, the, reads, newspaper)
Sean _____ every morning. 〈 　〉형식

3 너는 저녁 내내 TV를 봤니? (you, TV, did, watch)
_____ all evening? 〈 　〉형식

4 May는 그녀의 친구에게 목도리를 사주었다. (her, a scarf, friend, bought)
May _____. 〈 　〉형식

5 형이 나에게 생일 축하 카드를 보냈다. (birthday card, me, a, sent)
My brother _____. 〈 　〉형식

B 다음 ( ) 안의 말을 배열하여 대화를 완성하시오.

1 A: What does Mr. Kim teach you?
B: _____ (history, us, he, teaches)

2 A: What did you show her?
B: _____ (her, some, I, photos, showed)

3 A: How much did your brother lend you?
B: _____ (lent, he, 10 dollars, me)

4 A: What did you buy for your mom?
B: _____ (her, bought, necklace, I, a)

5 A: What did your parents give you for Christmas?
B: _____ (a, me, laptop, my, gave, parents)

4형식 문장 → 3형식 문장으로의 전환

■ 4형식 문장은 두 목적어의 위치를 바꾸고 간접목적어 앞에 전치사(to, for, of)를 써서 3형식 문장으로 전환할 수 있다.

> 4형식 문장: 주어+동사+간접목적어+직접목적어
>
> 3형식 문장: 주어+동사+직접목적어+전치사(to, for, of)+간접목적어

The man **showed us his paintings**. (4형식)

→ The man **showed his paintings to us**. (3형식)

■ 4형식 문장을 3형식 문장으로 전환할 때 사용되는 전치사는 수여동사에 따라 달라진다.

to를 사용하는 동사	for를 사용하는 동사	of를 사용하는 동사
give, teach, send, bring, show, tell, write, lend, pass 등	get, buy, make 등	ask (목적어가 a favor / a question인 경우)

★ **내신만점 TIP** 4형식을 3형식으로 전환할 때 전치사 to/for/of를 사용하는 동사를 알아두자.

A 다음 ( ) 안에서 알맞은 말을 고르시오.

1 Tommy lent his new bike (of / to) his sister.

2 Can you pass the cell phone (to / for) her?

3 My boyfriend bought some flowers (to / for) me.

4 I showed my test score (to my parents / my parents).

5 My grandmother made delicious hamburgers (for us / us).

B 다음 3형식 문장은 4형식 문장으로, 4형식 문장은 3형식 문장으로 바꾸어 쓰시오.

1 I'll tell you my life story.

→ I'll tell _____ .

2 Steve asked me a favor.

→ Steve asked _____ .

3 A lot of fans send letters to the movie star.

→ A lot of fans send _____ .

4 I'll get you a glass of water.

→ I'll get _____ .

5 Can you teach Spanish to me?

→ Can you _____ ?

6 I bought a toy car for my son.

→ I bought _____ .

5형식 문장의 목적격 보어 I

- 5형식 문장: 주어+동사+목적어+목적격 보어

Everyone thinks him kind.
　　주어　　동사　목적어　목적격 보어

- 5형식 문장에서 목적격 보어로 명사(구)나 형용사(구)가 올 수 있다. 이때 목적어와 목적격 보어는 의미상 〈목적어 = 목적격 보어〉 관계가 성립한다.

He calls **his teacher Mr. Clean**. (his teacher = Mr. Clean)
　　　　　　목적어　　　목적격 보어

A 다음 우리말과 같은 뜻이 되도록 ( ) 안에서 알맞은 말을 고르시오.

1 저를 혼자 내버려 두세요.
Please leave (alone me / me alone).

2 Nicole은 그 책이 유용하다는 것을 알았다.
Nicole found the book (useful / usefully).

3 그 남자와의 인터뷰는 나를 불안하게 만들었다.
My interview with the man made me (nervous / nervously).

4 우리는 우리의 애완 토끼를 'Oreo'라고 이름 지었다.
We named (our pet rabbit "Oreo" / "Oreo" our pet rabbit).

5 모든 사람이 에디슨을 위대한 발명가라고 생각한다.
Everyone thinks (Edison a great inventor / a great inventor Edison).

B 다음 우리말과 같은 뜻이 되도록 ( ) 안의 말을 배열하여 문장을 완성하시오.

1 그의 재능은 그를 유명한 음악가로 만들었다. (made, famous, him, a, musician)
His talent _____ .

2 안전띠가 너를 안전하게 지켜줄 것이다. (keep, safe, you)
The seat belt will _____ .

3 그 경험은 그녀를 다른 사람으로 만들었다. (a, person, made, her, different)
The experience _____ .

4 모든 사람이 나를 천재라고 부른다. (me, a, calls, genius)
Everyone _____ .

5 Brian은 그 온라인 게임이 재미있다는 것을 알았다.
(the, exciting, online, found, game)
Brian _____ .

5형식 문장의 목적격 보어 II

- 5형식 문장에서 want, allow, ask, tell, expect, advise, order 등의 동사가 사용될 경우 목적격 보어 자리에 to부정사가 온다.
I **want** you **to listen** carefully.
My teacher **allowed** me **to leave** early.

★ PLUS TIP   help는 동사원형과 to부정사를 모두 목적격 보어로 취할 수 있다.
I **helped** my dad **(to) take** out the garbage.

A 다음 ( ) 안의 말을 배열하여 문장을 완성하시오.

1 Harry promised me to come to the party.
I _____ soon.
(to, him, expect, come)

2 I like Mira.
But I don't want _____.
(to, anybody, know, it, about)

3 I caught a bad cold.
My doctor _____ a lot of water.
(drink, me, advised, to)

4 Kevin doesn't like science.
But his parents _____.
(him, be, a, want, scientist, to)

B 다음 우리말과 같은 뜻이 되도록 ( ) 안의 말을 이용하여 문장을 완성하시오.

1 형은 내가 그의 컴퓨터를 사용하는 것을 허락해 주었다. (allow, use)
My brother _____ _____ _____ his computer.

2 나는 그녀에게 과일을 먹으라고 말했다. (tell, eat)
I _____ _____ _____ _____ fruit.

3 Tim은 그 소포가 곧 도착할 거라고 예상한다. (expect, the package, arrive)
Tim _____ _____ _____ _____ _____ soon.

4 Amanda는 내게 집에 태워다 달라고 부탁했다. (ask, drive)
Amanda _____ _____ _____ _____ her home.

5 내가 바닥 청소하는 것을 도와줄 수 있니? (help, sweep)
Can you _____ _____ _____ _____ the floor?

5형식 문장의 목적격 보어 III

- 5형식 문장에 사역동사가 사용될 경우, 목적격 보어로 동사원형이 온다.
  - 사역동사: '~시키다', '~하게 하다'라는 의미의 동사로, make, have, let 등이 있다.
  He **made** me **move** his chair.
  My teacher never **lets** us **skip** class.

★ **PLUS TIP**
- get은 '~하도록 시키다'라는 사역의 의미를 가지고 있지만 목적격 보어로 to부정사를 취한다.
  He **got** her **to update** the files.
- 사역동사로 쓰인 have의 목적어와 목적격 보어의 관계가 수동이면 목적격 보어로 과거분사를 쓴다.
  I **had** my wisdom tooth **pulled**. (이가 뽑힌 것)

A 다음 〈보기〉에서 알맞은 말을 골라 빈칸에 적절한 형태로 써넣으시오. (단, 한 번씩만 사용할 것)

〈보기〉 cry   bring   keep   close   play

1 My parents make me _____ a diary.

2 The ending of the movie made me _____.

3 My sister got my puppy _____ her the newspaper.

4 My mom doesn't let me _____ outside on rainy days.

5 The old woman asked me _____ the window.

B 다음 우리말과 같은 뜻이 되도록 ( ) 안의 말을 이용하여 문장을 완성하시오.

1 엄마는 항상 내가 내 방을 청소하게 하신다. (make, clean)
My mom always _____ _____ _____ my room.

2 그녀는 그녀의 남편에게 토마토를 사 오게 했다. (have, buy)
She _____ _____ _____ _____ tomatoes.

3 그 선생님은 우리가 이야기하는 것을 허락하지 않으셨다. (let, talk)
The teacher _____ _____ _____ _____.

4 누나는 내가 누나의 카메라를 절대로 쓰지 못하게 한다. (let, use)
My sister never _____ _____ _____ her camera.

5 그들의 코치는 그들이 매일 팔굽혀펴기를 하게 한다. (have, do push-ups)
Their coach _____ _____ _____ _____ every day.

6 그 신발은 네가 키 커 보이게 한다. (make, look, tall)
Those shoes _____ _____ _____ _____.

7 아버지는 지난 주말 내가 파티에 가는 것을 허락하셨다. (let, go)
My father _____ _____ _____ to the party last weekend.

5형식 문장의 목적격 보어 IV

- 5형식 문장에 지각동사가 사용될 경우, 목적격 보어로 동사원형이 온다.
  - 지각동사: 감각 기관을 통해 우리가 인식하는 것을 표현하는 동사로, see, look at, watch, hear, listen to, feel, smell 등이 있다.
  I didn't **hear** you **call** me.
- 진행 중인 동작을 묘사할 경우, 목적격 보어로 현재분사(v-ing)를 쓰기도 한다.
  I **saw** the boy **crossing** the street.

★ 내신만점 *TIP*   5형식 문장의 목적격 보어는 동사에 따라 명사(구), 형용사(구), to부정사(구), 동사원형이 올 수 있다는 것을 기억하자.

A 다음 밑줄 친 부분을 어법에 맞게 고쳐 쓰시오.

1 Come here and listen to the birds <u>to sing</u>.

2 Did you see my grandparents <u>to take</u> a walk?

3 I watched my mom and dad <u>played</u> tennis.

4 Did you hear somebody <u>to come</u>?

5 She felt someone <u>touched</u> her arm.

6 He made me <u>to tell</u> him the secret.

B 다음 우리말과 같은 뜻이 되도록 (   ) 안의 말을 배열하여 문장을 완성하시오.

1 우리는 그 노인이 자신의 이야기를 반복해서 하는 것을 들었다.
(tell, old man, listened to, we, the)
_____ his story again and again.

2 나는 Jenny가 식당에서 혼자 밥을 먹고 있는 것을 보았다. (Jenny, saw, eating, I)
_____ alone at a restaurant.

3 그는 누군가가 자신을 보고 있는 것을 느꼈다. (someone, he, looking at, felt)
_____ him.

4 그들은 그들의 딸이 첼로를 연주하고 있는 것을 들었다.
(heard, playing, they, daughter, their)
_____ the cello.

5 사람들은 그 스턴트맨이 불타는 건물에서 뛰어내리는 것을 지켜보았다.
(the, jump, stuntman, watched, people)
_____ from a burning building.

6 나는 다른 방에서 불빛이 나오는 것을 볼 수 있었다. (the, see, light, I, coming, could)
_____ from the other room.

내신 대비 TEST

[01-03] 다음 빈칸에 알맞은 말을 고르시오.

01

The movie made him _____ a lot.

① laugh
② laughing
③ laughed
④ to laugh
⑤ be laughed

02

I want you _____ happy with him.

① be
② are
③ been
④ being
⑤ to be

03

My mom saw me _____ soccer with my friends.

① played
② to play
③ playing
④ be played
⑤ have played

04

다음 문장의 형태가 나머지와 <u>다른</u> 것은?

① Chris calls me his best friend.
② I showed Jane my album.
③ James passed me the ball.
④ He made her strawberry cake.
⑤ His teacher asked him his plan.

[05-06] 다음 빈칸에 들어갈 수 <u>없는</u> 말을 고르시오.

05

He _____ the novel to me.

① gave
② brought
③ showed
④ passed
⑤ bought

06

You look _____ in the red dress.

① nice
② pretty
③ lovely
④ beautifully
⑤ great

[07-08] 빈칸에 들어갈 말이 순서대로 알맞게 짝지어진 것을 고르시오.

07

• The roses smell so _____.
• Gary made his son _____ the dishes.

① well – wash
② well – to wash
③ good – wash
④ good – to wash
⑤ good – washed

08

• Tom wrote a letter _____ me.
• I asked her _____ me her phone number.

① of – give
② to – giving
③ to – to give
④ for – give
⑤ of – to give

09

- I _____ a sandcastle for him.
- He _____ me angry when he played games.

① made   ② saw
③ let   ④ had
⑤ helped

10

- I'll _____ you an interesting story.
- He will _____ them to be on time.

① tell   ② want
③ lend   ④ expect
⑤ show

11

다음 대화 중 자연스럽지 <u>않은</u> 것은?

① A: Did you see him running?
   B: Yes, he was very fast.
② A: What did she make for you?
   B: She made me feel happy.
③ A: Come here. I'll show you something.
   B: What is it?
④ A: What did you name your baby?
   B: We named him Matt.
⑤ A: What did you think of the test?
   B: I found it easy.

12

다음 우리말을 영어로 바르게 옮긴 것은?

나는 내 여동생이 노래 부르고 있는 것을 들었다.

① I heard my sister to sing a song.
② I heard my sister singing a song.
③ I heard my sister is singing a song.
④ I heard my sister sings a song.
⑤ I heard my sister to singing a song.

13

빈칸에 들어갈 말이 나머지와 <u>다른</u> 것은?

① She told a big secret _____ me.
② I will give a useful tip _____ you.
③ Will you send an email _____ us?
④ He taught music _____ his students.
⑤ Can you make some pasta _____ them?

14

다음 중 문장의 전환이 바르지 <u>않은</u> 것은?

① I couldn't write a letter to him.
   → I couldn't write him a letter.
② He passed a cup of water to her.
   → He passed her a cup of water.
③ Will you lend me your car, please?
   → Will you lend your car to me, please?
④ She brought board games to us.
   → She brought board games us.
⑤ Can you get me another pair of socks?
   → Can you get another pair of socks for me?

15

다음 밑줄 친 부분의 쓰임이 나머지와 다른 것은?

① Your joke <u>made</u> me upset.
② My little sister <u>made</u> me a snowman.
③ Travel can <u>make</u> you adventurous.
④ Recycling will <u>make</u> the world a better place.
⑤ Enjoying outdoor activities <u>makes</u> people healthy.

[16-17] 다음 중 어법상 틀린 것을 고르시오.

16

① Let me introduce myself.
② He solved the question easily.
③ The woman made me vanilla ice cream.
④ I expect him lend me some money.
⑤ She had her students work in a group.

17

① I will do it happily.
② Eric saw the leaves falling down.
③ The perfume smells like flowers.
④ Brian bought pajamas his parents.
⑤ I got him to buy me some food.

18

(A), (B), (C)의 괄호 안에서 알맞은 것끼리 바르게 짝지어진 것은?

(A) This pumpkin pie smells so [sweet / sweetly].
(B) She got me [wash / to wash] her new car.
(C) Jacob helped me [prepare / prepared] for the presentation.

	(A)	(B)	(C)
①	sweet	to wash	prepare
②	sweet	wash	prepare
③	sweet	to wash	prepared
④	sweetly	wash	prepared
⑤	sweetly	to wash	prepare

19

다음 중 어법상 옳은 것을 모두 고르면? (2개)

① You look wonderfully.
② Cathy gave a toy for her daughter.
③ She had her room cleaned.
④ It sounds a great idea.
⑤ I listened to him speak in front of people.

20

다음 중 〈보기〉와 같은 형식의 문장은?

〈보기〉 Exercising regularly keeps me healthy.

① These pineapples taste sweet.
② Nancy smiled brightly at that time.
③ James wants to watch a curling match.
④ My parents allowed us to go out for dinner.
⑤ Lucy taught her students the history of the Roman Empire.

서술형 따라잡기

01
주어진 말을 알맞게 배열하여 대화를 완성하시오.

A: You _____ .
(sad, really, look) What's up?
B: I failed my math test. My math teacher
_____ .
(grade, me, a, gave, low)

02
다음 두 문장이 같은 뜻이 되도록 빈칸에 알맞은 말을 쓰시오.

I'll get all of us free tickets.
→ I'll get _____ _____ _____
_____ _____ .

03
다음 그림을 보고, 〈보기〉에서 알맞은 말을 골라 문장을 완성하시오.

〈보기〉 talk   jump rope   water flowers

(1) I saw a girl _____ .

(2) I saw a boy _____ .

(3) I heard two women _____
to each other.

04
주어진 말을 이용하여 우리말과 뜻이 같도록 문장을 완성하시오.

(1) 나는 Jack이 똑똑하고 창의적이라는 것을 알았다.
(find, smart, creative)
→ _____ _____ _____ _____
_____ _____ .

(2) Keira는 그녀의 결혼 사진을 내게 보여주었다.
(show, her wedding picture)
→ Keira _____ _____ _____
_____ _____ _____ .

05
다음 표를 보고, 문장을 완성하시오.

DO	DON'T
(1) clean your room	(2) read comic books (3) play computer games

(1) Mom makes me _____ .

(2) Mom doesn't allow me _____ .

(3) Mom doesn't let me _____ .

기출응용

06
다음 〈보기〉와 같이 두 문장을 한 문장으로 쓰시오.

〈보기〉
I read an English book. Jamie wanted me to
do that.
→ Jamie wanted me to read an English book.

(1) I'll cook dinner. He'll get me to do that.
→ He'll get _____ .

(2) Mary will lend you her notebook. I'll tell
her to do so.
→ I'll tell _____ .

S E L F N O T E

핵심 포인트 정리하기

1 감각동사가 쓰인 2형식 문장 – 감각동사+① _____

- 감각동사: look, feel, smell, sound, taste 등과 같이 감각을 표현하는 동사

 이것만은 꼭! 〈감각동사+like+명사(구)〉 형태도 함께 기억하기!

2 4형식 문장 → 3형식 문장으로의 전환

- 4형식 문장을 3형식 문장으로 전환할 때 사용하는 전치사는 수여동사에 따라 달라짐

② _____를 쓰는 동사	③ _____를 쓰는 동사	④ _____를 쓰는 동사
give, teach, send, bring, show, tell, write, lend, pass 등	get, buy, make 등	ask (목적어가 a favor / a question일 때)

 이것만은 꼭! 4형식 문장을 3형식 문장으로 전환할 때 전치사 to/for/of를 쓰는 동사 구분하기!

3 5형식 문장의 목적격 보어

⑤ _____를 취하는 동사		want, allow, ask, tell, expect, advise, order 등
⑥ _____을 취하는 동사	⑦ _____ '~시키다', '~하게 하다'	make, have, let 등
	지각동사	see, look at, watch, hear, listen to, feel, smell 등 *진행 중인 동작을 묘사할 경우, 〈지각동사+목적어+⑧ _____〉

- get은 사역의 의미를 가지고 있지만 목적격 보어로 ⑨ _____를 취함
- 사역동사로 쓰인 have의 목적어와 목적격 보어의 관계가 수동이면 목적격 보어로 ⑩ _____를 씀

이것만은 꼭! 5형식 문장에서 목적격 보어로 to부정사/동사원형을 취하는 동사 알아두기!

문제로 개념 다지기

밑줄 친 부분이 어법상 맞으면 O, 틀리면 X 표시하고 바르게 고치시오.

1 Gordon <u>looks like</u> a superhero today.

2 This hot chocolate smells <u>sweetly</u>.

3 The man won't allow me <u>enter</u> the building.

4 My mother taught table manners <u>to me</u>.

5 I heard Mike <u>talking</u> on the phone.

6 He had me <u>to park</u> the car in the parking lot.

7 Could you make something delicious <u>to me</u>?

22 Chapter 01

CHAPTER 02
to부정사

My plan is <u>**to finish my homework tonight**</u>.　　　[명사적 용법]
　　　　　　　　　　보어

We have <u>something</u> <u>**to talk about**</u>.　　　[형용사적 용법]

He went to the store <u>**to buy clothes**</u>.　　　[부사적 용법]
　　　　　　　목적: ~하기 위해서

to부정사의 용법

to부정사는 문장 안에서 명사, 형용사, 부사의 역할을 할 수 있습니다. to부정사가 명사 역할을 할 경우 주어, 목적어, 보어로 쓰이는데, 특히 to부정사를 목적어로 취하는 동사들을 유념해 두어야 합니다. 형용사 역할을 할 경우 보통 명사를 뒤에서 수식하며, 부사 역할을 할 경우 문장 안에서 목적, 원인, 결과, 조건 등의 다양한 의미를 나타냅니다.

to부정사의 명사적 용법 I – 주어, 보어

- to부정사(to-v)는 문장 안에서 명사처럼 주어나 보어, 목적어 역할을 한다.
- to부정사가 주어로 쓰인 경우 '~하는 것은'으로 해석한다.

  To learn another language is not easy.

  * to부정사가 주어로 쓰인 경우, 그 자리에 가주어 It을 쓰고 to부정사는 문장의 뒤로 보내는 것이 일반적이다.

  To make a mistake isn't always bad. → **It** isn't always bad **to make a mistake**.
- to부정사가 보어로 쓰인 경우 '~하는 것(이다)'로 해석한다.

  My goal is **to win** the race.

★ **PLUS TIP** 주어로 쓰인 to부정사(구)는 3인칭 단수 취급한다.
To win a gold medal **is** my goal.

A 다음 두 문장이 같은 뜻이 되도록 문장을 완성하시오.

1 To say sorry is difficult.

→ It _____ _____ _____ _____ .

2 To build a house costs a lot of money.

→ It costs a lot of money _____ _____ _____ .

3 To swim here is not safe.

→ It _____ _____ _____ _____ .

4 It is impossible to save money now.

→ _____ _____ _____ _____ is impossible.

5 It is important to exercise every day.

→ _____ _____ _____ is important.

B 다음 우리말과 같은 뜻이 되도록 (   ) 안의 말을 배열하여 문장을 완성하시오.

1 그녀의 희망은 다시 연기하는 것이다. (again, hope, act, to, is, her)

_____

2 얼음 위를 걷는 것은 위험하다. (it, to, on the ice, walk, is, dangerous)

_____

3 이 문제를 해결하는 것은 쉽지 않다. (to, not, this, easy, problem, is, solve)

_____

4 그의 꿈은 대통령이 되는 것이었다. (become, was, dream, to, his, president)

_____

5 그의 목표는 많은 친구들을 사귀는 것이다. (his, to, goal, friends, make, is, many)

_____

to부정사의 명사적 용법 II – 목적어

- to부정사가 목적어로 쓰인 경우 '~하는 것'으로 해석한다.
  I want **to go** to bed early tonight.
- to부정사를 목적어로 취하는 동사에는 want, plan, decide, hope, expect, offer, need, promise, refuse, learn 등이 있다.
  They promised **to meet** at the shopping mall.

A 다음 〈보기〉에서 알맞은 말을 골라 빈칸에 적절한 형태로 써넣으시오. (단, 한 번씩만 사용할 것)

〈보기〉 go   ask   play   take   study   drive   meet

1 I'm learning _____ the drums.

2 My aunt hopes _____ to Europe next year.

3 Where's Jake? I need _____ him something.

4 He promised _____ carefully.

5 Cathy plans _____ abroad.

6 He decided _____ the subway.

7 I want _____ the writer someday.

B 다음 우리말과 같은 뜻이 되도록 (   ) 안의 말을 이용하여 문장을 완성하시오.

1 그녀는 올해 열심히 공부하기로 결심했다. (decide)
She _____ _____ _____ _____ this year.

2 나는 내일까지 그 책을 다 읽을 것으로 예상한다. (expect, finish)
I _____ _____ _____ the book by tomorrow.

3 그는 나에게 할인을 해 주겠다고 제안했다. (offer, give)
He _____ _____ _____ me a discount.

4 Steve는 그의 건강을 위해 운동을 할 필요가 있다. (need, exercise)
Steve _____ _____ _____ for his health.

5 그 아이는 채소 먹는 것을 거부했다. (refuse)
The child _____ _____ _____ vegetables.

6 나는 진실을 말할 것을 약속합니다. (promise, tell the truth)
I _____ _____ _____ _____ .

7 그녀는 인도로 여행갈 것을 계획했다. (plan, travel)
She _____ _____ _____ to India.

- 〈의문사+to부정사〉는 문장 안에서 명사적 용법으로 쓰이며, 주로 목적어 역할을 한다.
  - what to-v: 무엇을 ～할지
  - when to-v: 언제 ～할지
  - who(m) to-v: 누구를 ～할지
  - where to-v: 어디서 ～할지
  - how to-v: 어떻게 ～할지, ～하는 방법

  Please show me **how to use** this machine.

- 〈의문사+to부정사〉는 보통 〈의문사+주어+should+동사원형〉으로 바꾸어 쓸 수 있다.

  Do you understand **what to do**? → Do you understand **what you should do**?

A 다음 우리말과 같은 뜻이 되도록 〈보기〉에서 알맞은 의문사를 골라 문장을 완성하시오.

〈보기〉 how   when   what   where   whom

1 그녀는 누구를 도와야 할지 몰랐다.

She didn't know _____ _____ _____.

2 당신은 언제 이곳을 떠나야 할지 아시나요?

Do you know _____ _____ _____ here?

3 나는 휴가로 어디를 갈지 결정하지 못하겠다.

I can't decide _____ _____ _____ for my vacation.

4 Peter는 나에게 빵 만드는 방법을 가르쳐 주었다.

Peter taught me _____ _____ _____ bread.

5 저에게 다음에 무엇을 할지 말씀해 주세요.

Please tell me _____ _____ _____ next.

B 다음 문장을 〈보기〉와 같이 바꾸어 쓰시오.

〈보기〉 Now I understand how to use it.
→ Now I understand how I should use it.

1 I don't know where to start.

→ _____

2 She'll let you know how to dress for the party.

→ _____

3 I'm not sure when to call her.

→ _____

4 He asked me what to try first.

→ _____

to부정사의 형용사적 용법 I

- to부정사는 문장 안에서 형용사 역할을 하여 명사를 뒤에서 수식하고, '~하는', '~할'이라고 해석한다.
  Jack has a lot of work **to do** today.

- -thing, -one, -body로 끝나는 대명사를 형용사와 to부정사가 함께 수식하는 경우,
  〈-thing[-one / -body]+형용사+to부정사〉의 순서로 쓴다.
  I need **something warm to wear**.

A 다음 밑줄 친 부분을 어법에 맞게 고쳐 쓰시오.

1 We have no to rest time.

2 I want sweet something to eat.

3 She needs a pen black to use.

4 Do you have time have to a cup of tea?

5 There's nothing to watch interesting on TV.

B 다음 우리말과 같은 뜻이 되도록 ( ) 안의 말을 배열하여 문장을 완성하시오.

1 파리에는 방문할 미술관들이 많다. (visit, in Paris, many, to, museums)
There are _____.

2 나는 그에게 읽을 만화책 한 권을 주었다. (a, read, comic book, to, him)
I gave _____.

3 약 먹을 시간이다. (your, take, to, medicine)
It's time _____.

4 우리는 요리할 약간의 채소를 샀다. (some, to, vegetables, cook)
We bought _____.

5 그는 그녀를 행복하게 해 줄 무언가를 원했다. (something, her, make, to, happy)
He wanted _____.

6 나는 네게 보여줄 흥미로운 것을 갖고 있다. (exciting, to, something, you, show)
I have _____.

7 차가운 마실 것이 있습니까? (cold, anything, drink, to)
Do you have _____?

8 그녀는 그녀의 아기를 돌봐줄 누군가가 필요하다. (someone, look after, her, to, baby)
She needs _____.

Point 05 ─ to부정사의 형용사적 용법 II

- 형용사적 용법의 to부정사에 사용된 동사가 자동사일 경우, 뒤에 전치사를 빠뜨리지 않도록 주의한다.

  There's no chair **to sit** *in*.

  I don't have any friends **to talk** *with*.

  Seoul is an interesting city **to live** *in*.

- 〈자동사+전치사〉의 예

  - live in: ~에서 살다   - write with: ~로 쓰다

  - talk with: ~와 말하다   - sit on[in]: ~에 앉다

★ **내신만점 TIP** 〈자동사+전치사〉의 형태로 쓰는 to부정사의 형용사적 용법에 유의하자.

A 다음 ( ) 안에서 알맞은 말을 고르시오.

1 We bought a house (to live / to live in).

2 Give her something hot (to drink / to drink with).

3 Can you recommend some music (to listen / to listen to)?

4 I bought a magazine (to read / to read for).

5 We have an important issue (to talk / to talk about).

6 Could you lend me a pen (to write / to write with)?

B 다음 우리말과 같은 뜻이 되도록 ( ) 안의 말을 배열하여 문장을 완성하시오.

1 나는 함께 살 룸메이트를 구하고 있다. (live, a roommate, to, with)

  I'm looking for _____.

2 Jason은 가지고 놀 장난감이 거의 없다. (to, with, few toys, play)

  Jason has _____.

3 가지고 먹을 숟가락을 하나 주실 수 있나요? (eat, a spoon, with, to)

  Can you give me _____?

4 그 노부인은 앉을 의자가 필요하다. (to, a chair, in, sit)

  The old lady needs _____.

5 Mary는 머물 호텔을 결정했다. (in, to, stay, a hotel)

  Mary decided on _____.

6 그녀는 같이 춤을 출 파트너를 원한다. (with, a partner, dance, to)

  She wants _____.

7 너는 적을 종이를 좀 갖고 있니? (write, to, any paper, on)

  Do you have _____?

to부정사의 형용사적 용법 III

■ to부정사의 형용사적 용법 중에는 〈be+to부정사〉의 형태로 주어를 설명하여 예정, 의무, 가능, 운명, 의도 등의 의미를 나타내는 용법이 있다.
- 예정: John **is to take** a test tomorrow. (~할 예정이다)
- 의무: You**'re to finish** this work by eleven. (~해야 한다)
- 가능: No car **was to be** seen on the street. (~할 수 있다)
- 운명: I was **never to meet** the beautiful girl again. (~할 운명이다)
- 의도: If you **are to master** English, you should keep practicing. (~하려고 하다)

★ **PLUS TIP** to부정사의 부정형은 〈not[never]+to부정사〉의 형태로 쓴다.
To be or **not to be,** that is the question.

A 다음 두 문장이 같은 뜻이 되도록 문장을 완성하시오.

1 You have to follow the rules.
→ You ＿＿＿＿＿ ＿＿＿＿＿ ＿＿＿＿＿ the rules.

2 The president is going to visit France next month.
→ The president ＿＿＿＿＿ ＿＿＿＿＿ ＿＿＿＿＿ France next month.

3 If you intend to lose weight, you have to eat less.
→ If you ＿＿＿＿＿ ＿＿＿＿＿ ＿＿＿＿＿ weight, you have to eat less.

B 다음 우리말과 같은 뜻이 되도록 ( ) 안의 말과 〈be+to부정사〉를 이용하여 문장을 완성하시오.

1 그는 화가가 될 운명이었다. (become)
He ＿＿＿＿＿ ＿＿＿＿＿ ＿＿＿＿＿ a painter.

2 너는 여섯 시까지 파티에 와야 한다. (come)
You ＿＿＿＿＿ ＿＿＿＿＿ ＿＿＿＿＿ to the party by six.

3 그녀는 오늘 자신의 드레스를 세탁할 예정이다. (wash)
She ＿＿＿＿＿ ＿＿＿＿＿ ＿＿＿＿＿ her dress today.

4 그녀는 내일 그녀의 오랜 친구들을 만날 예정이다. (meet)
She ＿＿＿＿＿ ＿＿＿＿＿ ＿＿＿＿＿ her old friends tomorrow.

5 네가 자동차를 사려고 한다면, 돈을 저축해야 한다. (buy)
If you ＿＿＿＿＿ ＿＿＿＿＿ ＿＿＿＿＿ a car, you must save money.

6 Bella는 그와 결혼하지 못할 운명이었다. (get married to)
Bella ＿＿＿＿＿ ＿＿＿＿＿ ＿＿＿＿＿ ＿＿＿＿＿
＿＿＿＿＿ .

to부정사의 부사적 용법 I – 목적, 감정의 원인

- to부정사는 문장 안에서 부사처럼 동사, 형용사, 부사를 수식하는 역할을 한다.
- 부사적 용법의 to부정사는 목적이나 감정의 원인을 나타낼 수 있다.
  - 목적을 나타내는 경우 '~하기 위해', '~하러'로 해석한다.
  I saved some money **to buy** a new sports car.
  - 감정의 원인을 나타내는 경우 '~해서', '~하니'로 해석하며, 이때 to부정사는 주로 감정을 나타내는 형용사 뒤에 온다.
  I was glad **to get** your letter.

★ **PLUS TIP** ▶ 목적을 나타내는 to부정사의 부사적 용법은 의미를 명확하게 하기 위해 〈in order to-v〉 또는 〈so as to-v〉 형태로 쓰기도 한다.

A 다음 우리말과 같은 뜻이 되도록 문장을 완성하시오.

1 Tommy는 엄마를 돕기 위해 집을 청소했다.
Tommy cleaned the house _____ _____ his mom.

2 당신을 만나게 되어 매우 기쁩니다.
I'm so glad _____ _____ _____.

3 나는 새로운 단어를 배우기 위해 영어 소설을 읽는다.
I read English novels _____ _____ new words.

4 그 소식을 듣고 매우 유감스러웠습니다.
I was so _____ _____ _____ the news.

5 그는 그 대회에서 금메달을 따서 기뻤다.
He was _____ _____ _____ a gold medal in the contest.

6 Nancy는 영화 배우가 되기 위해서 고향을 떠났다.
Nancy left her hometown _____ _____ an actress.

B 다음 우리말과 같은 뜻이 되도록 ( ) 안의 말을 배열하여 문장을 완성하시오.

1 Yuna는 웅변대회에서 떨어져서 실망했다. (disappointed, was, lose, to)
Yuna _____ the speech contest.

2 David는 그의 친구인 Jina를 만나기 위해 한국으로 왔다. (Korea, to, meet, to, came)
David _____ his friend Jina.

3 나는 그곳에서 그를 보고 깜짝 놀랐다. (him, see, surprised, was, very, to)
I _____ there.

4 그는 시험에 합격하기 위해 열심히 공부했다. (hard, in order to, the exam, pass, studied)
He _____.

to부정사의 부사적 용법 II – 결과, 판단의 근거

- 부사적 용법의 to부정사는 결과나 판단의 근거를 나타내기도 한다.
  - 결과를 나타내는 경우 '(…해서) ~하다'로 해석한다.
  Justine grew up **to be** a pilot.
  - 판단의 근거를 나타내는 경우 '~하다니', '~하는 것을 보니'로 해석한다.
  You must like her **to say** so.

★ PLUS TIP   to부정사가 only와 함께 쓰여 결과의 의미를 나타내는 경우에는 '~지만 (결국) ~했다'로 해석한다.
I ran as fast as I could, **only to miss** the train. (→ I ran as fast as I could, but I missed the train.)

A   다음 우리말과 같은 뜻이 되도록 ( ) 안의 말을 배열하여 문장을 완성하시오.

1 지금까지 자는 것을 보니 Sam이 피곤한 게 틀림없다. (till, sleep, now, to)
Sam must be tired _____.

2 그녀에게 선물을 주는 것을 보니 Tim은 Lynne을 좋아하는 것이 틀림없다.
(her, a present, give, to)
Tim must like Lynne _____.

3 그녀는 자라서 유명한 소설가가 되었다. (novelist, be, to, famous, a)
She grew up _____.

4 경찰관은 그 아이를 구하려고 했지만 실패했다. (only, fail, to)
The policeman tried to save the child, _____.

5 매일 시간을 잘 지키는 것을 보니 그녀는 부지런한 게 틀림없다. (every day, be, on time, to)
She must be diligent _____.

B   다음을 〈보기〉와 같이 to부정사를 이용하여 바꾸어 쓰시오.

〈보기〉   He must be rich. He owns four cars.
       → He must be rich to own four cars.

1 I went to the department store, but I found it closed.
→ I went to the department store, _____.

2 He is on vacation. So he is happy.
→ He is happy _____.

3 She must be brave. She goes abroad by herself.
→ She must be brave _____.

4 Linda must be a big fan of that singer. She knows all of his songs.
→ Linda must be a big fan of that singer _____.

to부정사의 부사적 용법 III – 조건, 형용사 수식

- 부사적 용법의 to부정사는 조건을 나타내거나 형용사를 수식할 수도 있다.
  - 조건을 나타내는 경우 '만약 ～한다면'의 뜻으로, 주로 you would think 등의 표현과 함께 쓰인다.
  To hear him speak English, you would think that he was a native speaker.
  (→ If you heard him speak English, you would think that he was a native speaker.)
  - 형용사를 수식하는 경우 '～하기에'의 뜻으로 형용사를 뒤에서 수식한다.
  This water is safe **to drink**.

A 다음 주어진 문장과 같은 뜻이 되도록 to부정사를 이용하여 문장을 완성하시오.

1 If you tasted this cake, you would think it came from a bakery.
→ _____, you would think it came from a bakery.

2 If you smelled that cheese, you would think it tasted terrible.
→ _____, you would think it tasted terrible.

3 If you saw him run, you'd think he was the fastest kid in the school.
→ _____, you'd think he was the fastest kid in the school.

4 If you looked at him, you'd never guess he is thirty years old.
→ _____, you'd never guess he is thirty years old.

B 다음 우리말과 같은 뜻이 되도록 ( ) 안의 말을 이용하여 문장을 완성하시오.

1 이 음식은 만들기 간단하다. (simple)
This food is _____ _____ _____ .

2 러시아어는 배우기 어렵다. (difficult)
Russian is _____ _____ _____ .

3 그녀의 이야기를 들으면, 너는 그녀가 똑똑하다고 생각할 것이다. (story)
_____ , you would think she was smart.

4 이 앱은 사용하기 편리하다. (convenient)
This app is _____ _____ _____ .

5 그 도시는 혼자 여행하기에 위험하다. (dangerous)
The city is _____ alone.

6 내 고양이가 우는 것을 들으면, 너는 고양이가 사람처럼 말한다고 생각할 것이다. (cry)
_____ , you would think
he was speaking like a human.

to부정사의 의미상의 주어

- to부정사의 의미상의 주어가 문장의 주어 혹은 목적어와 일치하지 않을 경우, 일반적으로 to부정사 앞에
⟨for+목적격⟩을 사용하여 의미상의 주어를 나타낸다.
It was difficult for Jenny to learn how to tap dance.
- 사람에 대한 주관적인 평가를 나타내는 형용사(kind, nice, silly, foolish, wise, smart, clever, careless
등)가 보어로 쓰인 경우, to부정사 앞에 ⟨of+목적격⟩을 사용하여 의미상의 주어를 나타낸다.
It was careless of him to break the window.
- 의미상의 주어가 문장의 주어 혹은 목적어와 같거나 막연한 일반인인 경우에는 생략한다.

★ **내신만점 TIP** to부정사의 의미상의 주어가 ⟨for+목적격⟩과 ⟨of+목적격⟩의 형태로 제시되는 경우를 구분하자.

A 다음 우리말과 같은 뜻이 되도록 문장을 완성하시오.

1 뮤지컬을 보는 것이 나에게는 재미있다.
It's fun _____ _____ _____ _____ musicals.

2 내가 그런 소문을 믿은 것은 어리석었다.
It was stupid _____ _____ _____ _____ such a rumor.

3 네가 그렇게 말한 것은 현명했다.
It was wise _____ _____ _____ _____ so.

4 그 노부인을 돕다니 그는 매우 다정하다.
It's very friendly _____ _____ _____ the old lady.

5 우리가 그 절벽을 오르는 것은 위험하다.
It's dangerous _____ _____ _____ the cliff.

B 다음 우리말과 같은 뜻이 되도록 ( ) 안의 말을 배열하여 문장을 완성하시오.

1 사실대로 말하다니 Judy는 용감하다. (it's, of, to tell, brave, Judy, the truth)
_____

2 독일인들이 영어를 배우는 것은 쉽다. (to learn, it's, Germans, for, easy, English)
_____

3 그 아이들에게는 놀이공원에 가는 것이 즐겁다.
(to, the children, it's, for, to go, fun, the amusement park)
_____

4 나에게 너의 노트를 빌려주다니 너는 친절하다.
(your notebook, me, you, it's, of, kind, to lend)
_____

too ~ to-v

- ⟨too+형용사 / 부사+to-v⟩는 '…하기에는 너무 ~하다' 또는 '너무 ~해서 …할 수 없다'로 해석한다.
  Jim was **too tired to watch** the match.
- ⟨too+형용사 / 부사+to-v⟩는 ⟨so+형용사 / 부사+that+주어+can't[couldn't] ~⟩로 바꾸어 쓸 수 있다.
  I'm **too busy to meet** my friends. → I'm **so busy that I can't meet** my friends.
  It was **too heavy** for me **to carry**. → It was **so heavy that I couldn't carry** it.

A 다음 주어진 문장과 같은 뜻이 되도록 문장을 완성하시오.

1 This lesson is too difficult for them to follow.
→ This lesson is _____ .

2 It was too cold for us to go swimming.
→ It was _____ .

3 The water is so salty that she can't drink it.
→ The water is _____ .

4 Some English words are so strange that I can't understand them.
→ Some English words are _____ .

5 This room is so noisy that he can't study in it.
→ This room is _____ .

B 다음 우리말과 같은 뜻이 되도록 ( ) 안의 말과 to부정사를 이용하여 문장을 완성하시오.

1 너는 그 연극을 보기에는 너무 어리다. (young, watch)
You are _____ the play.

2 밖으로 나가기에는 날씨가 너무 춥다. (cold, go)
It's _____ outside.

3 그녀는 모델이 되기에는 키가 너무 작다. (short, be)
She is _____ a model.

4 나는 쇼핑하러 가기에는 너무 피곤하다. (tired, go)
I'm _____ shopping.

5 그 파이는 내가 먹기에는 너무 크다. (big, eat)
The pie is _____ .

6 그 역은 우리가 걸어가기에는 너무 멀다. (far, walk)
The station is _____ to.

~ enough to-v

- 〈형용사 / 부사+enough+to-v〉는 '…할 만큼 충분히 ~하다'로 해석한다.
  The child is **smart enough to understand** the book.
- 〈형용사 / 부사+enough+to-v〉는 〈so+형용사 / 부사+that+주어+can[could] ~〉로 바꾸어 쓸 수 있다.
  He is **tall enough to dunk** a basketball.
  → He is **so tall that he can dunk** a basketball.
  She was **slim enough to wear** the dress.
  → She was **so slim that she could wear** the dress.

★ 내신만점 *TIP* 〈too+형용사 / 부사+to-v〉와 〈형용사 / 부사+enough+to-v〉 구문에서 형용사와 부사의 위치를 구분하여 기억하자.

A 다음 밑줄 친 부분을 어법에 맞게 고쳐 쓰시오.

1 You didn't run <u>enough fast</u> to win the race.

2 She cooks well <u>enough be</u> a great cook.

3 Tom was <u>enough rich</u> to buy the boat.

B 다음 주어진 문장과 같은 뜻이 되도록 문장을 완성하시오.

1 The ice was thick enough for me to walk on.
→ The ice was _____ it.

2 My umbrella is small enough for me to carry anywhere.
→ My umbrella is _____ it anywhere.

3 James is so smart that he can go to Harvard.
→ James is _____ to Harvard.

4 Stacy is light enough for me to lift.
→ Stacy is _____ her.

C 다음 우리말과 같은 뜻이 되도록 ( ) 안의 말을 배열하여 문장을 완성하시오.

1 그는 공짜로 여행을 갈 만큼 운이 좋았다. (travel, enough, lucky, to)
He was _____ for free.

2 이 칼은 그 감자들을 썰 만큼 예리하지 않다. (cut, sharp, to, the potatoes, enough)
This knife isn't _____ .

3 그는 그 탁자를 혼자 옮길 만큼 힘이 세다. (move, to, strong, the table, enough)
He is _____ alone.

Chapter 02

[01-03] 다음 빈칸에 알맞은 말을 고르시오.

01

I was late, so I decided _____ a taxi.

① take　　　　　② to take
③ took　　　　　④ taking
⑤ to taking

02

It's difficult _____ me to get up early.

① for　　　　　② to
③ of　　　　　④ with
⑤ on

03

I don't have any friends to play _____.

① with　　　　　② to
③ of　　　　　④ for
⑤ on

기출응용

04

다음 밑줄 친 부분의 쓰임이 나머지와 다른 것은?

① It is not easy <u>to make</u> money.
② We decided <u>to go</u> to the festival.
③ My dream is <u>to have</u> a luxury car.
④ I really did my best <u>to win</u> that game.
⑤ <u>To go</u> skydiving is scary for me.

[05-06] 빈칸에 들어갈 말이 순서대로 알맞게 짝지어진 것을 고르시오.

05

- _____ is hard to get a job these days.
- _____ her dance, you would think she took lessons.

① It – Watch　　　　② It – If watch
③ It – To watch　　　④ This – Watch
⑤ This – To watch

06

- I'm not sure _____ to put my suitcase.
- He is _____ selfish to help others.

① what – so　　　　② where – too
③ what – too　　　　④ how – enough
⑤ where – enough

07

다음 빈칸에 들어갈 수 <u>없는</u> 말은?

I _____ to travel alone.

① planned　　　　② wanted
③ refused　　　　④ decided
⑤ enjoyed

08

다음 우리말을 영어로 바르게 옮긴 것은?

그녀는 그 청바지를 입을 만큼 충분히 날씬해.

① She is too slim to wear those jeans.
② She is too slim wear those jeans.
③ She is slim enough to wear those jeans.
④ She is enough slim to wear those jeans.
⑤ She is slim to enough wear those jeans.

[09-10] 다음 빈칸에 공통으로 들어갈 말을 고르시오.

09

- I need a true friend to talk _____.
- Ellie is looking for a pen to write _____.

① for   ② of
③ with   ④ to
⑤ on

10

- It is easy _____ me to draw his face.
- It was too late _____ him to say "I'm sorry."

① for   ② of
③ with   ④ to
⑤ on

11

다음 두 문장이 같은 뜻이 되도록 할 때 잘못된 것은?

① Please let me know how I should spell your name.
  → Please let me know how to spell your name.

② It is impossible to move the stone.
  → To move the stone is impossible.

③ I went to the grocery store to buy some fruit.
  → I went to the grocery store so as to buy some fruit.

④ I practiced hard, but I made many mistakes.
  → I practiced hard, only to make many mistakes.

⑤ She was so diligent that she could get up at six.
  → She was too diligent to get up at six.

[12-13] 다음 〈보기〉의 밑줄 친 부분과 쓰임이 같은 것을 고르시오.

12

〈보기〉 Do you have a lot of work <u>to do</u>?

① I was there <u>to help</u> my aunt.
② Sometimes it is necessary <u>to do</u> nothing.
③ Do you want <u>to eat</u> out tonight?
④ Do you have anything <u>to tell</u> me?
⑤ I was surprised <u>to see</u> you there.

13

〈보기〉 It isn't healthy <u>to stay up</u> late.

① I have running shoes <u>to wash</u>.
② She went out <u>to buy</u> some milk.
③ The rumor is hard <u>to believe</u>.
④ <u>To try</u> something new would be exciting.
⑤ <u>To hear</u> him play the trumpet, you would think he was a member of the orchestra.

14

다음 밑줄 친 부분이 어법상 틀린 것은?

① It was nice <u>to spend</u> time with you.
② It took me a long time <u>to get</u> ready.
③ It's a good idea <u>to go</u> on a picnic.
④ I hope <u>to see</u> your brother again.
⑤ It was kind <u>for him</u> to give me his gloves.

15

다음 〈보기〉의 문장과 의미가 같은 것은?

〈보기〉 He decided where to stay on his trip.

① He decided that he should stay on his trip.
② He decided where he stayed on his trip.
③ He decided where he is staying on his trip.
④ He decided where he should stay on his trip.
⑤ He decided what he should stay on his trip.

[16-18] 다음 중 어법상 틀린 것을 고르시오.

16

① It's nice of him to say so.
② It is always fun to go skiing.
③ Nick wanted to eat Italian food.
④ Can I get a piece of paper to write?
⑤ I don't know how to play the piano.

17

① He couldn't decide what to buy.
② She had funny something to tell me.
③ I have no candy to give to you.
④ Jun was glad to return to his hometown.
⑤ Jenny is to leave for Busan tomorrow.

18

① He brought some snacks to eat.
② He must be rich to drive that car.
③ It was kind of him to help me.
④ It is impossible for she to move the bed.
⑤ I'm wearing sunglasses to protect my eyes.

기출응용
19

다음 우리말과 같은 뜻이 되도록 주어진 말을 배열할 때 세 번째에 올 단어는?

어떤 실수도 하지 않도록 조심하세요.
(to, be, any, not, make, careful, mistakes)

① to   ② be   ③ not
④ make   ⑤ mistakes

고난도
20

다음 중 어법상 옳은 것끼리 짝지어진 것은?

(a) You are to be home by seven.
(b) He tried to meet her, only to fail.
(c) This is an easy question to answer it.
(d) How long will it take finish this work?
(e) She was standing there in order to see him.

① (a), (b), (c)   ② (a), (b), (e)
③ (b), (c), (d)   ④ (b), (d), (e)
⑤ (c), (d), (e)

서술형 따라잡기

01
주어진 말을 이용하여 우리말과 뜻이 같도록 문장을 완성하시오.

(1) 나는 이 소프트웨어를 사용하는 방법을 모른다.

→ I don't know _____ _____

_____ this software. (use)

(2) Gary는 그의 아버지를 다시 보지 못할 운명이었다.

→ Gary _____ _____ _____

_____ his father again. (see)

02
다음 주어진 문장과 같은 뜻이 되도록 빈칸에 알맞은 말을 쓰시오.

(1) To shout at people is rude.

→ _____ _____ _____

_____ _____ people.

(2) This cake is so big that I can share it with my neighbors.

→ This cake _____ _____ _____

_____ _____ _____

with my neighbors.

03
어법상 틀린 부분을 찾아 바르게 고쳐 쓰시오.

(1) We are to move at the end of the month. We should look for an apartment to live. (1군데)

(2) When I turned 20, I was too old to drive a car. So my father taught me what to drive. (2군데)

04
다음 그림을 보고, 주어진 말을 이용하여 문장을 완성하시오.

(1) He is _____ _____ _____

the cupboard. (tall, reach)

(2) She needs a chair _____ _____

_____. (sit)

05
다음 표를 보고, 〈보기〉와 같이 각 학생의 성격이나 상황을 설명하는 문장을 쓰시오.

Jane	kind	drive me home
(1) Mark	foolish	be late for school
(2) Justine	easy	solve math problems

〈보기〉 It is kind of Jane to drive me home.

(1) _____

(2) _____

06
다음 〈보기〉와 같이 'too ~ to' 구문을 이용하여 두 문장을 한 문장으로 만드시오.

〈보기〉 The box is very heavy.
Nobody can lift it.
→ The box is too heavy to lift.

(1) Sarah got up very late. She couldn't catch the train.

→ _____

(2) He was very short. He couldn't ride the roller coaster.

→ _____

핵심 포인트 정리하기

1 to부정사의 용법

명사적 용법	- 주어, 보어, ①_____역할 - 목적어로 to부정사를 취하는 동사: want, plan, decide, hope, expect 등 - 〈의문사+to부정사〉 → 〈의문사+주어+②_____+동사원형〉
형용사적 용법	- 명사를 뒤에서 수식하거나 주어를 설명 - 〈-thing[-one/-body]+③_____+to부정사〉 *to부정사의 동사가 자동사인 경우에는 동사 뒤에 전치사 필요 - 〈④_____〉: 예정, 의무, 가능, 운명, 의도 등의 의미 표현
부사적 용법	- 동사, 형용사, 부사 수식 - ⑤_____, 감정의 원인, 결과, 판단의 근거, 조건 등의 의미

 to부정사의 형용사적 용법에서 자동사 뒤에 오는 전치사를 빠뜨리지 말기!

2 to부정사의 의미상의 주어: 〈⑥_____+목적격〉 또는 〈of+목적격〉

- to부정사의 보어로 사람에 대한 주관적인 평가를 나타내는 형용사가 쓰인 경우 〈of + 목적격〉 사용

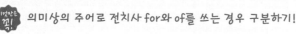 의미상의 주어로 전치사 for와 of를 쓰는 경우 구분하기!

3 〈too+형용사/부사+to-v〉: '너무 ~해서 …할 수 없다'

(→ so + 형용사/부사 + that + 주어 + can't[couldn't] ~)

4 〈형용사/부사+enough+to-v〉: '…할 만큼 충분히 ~하다'

(→ ⑦_____ + 형용사/부사 + that + 주어 + can[could] ~)

 〈too ~ to-v〉와 〈~ enough to-v〉 구문에서 형용사와 부사의 위치에 유의하기!

문제로 개념 다지기

밑줄 친 부분이 어법상 맞으면 O, 틀리면 X 표시하고 바르게 고치시오.

1 My goal is <u>to finishes</u> the race.

2 Anna didn't have any jellies <u>to eat</u>.

3 I didn't know <u>when I to meet him</u>.

4 My mother told me <u>to locking</u> the door before leaving home.

5 It's stupid of them <u>to not follow</u> the rules.

6 These clothes are <u>big too</u> for me to wear.

7 The bread was <u>soft enough for a child to chew</u>.

CHAPTER 03

동명사

Saving money is good for your future.
　　주어

Her job is **taking** care of children.
　　　　　보어

My sister likes **singing** traditional Korean songs.
　　　　　　　목적어

동명사의 역할

동명사는 <동사원형+-ing>의 형태로, 문장 안에서 명사처럼 주어, 보어, 목적어의 역할을 합니다. 동명사의 형태가 현재분사와 같아 혼동될 수도 있지만, 문장 안에서 하는 역할로 둘을 구분할 수 있답니다. 동명사가 문장 안에서 목적어로 쓰였을 때는 동사에 주목하세요. 동명사만을 목적어로 취하는 동사, to부정사만을 목적어로 취하는 동사, 동명사와 to부정사 둘 다를 목적어로 취하는 동사가 따로 있기 때문이죠.

동명사의 역할

■ 동명사는 〈동사원형+-ing〉의 형태로, 명사처럼 주어, 보어, 목적어의 역할을 한다.
- 주어로 쓰인 경우 '~하는 것은'으로 해석한다.
  Singing is my favorite hobby. (주어)
- 보어로 쓰인 경우 '~하는 것(이다)'으로 해석한다.
  My favorite hobby is **solving** puzzles. (보어)
■ 동사 또는 전치사의 목적어로 쓰인 경우 '~하는 것을'로 해석한다.
- 동사의 목적어로 쓰인 경우: I *enjoy* **learning** new languages.
- 전치사의 목적어로 쓰인 경우: She is interested *in* **helping** poor people.

★ PLUS TIP　동명사의 부정형은 〈not/never+v-ing〉의 형태로 쓴다.
I hate **not being** on time.

A　다음 〈보기〉에서 알맞은 말을 골라 빈칸에 적절한 형태로 써넣으시오.

〈보기〉　make　take　write　say　hear　climb　ride

1　_____ a shower will make you feel good.
2　Lisa is good at _____ mountains.
3　His goal was _____ a lot of money.
4　I couldn't finish _____ the report.
5　I'm tired of _____ the same story from him.
6　She left without _____ good-bye.
7　_____ my bicycle makes me happy.

B　다음 우리말과 같은 뜻이 되도록 ( ) 안의 말을 배열하여 문장을 완성하시오.

1　당신은 언제 일을 시작할 수 있나요? (working, when, you, start, can)
　　_____

2　내 직업은 야생 동물들을 보호하는 것이다. (wild animals, job, is, protecting, my)
　　_____

3　나는 영화 동아리에 가입하는 것에 대해 생각 중이다.
　　(movie club, thinking, a, joining, I'm, about)
　　_____

4　운동을 하는 것은 당신의 건강에 좋다. (health, your, good, is, exercising, for)
　　_____

5　약속을 지키지 않아서 미안해. (my promise, I'm, not, for, keeping, sorry)
　　_____

자주 쓰이는 동명사 표현

be busy v-ing	~하느라 바쁘다	be worth v-ing	~할 가치가 있다
go v-ing	~하러 가다	feel like v-ing	~하고 싶다
look forward to v-ing	~하기를 고대하다	be used to v-ing	~하는 데 익숙하다
It is no use v-ing	~해도 소용없다	on[upon] v-ing	~하자마자 (= as soon as+주어+동사)
How[What] about v-ing?	~하는 것은 어때?	cannot help v-ing	~하지 않을 수 없다 (= cannot (help) but+동사원형)

A 다음 ( ) 안에서 알맞은 말을 고르시오.

1 I go (hike / hiking) every Sunday.

2 She looked forward to (visit / visiting) her hometown.

3 I could not help (to laugh / laughing) at his joke.

4 I don't feel like (eating / eat) breakfast.

5 My mom wants (to make / making) cookies.

6 On (hear / hearing) the news, he started to cry.

B 다음 우리말과 같은 뜻이 되도록 위의 표현들과 ( ) 안의 말을 이용하여 문장을 완성하시오.

1 영화 보러 가는 것은 어때? (go to a movie)

_____

2 Laura는 취업 설명회를 준비하느라 바쁘다. (prepare for the job fair)

_____

3 나는 그녀를 그리워하지 않을 수 없다. (miss)

_____

4 그 책은 두 번 읽을 가치가 있다. (read twice)

_____

5 그것에 대해 걱정해도 소용없다. (worry about)

_____

6 나는 내 개와 산책하고 싶다. (take a walk)

_____

7 그녀는 그 기계를 다루는 데 익숙하다. (handle the machine)

_____

8 그가 당신을 다음 달에 만나기를 고대합니다. (meet)

_____

동명사와 현재분사 I

- 동명사와 현재분사는 모두 〈동사원형+-ing〉의 형태이지만 동명사는 명사의 역할을, 현재분사는 형용사의 역할을 한다.
- 〈v-ing〉가 be동사 뒤에 오는 형태
  - 동명사로 쓰인 경우 '~하는 것(이다)'로 해석한다.
    My favorite activity is **acting** on the stage.
  - 현재분사로 쓰인 경우 진행형의 문장에서 '~하고 있는'으로 해석한다.
    A beautiful actress is **acting** on TV.

★ 내신만점 TIP 〈be동사+동명사〉가 쓰인 문장에서 주어와 보어는 동격 관계임을 기억하자.
My dream is **climbing** the world's tallest mountains. (my dream = climbing the world's tallest mountains)

A 다음 밑줄 친 부분이 동명사인지 현재분사인지 〈 〉안에 써넣으시오.

1 They were <u>taking</u> a break. 〈   〉

2 My boyfriend is <u>waiting</u> for me. 〈   〉

3 He has a bad habit of <u>eating</u> late at night. 〈   〉

4 Her job is <u>answering</u> calls from customers. 〈   〉

5 She is <u>using</u> scissors to cut the paper. 〈   〉

6 My brother's hobby is <u>playing</u> computer games. 〈   〉

B 다음 우리말과 같은 뜻이 되도록 ( ) 안의 말을 이용하여 문장을 완성하시오.

1 그 과학자의 일은 로봇을 만드는 것이었다. (make, robots)
The scientist's job _____ _____ _____.

2 내가 가장 좋아하는 활동은 음악을 듣는 것이다. (listen to music)
My favorite activity _____ _____ _____ _____.

3 그는 친구와 통화 중이다. (talk, on the phone)
He _____ _____ _____ _____ _____ with his friend.

C 다음 문장을 밑줄 친 부분에 유의하여 우리말로 해석하시오.

1 He is <u>washing his car</u>.
_____

2 Her job is <u>designing clothes</u>.
_____

3 A baby was <u>sleeping on the bed</u>.
_____

- 〈v-ing〉가 명사 앞에 오는 형태
  - 동명사로 쓰인 경우 '~을 위한', '~로 사용되는'으로 해석하며, 뒤에 오는 명사의 용도나 목적을 나타낸다.

    The girl is wearing **dancing shoes**.

    (dancing shoes → shoes for dancing)
  - 현재분사로 쓰인 경우 '~을 하고 있는'으로 해석하며, 수식하는 명사의 진행 및 능동을 나타낸다.

    Look at the **dancing girl**. (the dancing girl → the girl is dancing)

A   다음 밑줄 친 부분이 동명사인지 현재분사인지 〈 〉 안에 써넣으시오.

1 Who is the crying boy? 〈　　〉

2 I burned my finger with boiling water. 〈　　〉

3 I use paper bags instead of shopping bags. 〈　　〉

4 These running shoes are really comfortable. 〈　　〉

5 Look at the singing birds. They're so small. 〈　　〉

6 These are non-smoking seats. 〈　　〉

7 There are too many people in the waiting room. 〈　　〉

8 Yesterday, I watched the rising sun. 〈　　〉

9 The firefighters saved a man from the burning building. 〈　　〉

10 I'll buy some cooking tools at the shop. 〈　　〉

11 The barking dog scared the children. 〈　　〉

12 I bought some food and drinking water. 〈　　〉

B   다음 짝지어진 문장들의 밑줄 친 부분에 유의하여 우리말로 해석하시오.

1 (a) I like that swimming dolphin.

     (b) There are many children in the swimming pool.

2 (a) This sleeping baby is cute.

     (b) Don't forget to bring your sleeping bag.

3 (a) We should respect all living things.

     (b) The woman guided us to the living room.

4 (a) We called him a "walking dictionary."

     (b) The elderly woman can't walk without a walking stick.

동명사와 to부정사 I

■ 동사에 따라 동명사나 to부정사 중 하나만을 목적어로 취하기도 하고, 둘 다 취하기도 한다.

동명사	enjoy, consider, mind, finish, keep, practice, deny, avoid, give up 등
to부정사	want, hope, wish, expect, decide, plan, promise, agree, refuse 등
동명사와 to부정사	like, love, hate, begin, start, continue 등

I couldn't **finish reading** the book.
She **wants to know** his name.
Students **began taking** the test. (= Students **began to take** the test.)

A 다음 ( ) 안에서 알맞은 말을 고르시오.

1 When do you plan (studying / to study) abroad?

2 My mother enjoys (watching / to watch) talk shows on TV.

3 They agreed (leaving / to leave) early in the morning.

4 Julie decided (renting / to rent) a bigger apartment next year.

5 You are too young to consider (getting / to get) married.

6 It was a nice day, so we kept (walking / to walk) along the street.

7 She gave up (trying / to try) to memorize their names.

8 Jamie promised (bringing / to bring) his camera tomorrow.

9 Don't hurry. I don't mind (waiting / to wait).

10 I hope (making / to make) my own movie someday.

B 다음 우리말과 같은 뜻이 되도록 ( ) 안의 말을 배열하여 문장을 완성하시오.

1 내가 너를 여기에서 만날 거라고는 예상하지 못했다. (expect, didn't, here, to, I, see, you)

_____

2 그는 새로운 사람들을 만나는 것을 싫어한다. (people, meeting, hates, new, he)

_____

3 그 아이들은 주변의 쓰레기를 줍기 시작했다.
(the trash, the children, pick up, around them, to, started)

_____

4 Keira는 이번 달에 스페인어를 배우기 시작했다.
(learning, Keira, this month, Spanish, began)

_____

5 나는 이 회사에서 계속 일할 것이다. (work, continue, at this company, I'll, to)

_____

동명사와 to부정사 II

■ 다음의 동사들은 동명사와 to부정사 둘 다를 목적어로 취할 수 있지만, 각각 의미가 다르므로 주의해야 한다.

목적어 \ 동사	remember	forget	try	stop
동명사	~한 것을 기억하다	~한 것을 잊다	(시험 삼아) ~해 보다	~하는 것을 멈추다
to부정사	~할 것을 기억하다	~할 것을 잊다	~하려고 노력하다	*~하기 위해 멈추다

* 〈stop+to-v〉는 목적을 나타내는 부사적 용법의 to부정사이다.

★ 내신만점 TIP   동명사와 to부정사 모두 목적어로 취할 수 있는 동사 중 의미 차이가 없는 동사와 있는 동사를 구분해서 기억하자.

A 다음 우리말과 같은 뜻이 되도록 〈보기〉에서 알맞은 말을 골라 빈칸에 적절한 형태로 써넣으시오.

〈보기〉 open   eat   buy   give   live   lock

1 그는 8살 때 암스테르담에서 살았던 것을 기억한다.
He remembers _____ in Amsterdam when he was eight.

2 Ross에게 이 책 주는 것을 기억해라.
Remember _____ Ross this book.

3 외출할 때 문 잠그는 것을 잊지 마라.
Don't forget _____ the door when you go out.

4 그녀는 꽃을 사기 위해 멈췄다.
She stopped _____ some flowers.

5 우리는 그 창문을 열려고 노력했지만 그럴 수가 없었다.
We tried _____ the window, but we couldn't.

6 나는 5년 전에 패스트푸드 먹는 것을 그만두었다.
I stopped _____ fast-food five years ago.

B 다음 문장을 밑줄 친 부분에 유의하여 우리말로 해석하시오.

1 I remember watching this movie long ago.
_____

2 They forgot seeing her at the party last year.
_____

3 She tried putting on the shoes.
_____

4 Because I was very tired, I stopped to rest at the park.
_____

내신대비 TEST

[01-03] 다음 빈칸에 알맞은 말을 고르시오.

01

_____ new places is a lot of fun.

① Visit   ② Visited   ③ Visits
④ Visiting   ⑤ To visiting

02

Julie is busy _____ for the final exam.

① prepare   ② preparing   ③ prepared
④ prepares   ⑤ to preparing

03

We agreed _____ at the library.

① met   ② meet   ③ meeting
④ being met   ⑤ to meet

04
다음 밑줄 친 ⓐ와 ⓑ의 형태로 알맞은 것은?

ⓐ <u>Drink</u> a lot of water is very important when you exercise. So, don't forget to bring some ⓑ <u>drink</u> water to the gym.

① Drink[drink]   ② Drinks[drinks]
③ Drunk[drunk]   ④ Drinking[drinking]
⑤ To drink[to drink]

[05-06] 다음 빈칸에 들어갈 수 <u>없는</u> 말을 고르시오.

05

I _____ to make a new garden.

① refused   ② hoped   ③ decided
④ planned   ⑤ considered

06

She _____ watching sports on TV.

① kept   ② finished   ③ promised
④ enjoyed   ⑤ gave up

[07-08] 빈칸에 들어갈 말이 순서대로 알맞게 짝지어진 것을 고르시오.

07

A: Shall we eat at home or go to a restaurant?
B: I don't mind _____ to a restaurant. It's up to you.
A: I want _____ at home.

① go – to eat   ② to go – eat
③ going – eating   ④ to go – eating
⑤ going – to eat

08

A: Did you remember _____ your mother?
B: Oh no, I forgot _____ her. It's not late, so I should do it now.

① call – call   ② to call – to call
③ calling – calling   ④ to call – calling
⑤ calling – to call

09

① Her job is <u>teaching</u> English.
② His goal is <u>winning</u> the contest.
③ My hobby is <u>collecting</u> stickers.
④ She is <u>watching</u> TV in the room.
⑤ My favorite activity is <u>playing</u> soccer.

10

① I hate <u>taking</u> tests.
② I like <u>walking</u> in the park.
③ I cannot give up <u>drinking</u> coffee.
④ You cannot avoid <u>making</u> mistakes.
⑤ The teacher woke up <u>sleeping</u> students.

11

다음 우리말을 영어로 옮긴 것 중 <u>잘못된</u> 것은?

① 나는 시험 삼아 그의 차를 운전해 보았다.
   I tried to drive his car.
② 우리는 당신과 함께 일하기를 고대하고 있다.
   We are looking forward to working with you.
③ 이번 주말에 하이킹하러 갈래?
   Shall we go hiking this weekend?
④ 나는 그 포스터를 쳐다보지 않을 수 없다.
   I cannot help looking at the poster.
⑤ 그 나라는 방문할 가치가 있다.
   That country is worth visiting.

12

① A: This machine doesn't work.
   B: Try pressing the green button.
② A: Did you send the card?
   B: Sorry, I forgot to send it.
③ A: Stop to play the game!
   B: Let me just play one more time.
④ A: What is the man doing?
   B: He is trying to fix my car.
⑤ A: You lent me 10 dollars a week ago.
   B: Did I? I don't remember lending you any
      money.

13

① A: What is Carol doing?
   B: She is busy taking pictures.
② A: Do you want to take a taxi?
   B: No, I feel like walking.
③ A: Did you like the concert?
   B: Yes, I still remember to see it.
④ A: I went to the new museum yesterday.
   B: Is it worth going there?
⑤ A: How about ordering a pizza?
   B: That sounds good.

14

다음 우리말과 같은 뜻이 되도록 빈칸에 들어갈 말로 알맞은 것은?

그 아기는 우는 것을 멈추고 나를 쳐다보았다.
→ The baby stopped _____ and looked
   at me.

① to cry   ② cry   ③ cried
④ crying   ⑤ to be crying

[15-16] 다음 밑줄 친 부분이 어법상 틀린 것을 고르시오.

15

① Nick planned to buy a new car.
② He stopped talking and walked out.
③ It's a machine for cutting grass.
④ All the students agreed wearing school uniforms.
⑤ Don't forget to turn off the light when you leave.

16

① He hoped meeting a pretty girl.
② Getting up early is difficult for me.
③ Do you mind opening the window?
④ I remembered putting my hairpin in the box.
⑤ My mom keeps telling me to study more.

17

(A), (B), (C)의 괄호 안에서 알맞은 것끼리 바르게 짝지어진 것은?

(A) My dad promised [to drive / driving] me to school.
(B) It is no use [to ask / asking] for help.
(C) Here's the trash. Don't forget [to take / taking] it out.

	(A)	(B)	(C)
①	to drive	to ask	to take
②	to drive	asking	to take
③	driving	asking	taking
④	driving	to ask	taking
⑤	driving	to ask	to take

기출응용
18

다음 〈보기〉의 밑줄 친 부분과 쓰임이 같은 것은?

〈보기〉 Look at the swimming boy.

① There's a barking dog outside.
② Can you please stop walking around?
③ I'm interested in drawing cartoons.
④ I couldn't help falling asleep in class.
⑤ My puppy likes playing with a ball.

19

다음 짝지어진 두 문장의 의미가 같지 않은 것은? (2개)

① We stopped to have dinner.
   → We stopped having dinner.
② Oliver hates to speak in front of people.
   → Oliver hates speaking in front of people.
③ I forgot to watch the movie with him.
   → I forgot watching the movie with him.
④ The man continued to ride his bike.
   → The man continued riding his bike.
⑤ The pigeons started to come near me.
   → The pigeons started coming near me.

고난도
20

다음 중 어법상 옳은 문장의 개수는?

(a) Holly is afraid of go in the water.
(b) Anna kept chopping the vegetables.
(c) I don't mind to give you a ride to the station.
(d) He didn't expect passing the job interview.
(e) You should avoid using elevators when a fire breaks out.

① 1개   ② 2개   ③ 3개   ④ 4개   ⑤ 5개

01

주어진 말을 알맞게 배열하여 우리말과 뜻이 같도록 문장을 완성하시오.

(1) 나는 매운 음식을 먹는 것이 익숙하다.

(eating, spicy food, am, to, I, used)

→ _____

(2) 이 동아리에 가입하는 게 어때?

(about, joining, what, this club)

→ _____

02

다음 두 문장이 같은 뜻이 되도록 빈칸에 알맞은 말을 쓰시오.

(1) As soon as I saw him, I hugged him.

→ _____ _____ him, I hugged him.

(2) I cannot but be proud of my son.

→ I _____ _____ _____ proud of my son.

03

다음 대화를 읽고, 〈보기〉에서 알맞은 말을 골라 적절한 형태로 써넣으시오.

〈보기〉 ask   bring   go   prepare

A: What do you want to do this weekend?

B: I feel like _____ to the park.

A: That's a good idea. What about taking Jenny with us?

B: She is busy _____ for an exam. It is no use _____ her.

A: Okay. Oh, remember _____ your hat.

B: All right.

04

〈기출응용〉

다음 〈보기〉와 같이 주어진 문장을 바꾸어 쓸 때, 빈칸에 알맞은 말을 쓰시오.

〈보기〉 She sailed on a boat. She remembered it.
→ She remembered sailing on a boat.

(1) I asked them to build an opera house. But they refused.

→ They _____ _____ _____ an opera house.

(2) He forgot that he picked some apples.

→ He _____ _____ some apples.

05

어법상 틀린 부분을 모두 찾아 바르게 고쳐 쓰시오. (2군데)

I decided losing weight. So I stopped eating chocolate. And I'm thinking about to work out at a gym.

06

다음 진희에 대한 정보를 나타낸 표를 보고, 문장을 완성하시오.

Interest	Help poor people
Like	Take walks
Plan	Take a vacation to Jeju Island
Bad Habit	Go to sleep late at night

Jinhee is interested in _____ _____. She likes _____ and plans _____ _____ _____ _____ to Jeju Island. This year, she will stop _____ _____ at night.

핵심 포인트 정리하기

1 동명사의 역할

- 형태: 〈① _____ + _____ 〉
- 역할: 주어/보어/동사나 전치사의 목적어

2 동명사와 현재분사

- 동명사: ② _____ 역할, '~하는 것'이라는 의미, 또는 명사 앞에 쓰인 경우 '~을 위한', '~로 사용되는'의 의미
- 현재분사: ③ _____ 역할, '~하고 있는'의 의미

 동명사와 현재분사의 쓰임 구분하기!

3 동명사와 to부정사

- ④ _____ 만 목적어로 취하는 동사: enjoy, consider, mind, finish, keep, practice, deny 등
- ⑤ _____ 만 목적어로 취하는 동사: want, hope, wish, expect, decide, plan, promise 등
- 동명사와 to부정사 둘 다를 목적어로 취하는 동사
  - 의미 차이가 없는 경우: like, love, hate, begin, start, continue 등
  - 의미 차이가 있는 경우

remember	동명사	⑥ '_____'
	to부정사	'~할 것을 기억하다'
forget	동명사	'~한 것을 잊다'
	to부정사	⑦ '_____'
try	동명사	⑧ '_____'
	to부정사	'~하려고 노력하다'
stop	동명사	⑨ '_____'
	to부정사	⑩ '_____'

 동명사와 to부정사를 각각 목적어로 취하는 동사 기억하기!
동명사와 to부정사를 목적어로 취할 때 의미가 달라지는 동사 알아두기!

문제로 개념 다지기

밑줄 친 부분이 어법상 맞으면 O, 틀리면 X 표시하고 바르게 고치시오.

1 Her favorite hobby is <u>traveling</u> all around the world.

2 Thank you for <u>call</u> me.

3 They kept <u>to talk</u> about their new teacher.

4 I feel like <u>to eat</u> out with you.

5 Dad promised <u>buying</u> me a new jacket.

6 Peter denied <u>stealing</u> our ideas.

food truck

CHAPTER 04

대명사

개념 쏙쏙

Some want to go skiing, but **others** want to go ice skating.   [부정대명사]

He fell off the ladder, but he didn't hurt **himself**.   [재귀대명사]

대명사의 종류

대명사의 종류에는 사람을 가리키는 인칭대명사, 특정한 사람이나 사물을 가리키는 지시대명사가
있습니다. 또한 some, any, another 등과 같이 막연한 사람이나 사물을 나타내는 부정대명사와
인칭대명사의 소유격이나 목적격에 -self[-selves]를 붙인 형태의 재귀대명사도 있답니다.

부정대명사 one

- 부정대명사: 막연한 사람이나 사물을 가리키는 대명사로, 대표적인 것에는 one이 있다. 복수형은 ones이다.
- one의 쓰임
  - 앞에 언급된 명사와 같은 종류의 사람이나 사물을 가리킬 때
    I don't have a pen. Will you lend me **one**? (one = a pen)
    There are many gloves. I like the red **ones**. (ones = gloves)
  - we, you와 같이 일반인을 총칭할 때
    One should follow traffic rules.

★ **PLUS TIP** 대명사 it의 경우, 앞에 언급된 특정한 대상을 가리킨다.
I like your ring. Can I see **it**? (it = your ring)

A 다음 빈칸에 one, ones, it 중 알맞은 말을 쓰시오.

1 Which bag is yours, this _____ or that _____?

2 Did you see my blue sweater? I can't find _____.

3 What do you think of this watch? If you like it, I'll buy _____.

4 These apples are too small. I want bigger _____.

5 I don't like the yellow umbrella, but I like the green _____.

6 This cup is dirty. Can you bring me a clean _____?

7 I lost my car key. Can you help me to find _____?

8 Can I borrow your bike? I'll return _____ by noon.

9 _____ should respect elderly people.

10 A: Is there a bank near here?
   B: Yes, there is _____ on Oak Street.

B 다음 우리말과 같은 뜻이 되도록 ( ) 안의 말을 이용하여 문장을 완성하시오.

1 사람은 항상 최선을 다해야 한다. (should)
   _____ _____ always do one's best.

2 나는 헌 책들을 팔고 새것들을 샀다. (buy)
   I sold my old books and _____ _____ _____.

3 엄마가 내게 새 책상을 사 주셨지만, 나는 그것이 마음에 들지 않는다. (like)
   My mom bought me a new desk, but I _____ _____ _____.

4 나는 세 개의 남는 쿠폰을 갖고 있어. 한 개를 고르면 그것을 너에게 줄게. (give)
   I have three extra coupons. Pick _____, and I'll _____ _____ to you.

부정대명사 all / both

| all | 모두, 모든 (것) | **All** of my friends live in Busan. |
| both | 둘 다, 양쪽(의) 〈복수 취급〉 | **Both** of them are tall and handsome. |

★ **PLUS TIP** 대명사 all은 사람을 나타낼 때는 복수, 사물이나 상황을 나타낼 때는 단수 취급한다.
단, 〈all (of)+명사〉인 경우 뒤에 오는 명사의 수에 동사를 일치시킨다.
All *were* present at the meeting. / **All** *was* calm in the town.
All five people *were* hurt in the accident.

A 다음 우리말과 같은 뜻이 되도록 문장을 완성하시오.

1 우리 둘 다 수학에 흥미가 있다.

_____ _____ _____ are interested in mathematics.

2 오늘 양쪽 팀 모두 경기를 잘했다.

_____ _____ played well today.

3 우리 부모님 두 분 모두 내 가장 친한 친구를 좋아하신다.

_____ _____ _____ _____ like my best friend.

4 그의 자녀들 모두 그를 격려하러 경기장에 왔다.

_____ _____ _____ _____ came to the stadium to encourage him.

B 다음 문장에서 <u>틀린</u> 부분을 찾아 어법에 맞게 고쳐 쓰시오.

1 All students hates tests.

2 Both six classmates in my group thought the museum was boring.

3 Both of them wants to go to that art gallery.

4 There are four members in the band. Both of them love music.

5 All the boys in my club likes her.

C 다음 우리말과 같은 뜻이 되도록 ( ) 안의 말을 배열하여 문장을 완성하시오.

1 저는 여러분 모두에게 감사드리고 싶습니다. (I, you, want, thank, to, of, all)

_____

2 우리는 둘 다 17살이다. (seventeen, are, us, both, of, old, years)

_____

3 내 돈은 전부 내 주머니에 있었다. (was, my money, in, all, my pocket, of)

_____

Point 03 · 부정대명사 some / any / each / every

some	약간(의), 몇몇(의)	**Some** of them agree with him.
any	약간(의), 조금(의)	Do you have **any** coins? – No, I don't have **any**.
each	각각(의) 〈단수 취급〉	**Each** of them was happy to see him.
every	모든, ~마다 〈단수 취급〉 (형용사로만 사용)	**Every** parent loves his or her children. I volunteer here **every** two weeks.

- some은 주로 긍정문이나 권유문에, any는 주로 부정문, 의문문, 조건문에 쓰인다.
- each는 전체를 구성하는 개별적인 것에 초점을 두는 반면, every는 개별적인 것들의 전체에 초점을 둔다.

★ **내신만점 TIP** 〈all, both, each, every+명사〉가 문장의 주어로 쓰일 때 동사의 수 일치에 유의하자.

A 다음 우리말과 같은 뜻이 되도록 〈보기〉에서 알맞은 말을 골라 문장을 완성하시오.

〈보기〉 some   any   each   every

1 그녀의 이야기 중 몇몇은 진실이다.
_____ of her stories are true.

2 너는 좋은 영화관을 좀 알고 있니?
Do you know _____ good movie theaters?

3 우리는 모두 다르기 때문에 우리들 각각은 특별하다.
_____ of us is special, because we are all different.

4 월드컵은 4년마다 열린다.
The World Cup is held _____ four years.

5 이 방에는 세 사람이 있다. 각각의 사람은 다른 언어를 말한다.
There are three people in this room. _____ person speaks a different language.

6 나는 머핀 몇 개를 사려고 갔으나, 그 빵집에는 조금도 없었다.
I went to buy _____ muffins, but the bakery didn't have _____.

B 다음 문장에서 <u>틀린</u> 부분을 찾아 어법에 맞게 고쳐 쓰시오.

1 Any frogs woke up.

2 All of the employees works hard for the company.

3 Every player do his or her best.

4 A: Would you like any tea?
B: No, thanks. I already had some.

5 Each student have his or her own ID card.

6 Don't buy some clothes. You already have enough.

부정대명사 another / one ~ the other …

another	또 하나 다른 것(의), 또 하나(의) 〈같은 종류의 것을 가리킬 때〉	This skirt is not my style. Can you show me **another**?
one ~ the other …	(둘 중의) 하나는 ~ 나머지 하나는 … 〈두 개를 차례로 가리킬 때〉	I have two pets. **One** is a cat and **the other** is a dog.

★ PLUS TIP 셋 중 하나는 one, 또 다른 하나는 another, 나머지 하나는 the other로 표현한다.

A 다음 빈칸에 another, one, the other 중 알맞은 말을 쓰시오.

1 이 펜은 안 나와요. 또 다른 펜 있나요?
This pen doesn't work. Do you have _____?

2 사람들은 그녀를 Tina라고 부르지만, 그녀는 또 다른 이름이 있다.
People call her Tina, but she has _____ name.

3 저기 있는 두 소년을 봐. 한 명은 우리 오빠고 나머지 한 명은 오빠의 친구야.
Look at the two boys over there.
_____ is my brother and _____ is his friend.

4 그 아이는 두 개의 장난감을 집었다. 하나는 인형이었고 나머지 하나는 자동차였다.
The child picked up two toys. _____ was a doll and _____
was a car.

5 그에게는 세 명의 친구가 있다. 한 명은 미국인이고, 또 한 명은 중국인, 나머지 한 명은
러시아인이다.
He has three friends. _____ is American, _____ is Chinese,
and _____ is Russian.

B 다음 우리말과 같은 뜻이 되도록 (   ) 안의 말을 배열하여 문장을 완성하시오.

1 커피 한 잔 더 드시겠습니까? (cup, coffee, of, another)
Would you like _____?

2 그곳에 가는 또 다른 방법이 있나요? (way, there, get, to, another)
Is there _____?

3 나는 생일에 두 개의 선물을 받았다. 하나는 부모님에게서, 나머지 하나는 Kelly에게서
받았다. (from, was, other, the, Kelly)
I got two presents on my birthday. One was from my parents and _____
_____.

부정대명사 some~others …/each other/one another

some ~ others …	어떤 것[사람]들은 ~, 또 어떤 것[사람]들은 …	**Some** like horror movies and **others** like action movies.
each other	서로 〈둘일 때〉	Ross and Rachael love **each other**.
one another	서로 〈셋 이상일 때〉	Three girls were talking to **one another**.

★ PLUS TIP
· 〈some ~ the others …〉는 '어떤 것[사람]들은 ~, 나머지 모든 것[사람]들은 …'이라는 의미이다.
· 현대영어에서는 each other와 one another를 구별 없이 사용하기도 한다.

A 다음 우리말과 같은 뜻이 되도록 〈보기〉에서 알맞은 말을 골라 빈칸에 쓰시오.

〈보기〉 one another   each other   some   others

1 저 두 소녀는 온종일 서로 말을 하지 않았다.
Those two girls didn't talk to _____ all day.

2 너희 셋은 서로 어떻게 만났니?
How did the three of you meet _____?

3 어떤 버섯은 먹으면 위험하다. 하지만 또 어떤 것들은 그렇지 않다.
_____ mushrooms are dangerous to eat. But _____ are not.

4 Brian과 Jennifer는 서로를 쳐다보고 미소를 지었다.
Brian and Jennifer looked at _____ and smiled.

5 그 세 명의 아이들은 서로 공을 패스하고 있었다.
The three children were passing a ball to _____.

6 어떤 학생들은 에세이를 제출했고, 또 어떤 학생들은 제출하지 않았다.
_____ students handed in the essay and _____ didn't.

B 다음 우리말과 같은 뜻이 되도록 ( ) 안의 말을 이용하여 문장을 완성하시오.

1 Jessica와 나는 서로 자주 전화한다. (call)
Jessica and I often _____ _____ _____.

2 그 다섯 명의 선수들은 서로 안다. (know)
The five players _____ _____ _____.

3 어떤 사람들은 '네'라고 대답했고, 또 어떤 사람들은 '아니오'라고 말했다. (answer)
_____ _____ "yes" and _____ said "no."

4 어떤 관광객은 쇼핑을 갔고, 나머지 모든 관광객은 쉬었다. (rest)
_____ tourists went shopping and _____ _____ _____.

재귀대명사의 재귀 용법

- 재귀대명사: 인칭대명사의 소유격이나 목적격에 -self나 -selves를 붙여 만든 형태로, '~ 자신'이라는 뜻이다.
- 재귀 용법: 주어가 하는 동작의 대상이 주어 자신일 때 사용하며, 재귀대명사가 동사나 전치사의 목적어로 올 수 있다.
  - 동사의 목적어: I *made* **myself** a nice pair of gloves.
  - 전치사의 목적어: Look *at* **yourself** in the mirror.

★ 내신만점 TIP 재귀 용법으로 쓰인 재귀대명사는 생략할 수 없음을 기억하자.

A 다음 밑줄 친 부분을 어법에 맞게 고쳐 쓰시오.

1 They called <u>theirselves</u> Super Band.

2 The door is open. Let <u>you</u> in.

3 We must love <u>ourself</u> before we love others.

4 Sean asked <u>myself</u> about the movie. And I told him it was good.

5 Matt is selfish. He only thinks about <u>him</u>.

6 Don't give up, and you'll feel good about <u>you</u>.

B 다음 우리말과 같은 뜻이 되도록 ( ) 안의 말을 이용하여 문장을 완성하시오.

1 Jake, 반 친구들에게 네 소개를 해 주겠니? (introduce)
Jake, can you _____ _____ to the class?

2 반 고흐는 37세의 나이에 자살했다. (kill)
Van Gogh _____ _____ at the age of 37.

3 "넌 할 수 있어!" Tara는 그녀 자신에게 말했다. (say to)
"You can do it!" Tara _____ _____ _____.

4 나는 또 지각을 했다. 나는 정말 나 자신에게 화가 난다. (angry with)
I was late again. I'm really _____ _____.

5 우리는 우리 자신을 믿어야 한다. (believe in)
We should _____ _____ _____.

6 우리 어머니는 요리하는 도중에 화상을 입으셨다. (burn)
My mother _____ _____ while she was cooking.

7 Sam은 대형 화면 속의 자기 자신을 보았다. (look at)
Sam _____ _____ _____ on the big screen.

8 그는 마침내 자기 자신을 돌봐야 한다는 것을 깨달았다. (take care of)
He finally realized that he should _____ _____ _____.

재귀대명사의 강조 용법

- 강조 용법: 주어나 목적어의 뜻을 강조할 때 사용하며, 이때 재귀대명사는 생략할 수 있다.
  I **myself** wrote the song. / I wrote the song **myself**. (주어 강조)
  He loved the woman **herself**, not her money. (목적어 강조)

★ PLUS TIP 주어를 강조하는 재귀대명사는 주어 다음이나 문장 끝에 올 수 있다.

A 다음 우리말과 같은 뜻이 되도록 문장을 완성하시오.

1 내가 직접 이 스파게티를 요리했다.
   I _____ this spaghetti _____.

2 대통령이 직접 그녀에게 상을 주었다.
   The president _____ gave her the prize.

3 그 아이들이 직접 이 샌드위치를 만들었다.
   The children made these sandwiches _____.

4 네 방 청소는 네가 직접 해야 한다.
   You should clean your room _____.

5 우리가 직접 여행 계획을 세우자.
   Let's make our travel plans _____.

6 그녀는 가르치는 것 자체는 즐겼지만, 학교에서 일하는 것은 즐기지 않았다.
   She enjoyed _____ _____, but not working at the school.

7 나는 그 영화 자체는 좋아하지 않았지만, 거기 나온 주연 배우가 좋았다.
   I didn't like _____ _____ _____, but I liked the main actor in it.

B 다음 우리말과 같은 뜻이 되도록 ( ) 안의 말을 배열하여 문장을 완성하시오.

1 나는 지배인 본인과 이야기하고 싶다. (himself, speak, the manager, to)
   I want to _____.

2 그녀는 직접 나에게 그 소식을 전했다. (herself, news, the, me)
   She told _____.

3 Tony가 직접 우리에게 공 던지는 법을 보여 주었다. (us, to, himself, throw, how, a ball)
   Tony showed _____.

4 나는 영어 자체는 싫지만, 우리 영어 선생님은 좋다. (English, hate, I, itself)
   _____, but I like my English teacher.

5 내가 너를 위해 직접 이 초콜릿 케이크를 만들었다. (you, for, myself, chocolate cake, this)
   I made _____.

■ 재귀대명사를 포함한 관용적인 표현에는 다음과 같은 것들이 있다.
- by oneself: 혼자서, 혼자 힘으로
- in itself: 본래, 그 자체가
- beside oneself: 제정신이 아닌
- enjoy oneself: 즐거운 시간을 보내다
- for oneself: 스스로, 스스로를 위해
- between ourselves: 우리끼리 얘기지만
- help oneself (to ~): (~을) 마음껏 먹다
- make oneself at home: 편히 지내다

A 다음 우리말과 같은 뜻이 되도록 할 때, 틀린 부분을 어법에 맞게 고쳐 쓰시오.

1 나는 이것을 혼자서 끝내야 한다.
I should finish this of myself.

2 이 음식을 마음껏 드세요. 당신을 위해 만들었어요.
Help itself to this food. I made it for you.

3 우리끼리 얘기지만, 나는 누가 그 악성 댓글을 남겼는지 알아.
In ourselves, I know who left the bad comments.

4 축구 팬들은 흥분해서 제정신이 아니었다.
The soccer fans were by themselves with excitement.

5 그들은 함께 있을 때면 즐거운 시간을 보낸다.
They enjoy oneself when they are together.

B 다음 우리말과 같은 뜻이 되도록 위의 표현들을 이용하여 문장을 완성하시오.

1 그것은 그 자체로 훌륭한 생각이다.
That is a great idea _____ _____.

2 그는 탁자 위에 있는 과일들을 마음껏 먹었다.
He _____ _____ to the fruit on the table.

3 우리는 놀이공원에서 즐거운 시간을 보냈다.
We _____ _____ at the amusement park.

4 그녀는 행복과 기쁨으로 제정신이 아니었다.
She was _____ _____ with happiness and joy.

5 그는 이 집을 혼자서 지었다.
He built this house _____ _____.

6 와 주셔서 감사합니다. 편히 계세요.
Thank you for coming. _____ _____ _____ _____.

내신대비 TEST

[01-03] 다음 빈칸에 알맞은 말을 고르시오.

01

A: What would you like to have?
B: I'll have a pizza. A small _____, please.

① one   ② ones   ③ some
④ any   ⑤ it

02

I gave my sister some money, but she didn't spend _____.

① one   ② ones   ③ some
④ any   ⑤ another

03

Some students like to play soccer and _____ like to play basketball.

① other   ② the other   ③ another
④ others   ⑤ all

04

다음 밑줄 친 부분의 쓰임이 잘못된 것은?

① I wasn't able to express meself.
② He made the chicken soup himself.
③ Please help yourself to the cookies.
④ My sister should take care of herself first.
⑤ Lucy enjoyed herself during the winter vacation.

[05-07] 다음 빈칸에 공통으로 들어갈 말을 고르시오.

05

• We missed the train, so we took the next _____.

• _____ should not steal things.

① it[It]   ② one[One]
③ ones[Ones]   ④ others[Others]
⑤ the other[The other]

06

• Would you like _____ water?
• A: What did you eat for lunch?
  B: I ate _____ spaghetti.

① any   ② each   ③ every
④ other   ⑤ some

07

• I made some cake for you. Help _____.
• Be careful! You may hurt _____.

① yourself   ② myself   ③ you
④ itself   ⑤ ourselves

[08-10] 빈칸에 들어갈 말이 순서대로 알맞게 짝지어진 것을 고르시오.

08

• _____ of them have curly hair.
• Ted and Jane like _____.

① All – the others   ② Each – each other
③ Each – one another   ④ Both – the others
⑤ Both – each other

09

- Please make yourself _____ home.
- _____ ourselves, I don't think their idea is good.

① for – Between　　② to – With
③ at – For　　④ beside – With
⑤ at – Between

10

I have three sons. _____ is a lawyer, _____ is a teacher and _____ is a student.

① One – the other – other
② One – another – the other
③ One – another – other
④ Some – the other – another
⑤ Some – another – the other

11
다음 밑줄 친 부분의 용법이 나머지와 다른 것은?

① I taught myself Japanese.
② The man hurt himself.
③ Why don't you do it yourself?
④ Jenny made herself a nice hair pin.
⑤ We should respect ourselves.

[12-13] 다음 밑줄 친 부분이 어법상 틀린 것을 고르시오.

12
① Every person have problems.
② All runners are standing at the starting line.
③ Both Nancy and Lisa love Jim.
④ Some were dead and others were alive.
⑤ Each person in this class has a different last name.

13
① I bought some apples at a low price.
② Do you have any books to read?
③ There isn't some food at home.
④ This shirt is too small for me. Do you have a bigger one?
⑤ If you have any questions, let me know.

14
다음 우리말을 영어로 옮긴 것 중 잘못된 것은?

① Ron은 음악 자체를 좋아한다.
　Ron likes the music itself.
② 나는 가끔 혼잣말을 한다.
　I sometimes talk to myself.
③ 두 명의 남자가 있다. 한 명은 모델이고 나머지 한 명은 작가이다.
　There are two men. One is a model and other is a writer.
④ 너희 셋은 서로 도와야 한다.
　The three of you should help one another.
⑤ 어떤 사람들은 경기를 즐겼지만, 나머지 모든 사람들은 그러지 못했다.
　Some people enjoyed the game, but the others didn't.

15
다음 중 밑줄 친 부분을 생략할 수 있는 것은?

① She is proud of <u>herself</u>.
② I hate <u>myself</u> for doing such a thing.
③ He dried <u>himself</u> with a towel.
④ Lola made beautiful candles <u>herself</u>.
⑤ Those people always speak about <u>themselves</u>.

16
다음 대화 중 자연스럽지 <u>않은</u> 것은?

① A: Who wrote this poem?
   B: Believe it or not, I wrote it myself.
② A: What was he doing?
   B: He was teaching some students.
③ A: Oh, you bought a new laptop.
   B: Yes. You can use one if you want.
④ A: This coat doesn't look good on me.
   B: Then I'll show you another.
⑤ A: I want to try these sunglasses on.
   B: Which ones do you mean?

17
다음 (A), (B), (C)의 빈칸에 들어갈 말로 바르게 짝지어진 것은?

(A) Life in _____ is worth living.
(B) Every song on the band's album
    _____ great.
(C) My shoes are old. I have to buy new
    _____.

	(A)		(B)		(C)
①	it	⋯⋯	are	⋯⋯	ones
②	itself	⋯⋯	is	⋯⋯	ones
③	it	⋯⋯	is	⋯⋯	them
④	itself	⋯⋯	is	⋯⋯	them
⑤	it	⋯⋯	are	⋯⋯	them

기출응용
18
다음 중 어법상 <u>틀린</u> 문장의 개수는?

(a) The two students taught each others.
(b) Some kids like sweets, but another don't.
(c) This car is expensive. I want to see another.
(d) I have two dogs. One is shy and the other is active.
(e) Let us introduce ourselves to you.

① 1개   ② 2개   ③ 3개   ④ 4개   ⑤ 5개

고난도
19
다음 중 어느 빈칸에도 들어갈 수 <u>없는</u> 것은?

(a) _____ is well.
(b) I don't have _____ problems.
(c) _____ activities are exciting.
(d) _____ of them are ready to run.

① all   ② both
③ some   ④ any
⑤ each

고난도
20
다음 중 어법상 옳은 것을 모두 고르면? (2개)

① I dressed me up for the party.
② Nicky met with the CEO himself.
③ Each girl has her own desk.
④ I like white cars more than black one.
⑤ She has two boxes. One is big and the others are small.

서술형 따라잡기

01
주어진 문장과 같은 뜻이 되도록 빈칸에 알맞은 말을 쓰시오.

(1) Many people in this city live alone.
 → Many people in this city live _____ _____.

(2) John is sitting next to Mary, and Mary is sitting next to John.
 → John and Mary are sitting next to _____ _____.

02
우리말과 같은 뜻이 되도록 ( ) 안의 말을 배열하여 문장을 완성하시오.

그들은 둘 다 편히 있었다.
(home, made, them, of, themselves, at, both)

→ _____

03
다음 학급별 활동표를 보고, 빈칸에 알맞은 대명사를 쓰시오.

Activity Class	Draw pictures	Read books	Solve math problems
Class A	11	9	0
Class B	9	9	4

(1) There are 20 students in class A.
 _____ are drawing pictures and _____ are reading books.

(2) There are 22 students in class B.
 _____ are drawing pictures and _____ are reading books. The rest are solving math problems.

04
주어진 말을 이용하여 우리말과 뜻이 같도록 문장을 완성하시오.

(1) 우리 모두는 제정신이 아니었다. (be, beside)
 All of us _____ _____ _____.

(2) 나는 세 명의 소설가를 좋아한다. 각각은 서로 다른 작문 스타일을 갖고 있다. (one, have)
 I like three novelists. _____ _____ _____ different style of writing.

05
다음 그림을 보고, 문장을 완성하시오.

There are three boys. _____ is wearing a hat, _____ is wearing a scarf, and _____ _____ is wearing gloves.

고난도
06
다음 대화에서 어법상 틀린 부분을 모두 찾아 바르게 고쳐 쓰시오. (3군데)

A: You look cold. Look! Every student are wearing a coat.
B: Yes. All of them look warm in their coats.
A: Don't you have a coat?
B: I bought one last week, but I left one at home.
A: Today is a cold day. Take care of you.
B: Thank you.

핵심 포인트 정리하기

1 부정대명사

- one: 앞에 언급된 명사와 같은 종류의 사람이나 사물을 지칭하거나 일반인을 총칭
- ① _____ : '모두', '모든 (것)'
- both: '둘 다', '양쪽(의)' — 복수 취급
- some / any: '약간(의)', '몇몇(의)'/ '약간(의)', '조금(의)'
- each: '각각(의)' — 단수 취급
- ② _____ : '모든', '~마다' — 단수 취급

 부정대명사가 명사와 함께 쓰일 때 동사의 수 일치를 주의 깊게 보기!

another	'또 하나 다른 것(의)', '또 하나(의)' 〈같은 종류〉
one ~ ③ _____ …	'(둘 중의) 하나는 ~ 나머지 하나는 …'
one, another, the other	'(셋 중에) 하나는', '또 다른 하나는', '나머지 하나는'
some ~ ④ _____ …	'어떤 것[사람]들은 ~, 또 어떤 것[사람]들은 …'
some ~ the others …	'어떤 것[사람]들은 ~, 나머지 모든 것[사람]들은 …'
each other	'서로' 〈둘일 때〉
⑤ _____	'서로' 〈셋 이상일 때〉

2 재귀대명사

- 재귀 용법: 동사나 전치사의 ⑥ _____ (생략 X)
- 강조 용법: 주어, 목적어의 뜻 강조 (생략 O)

 문장의 주어가 무엇인지 먼저 파악하기!
재귀대명사를 포함하는 관용표현 외우기!

문제로 개념 다지기

다음 ( ) 안에서 알맞은 말을 고르시오.

1 I've lost my favorite bag. I need a new (one / it).

2 All of the pictures (was / were) hanging in the gallery.

3 Both of the men in the room (is / are) German.

4 I have two cats. One has brown fur and (the other / another) has white fur.

5 Some birds can fly but (the other / others) can't.

6 The boy broke the window. He was very angry with (himself / itself).

7 Students must get to the airport by (theirselves / themselves).

CHAPTER

05

시제

Sue **has** never **been** to Europe before.　　　[경험: '~한 적이 있다']

I've just **checked** your messages.　　　[완료: '막 ~했다']

They **have used** this car for 10 years.　　　[계속: '(지금까지 계속) ~해 왔다']

He **has gone** to school by bus.　　　[결과: '~해 버렸다']

현재완료

<have[has]+v-ed>의 형태로, 과거에 일어난 일이 현재까지 영향을 미치고 있는 경우에 사용합니다.
문맥에 따라 다음의 4가지 의미를 나타냅니다.

1) 현재까지의 경험
2) 과거의 동작이 현재에 막 완료됨
3) 과거부터 현재까지 어떤 일이 계속되고 있음
4) 과거에 일어난 일의 결과가 현재까지 영향을 미치고 있음

- 현재진행형: 〈am[are/is]+v-ing〉의 형태로 현재 진행 중인 일을 나타내며, '~하고 있다', '~하는 중이다'로 해석한다.
It **is raining** outside, and people **are holding** umbrellas.
- 현재진행형은 가까운 미래에 일어날 일이나 최근에 일어나고 있는 일을 말할 때도 쓴다.
We **are going** on a picnic tomorrow. / I **am studying** Japanese these days.
- 과거진행형: 〈was[were]+v-ing〉의 형태로 과거 특정 시점에 진행 중이던 일을 나타내며, '~하고 있었다'로 해석한다.
Two students **were fighting** when the teacher came in.

 소유, 감각, 감정, 인지 등을 나타내는 동사(have, see, hear, like, know, think, believe 등)는 진행형으로 쓰지 않음에 유의하자. 단, have가 '먹다', think가 '고려하다'의 의미일 때는 진행형으로 쓸 수 있다.

A 다음 우리말과 같은 뜻이 되도록 할 때, <u>틀린</u> 부분을 어법에 맞게 고쳐 쓰시오.

1 너는 왜 내 책상에 앉아 있니?
Why are you sit at my desk?

2 초인종이 울렸을 때, 나는 샤워를 하고 있었다.
When the bell rang, I am taking a shower.

3 엄마가 도착했을 때, 부엌에서 무엇인가가 타고 있었다.
Something burns in the kitchen when my mom arrived.

B 다음 ( ) 안의 말을 이용하여 현재진행형과 과거진행형 중 적절한 형태로 문장을 완성하시오.

1 Look at the elephants! They _____ _____ water. (drink)

2 David _____ _____ with his teacher at that time. (talk)

3 Laura _____ _____ for the bus. She looks bored. (wait)

C 다음 우리말과 같은 뜻이 되도록 ( ) 안의 말을 이용하여 문장을 완성하시오.

1 너는 무슨 말을 하고 있는 거니? (talk about)
What _____ _____ _____ _____?

2 우리는 이번 일요일에 낚시하러 갈 것이다. (go fishing)
_____ _____ _____ _____ this Sunday.

3 그가 문을 열었을 때, 그녀는 테이블을 치우고 있었다. (clean)
When he opened the door, _____ _____ _____ the table.

4 Peter는 Bella에게 줄 선물을 고르고 있었다. (choose, a present)
Peter _____ _____ _____ _____ for Bella.

과거시제와 현재완료

- **과거시제**: 과거 특정 시점에 일어난 동작이나 상태를 나타낸다.
  I **was** sick yesterday. (지금 아픈지 알 수 없음)
- **현재완료**: 과거에 일어난 일이 현재까지 영향을 미치고 있는 상태를 나타내며 〈have[has]+v-ed〉의 형태로 쓴다. 부정형은 〈have[has]+not+v-ed〉, 의문형은 〈Have[Has]+주어+v-ed ~?〉이다.
  I **have been** sick since yesterday. (지금까지 아픈 상태)
  We **have not[haven't] decided** where to go yet.
  Have you ever **been** to Croatia? — Yes, I have. / No, I haven't.

★ **내신만점 TIP** ▶ when이나 yesterday, ago, last week 등 특정 과거 시점을 나타내는 말은 현재완료와 함께 쓰지 않는다는 것을 기억하자.

A 다음 ( ) 안에서 알맞은 말을 고르시오.

1 Ray (lost / has lost) his ring yesterday.
2 Judy (read / has read) a storybook last month.
3 (Did you go / Have you gone) to Laos last vacation?
4 I (don't play / haven't played) table tennis before.
5 Susan (heard / has heard) the news an hour ago.

B 다음 〈보기〉에서 알맞은 말을 골라 빈칸에 적절한 형태로 써넣으시오.

〈보기〉 know   be   change   have   come

1 Where _____ you born?
2 He _____ his name a few years ago.
3 I _____ him since I was ten.
4 When I _____ home yesterday, I was very tired.
5 She _____ a headache in the morning.

C 다음 우리말과 같은 뜻이 되도록 ( ) 안의 말을 배열하여 문장을 완성하시오.

1 그 식물이 얼마나 자랐는지 봐라. (grown, the plant, has)
   Look how much _____.

2 그녀는 도서관에 책을 빌리러 가서 지금 여기에 없다.
   (borrow, to, she, a book, gone, has)
   _____ at the library, so she's not here now.

3 그는 10년 동안 이 식당에서 일해 왔다. (this restaurant, he, worked, at, has)
   _____ for ten years.

현재완료의 용법 – 경험

- 현재까지의 경험을 나타낼 때 쓰며, '~한 적이 있다'라고 해석한다.
- 경험을 나타내는 현재완료는 주로 before, ever, never, once 등과 함께 쓴다.
  I **have never seen** such a kind man.

A 다음 우리말과 같은 뜻이 되도록 〈보기〉에서 알맞은 말을 골라 빈칸에 적절한 형태로 써넣으시오.

〈보기〉 travel   miss   eat   take   be   see

1 너는 전에 멕시코 음식을 먹어본 적이 있니?
_____ you _____ Mexican food before?

2 우리는 전에 이 그림을 본 적이 있다.
We _____ _____ this painting before.

3 우리 가족은 싱가포르로 여행한 적이 있다.
My family _____ _____ to Singapore.

4 Linda는 불어 수업을 수강한 적이 있다.
Linda _____ _____ a French class.

5 나는 야구 경기를 놓친 적이 없다.
I _____ _____ _____ a baseball game.

6 너는 디즈니랜드에 가 본 적이 있니?
_____ you ever _____ to Disneyland?

B 다음 우리말과 같은 뜻이 되도록 ( ) 안의 말을 배열하여 문장을 완성하시오.

1 너는 아이스하키를 해 본 적이 있니? (ever, played, you, have)
_____ ice hockey?

2 나는 수족관에 한 번 가 본 적이 있다. (been, have, the aquarium, I, to)
_____ once.

3 그 팀은 경기에서 단 한 번도 져 본 적이 없다. (has, lost, the team, never)
_____ a game.

4 Sean은 이전에 반려동물을 키워 본 적이 없다. (a pet, never, has, had, Sean)
_____ before.

5 그 가수는 전에 이 도시에서 콘서트를 두 번 개최한 적이 있다.
(in, held, the singer, this city, a concert, has)
_____ twice before.

현재완료의 용법 – 완료

- 과거에 시작한 어떤 동작이 현재에 막 완료되었음을 나타낼 때 현재완료를 쓴다. '벌써/이미/막 ~했다' 또는 '아직 ~하지 않았다'로 해석한다.
- 완료를 나타내는 현재완료는 주로 already, just, yet 등과 함께 쓴다.
  I **have just bought** a birthday present for him.

★ *PLUS TIP* already와 just는 보통 have[has]와 v-ed 사이에, yet은 문장 맨 끝에 쓴다.

A 다음 문장을 우리말로 해석하고, 현재완료가 '경험'과 '완료' 중 어떤 용법으로 쓰였는지 〈 〉 안에 써넣으시오.

1 Have you already done your homework? 〈   〉

_____

2 I have been to New York once. 〈   〉

_____

3 They have just moved into this apartment. 〈   〉

_____

B 다음 ( ) 안의 말을 알맞게 배열하여 대화를 완성하시오.

1 A: Can I take away your plate, sir?
B: No, I _____. (eating, finished, yet, haven't)

2 A: Is Rick still in the bathroom?
B: No, he _____. (out, just, has, come)

3 A: Did you buy the book?
B: No, _____. (opened, the store, yet, hasn't)

C 다음 우리말과 같은 뜻이 되도록 ( ) 안의 말을 이용하여 문장을 완성하시오.

1 그녀는 아직 그 새 옷을 입어보지 않았다. (wear)
She _____ _____ the new clothes yet.

2 Eric은 자신의 여자친구에 대해 아직 아무에게도 말하지 않았다. (tell, anyone)
Eric _____ _____ _____ about his girlfriend yet.

3 나는 방금 Sue로부터 전화를 받았다. (get a call)
I _____ just _____ _____ _____ from Sue.

4 너는 벌써 양치했니? (brush one's teeth)
_____ _____ already _____ _____ _____?

현재완료의 용법 – 계속

- 과거의 어느 시점부터 현재까지 어떤 일이 계속되고 있음을 나타낼 때 현재완료를 쓴다. '(지금까지 계속) ~해 왔다'로 해석한다.
- 계속을 나타내는 현재완료는 for, since, how long 등과 함께 자주 쓴다.
  They **have been** friends **for** three years.
  I **have lived** here **since** I was five.

★ **PLUS TIP** for(~ 동안) 뒤에는 동작·상태가 지속된 기간이 오고, since(~ 이래로) 뒤에는 동작·상태가 시작된 시점이 온다.

A 다음 〈보기〉와 같이 for나 since를 이용하여 두 문장을 한 문장으로 만드시오.

〈보기〉 I started working here three years ago. I still work here.
→ I have worked here for three years.

1 I loved Mina when I was a child. I still love her.
→ I _____ I was a child.

2 I bought this sofa five years ago. I still have it.
→ I _____ five years.

3 He was sick on Monday. He is still sick.
→ He _____ Monday.

4 Stephen moved to this house ten years ago. He still lives here.
→ Stephen _____ ten years.

B 다음 우리말과 같은 뜻이 되도록 ( ) 안의 말을 배열하여 문장을 완성하시오.

1 Randy는 캐나다에서 2년째 공부하고 있다. (for, in, has, two, studied, years, Canada)
Randy _____.

2 나는 6살 이후로 안경을 써 왔다. (glasses, worn, since, have, I)
_____ I was six.

3 너희는 얼마나 오랫동안 서로 알고 지냈니? (long, you, have, how, known)
_____ each other?

4 Molly는 어렸을 때부터 춤추는 것을 좋아했다. (dance, to, liked, since, has)
Molly _____ she was young.

5 Bob은 지난 수요일 이후로 Sally를 보지 못했다. (Sally, seen, since, hasn't)
Bob _____ last Wednesday.

현재완료의 용법 – 결과

- 과거에 일어난 일의 결과가 현재까지 영향을 미칠 때 현재완료를 쓴다. '~해 버렸다 (그래서 지금은 ~하다)'로 해석한다.
- 결과를 나타내는 현재완료는 현재 상태가 어떠한지 알 수 있다는 점에서 과거시제와 구분된다.
Carl **has lost** his watch. (→ Carl lost his watch. So he doesn't have it now.)

★ 내신만점 *TIP* have[has] gone to는 '~에 가고 (지금 여기에) 없다'라는 의미로 〈결과〉의 현재완료이고, have[has] been to는 '~에 가 본 적이 있다'라는 의미로 〈경험〉의 현재완료임을 알아두자.

A 다음 ( ) 안의 말을 이용하여 대화를 완성하시오.

1 A: Where is Jim? I haven't seen him lately.
B: He _____ _____ to Busan. (go)

2 A: Why is Julian in the hospital?
B: He _____ _____ his leg. (break)

3 A: Do you have anything to eat?
B: No, David _____ _____ all the candy bars. (eat)

4 A: Could you lend me your notebook?
B: Sorry, I _____ _____ it at home. (leave)

5 A: Why are you on a diet?
B: I _____ _____ a lot of weight this year. (gain)

B 다음 〈보기〉와 같이 두 문장을 한 문장으로 만드시오.

〈보기〉 He went to meet Brian. So he is not here now.
→ He has gone to meet Brian.

1 Steve lost his key. So he doesn't have it now.
→ _____

2 I sold my old books. So I don't have them now.
→ _____

3 Sarah left her bag on the bus. So she doesn't have it now.
→ _____

4 My father went to Hong Kong on business. So he isn't here now.
→ _____

Chapter 05

내신대비 TEST

[01-03] 다음 빈칸에 알맞은 말을 고르시오.

01

A: Have you _____ John today?
B: Yes, I saw him a minute ago.

① see   ② saw
③ seen   ④ to see
⑤ seeing

02

I was _____ the dishes when he called.

① wash   ② washed
③ washing   ④ to wash
⑤ have washed

03

A: Is the car in the garage theirs?
B: Yes, they _____ it last week.

① buy   ② bought
③ buying   ④ have bought
⑤ to buy

04

다음 밑줄 친 부분의 쓰임이 **잘못된** 것은?

① Shakespeare wrote a lot of plays.
② I have slept for three hours last night.
③ Have you heard from him recently?
④ He has enjoyed traveling since he was young.
⑤ My uncle is coming to our town this afternoon.

[05-07] 빈칸에 들어갈 말이 순서대로 알맞게 짝지어진 것을 고르시오.

05

A: Have you ever _____ to Australia?
B: No, I _____.

① been – have   ② gone – hasn't
③ been – haven't   ④ went – have
⑤ gone – have

06

A: Haven't Tom and Jerry arrived _____?
B: They've _____ arrived. They are
   drinking coffee downstairs.

① already – yet   ② still – already
③ just – yet   ④ already – still
⑤ yet – already

07

A: Have you skated _____ more than 10
   years?
B: Yes, I have skated _____ I was an
   elementary school student.

① for – for   ② for – since
③ since – for   ④ since – before
⑤ before – since

08

다음 두 문장을 한 문장으로 만들 때, 빈칸에 들어갈 말로 알맞은 것은?

My parents went to the beach. So they are not here now.
→ My parents _____ to the beach.

① were going
② are gone
③ have been
④ have gone
⑤ have been going

[09-11] 다음 〈보기〉의 밑줄 친 부분과 쓰임이 같은 것을 고르시오.

09

〈보기〉 I have never played the guitar before.

① She has been to Japan.
② Sam has found his wallet.
③ He has just come back home.
④ My dad has lived here all his life.
⑤ I haven't told my mom the truth yet.

10

〈보기〉 They have been married for 20 years.

① He has loved her since he was nine.
② Lynn has never danced before.
③ Vicky hasn't decided what to do.
④ She has gone to her house.
⑤ I've just met her at the library.

11

〈보기〉 The singer has just arrived at the concert hall.

① Ted has lost his memory.
② Peter hasn't finished cooking yet.
③ Erica has studied Korean since 2010.
④ I have swum in the sea once.
⑤ Willy has never called me.

[12-13] 다음 대화 중 자연스럽지 않은 것을 고르시오.

12

① A: Have you ever tried raw fish?
   B: Yes, I've tried it once.
② A: How long have you collected these dolls?
   B: Since I was seven.
③ A: Where have you been?
   B: I've gone to the bathroom.
④ A: Why is it so cold in here?
   B: Somebody has opened the window.
⑤ A: Have you started your homework?
   B: Not yet.

13

① A: What are you looking for?
   B: I'm looking for my passport.
② A: Are you listening to me?
   B: Yes, I am.
③ A: Can I speak to Victor?
   B: Sorry, but he has just left.
④ A: How long have you lived in Italy?
   B: I've lived there before.
⑤ A: What was he doing when you saw him?
   B: He was washing his hands.

14

다음 우리말을 영어로 바르게 옮긴 것은?

나는 작년부터 다섯 권의 책을 읽었다.

① I'm reading five books for last year.
② I was reading five books since last year.
③ I have read five books for last year.
④ I read five books for last year.
⑤ I have read five books since last year.

15

다음 밑줄 친 부분을 묻는 의문문으로 알맞은 것은?

Julie has worked here for six months.

① How long did Julie work here?
② How much has Julie worked here?
③ How long has Julie worked here?
④ How long have Julie worked here?
⑤ When have Julie worked here?

기출응용

16

다음 중 어법상 옳은 것끼리 짝지어진 것은?

(a) I'm thinking that you have a great idea.
(b) He was looking at the stars in the sky.
(c) Many children are liking cotton candy.
(d) They are having steak with mashed potatoes.
(e) She is going to Jenny's party tonight.

① (a), (b), (c)　　② (a), (c), (e)
③ (b), (c), (d)　　④ (b), (d), (e)
⑤ (c), (d), (e)

17

다음 밑줄 친 부분의 용법이 나머지와 다른 것은?

① She has flown in a plane once.
② We have never made a mistake.
③ They have been on TV three times.
④ He has run in a marathon before.
⑤ I have worked at the grocery for two years.

[18-19] 다음 중 어법상 틀린 것을 고르시오.

18

① It hasn't rained this week.
② When did you meet Joe?
③ Where were you yesterday?
④ He has never seen her face.
⑤ I've bought new clothes two months ago.

19

① He's not taking an art class.
② It was very cold last month.
③ I'm just looking out the window.
④ Billy is studying when I visited him.
⑤ I haven't eaten anything today.

고난도

20

다음 대화의 밑줄 친 부분 중 어법상 틀린 것은?

A: Hey, Mary. ① Have you seen Eric today?
B: He ② has gone to the library. He ③ is preparing for an exam.
A: Oh, no! I ④ haven't finished my Spanish homework yet. I need his help.
B: I ⑤ have lived in Spain when I was young. If you don't mind, I can help you.

서술형 따라잡기

01
다음 두 문장을 한 문장으로 만들 때, 빈칸에 알맞은 말을 쓰시오.

(1) Paul started teaching math ten years ago.
   He still teaches it.
   → Paul _____ _____ math for ten years.

(2) Nina moved to Russia last year.
   So she's not here in Seoul.
   → Nina _____ _____ to Russia.

02
다음 우리말과 뜻이 같도록 주어진 말을 이용하여 대화를 완성하시오.

(1) A: Did you see Tom today?
   B: Yes, _____ _____ _____
   _____ with his friends. (eat lunch)
   (응, 그는 친구들과 점심을 먹고 있었어.)

(2) A: Where is your sister?
   B: She'll be right here in a moment. She
   _____ _____ _____. (arrive)
   (그녀는 아직 도착하지 않았어.)

03
주어진 말을 알맞게 배열하여 우리말과 뜻이 같도록 문장을 완성하시오.

(1) 너는 그곳에 얼마나 오랫동안 있었니?
   (been, have, long, there, you, how)
   → _____

(2) 나는 6살 이후로 쭉 피아노를 쳐 왔다.
   (have, I, six, since, was, played, I, the piano)
   → _____

04
다음 그림을 보고, 주어진 말을 이용하여 Jack의 경험을 나타내는 문장을 완성하시오.

(1) visit France (2) sing on stage (3) make a cake

(1) Jack _____ before.

(2) Jack _____ three times.

(3) Jack _____ once.

05
다음 Ken의 수첩을 보고, 문장을 완성하시오.

Mon.	Tue.	Wed.	Thur.	Fri. (today)
	Have a party			
		Practice dancing		

(1) Ken _____ on Tuesday.

(2) Ken _____ for three days.

고난도

06
다음 대화를 읽고, 어법상 틀린 부분을 모두 찾아 바르게 고쳐 쓰시오. (2군데)

A: Where have you been last weekend?
B: I went to the night market with my cousins from the U.S.
A: I've been there before. It was really exciting. So, when are your cousins going back to the U.S.?
B: They have left tomorrow.

핵심 포인트 정리하기

1 진행형

- 형태: 〈① _____ + _____〉
  - 현재진행형: 〈be동사의 현재형 + v-ing〉 / 현재 진행 중인 일 '~하고 있다', '~하는 중이다'
  - 과거진행형: 〈be동사의 과거형 + v-ing〉 / 과거 특정 시점에 진행 중이던 일 '~하고 있었다'
  - *현재진행형은 가까운 미래에 일어날 일이나 최근에 일어나고 있는 일을 나타내기도 함

 진행형으로 쓰지 않는 동사 확인하기!

2 현재완료

- 의미: 과거에 일어난 일이 현재까지 영향을 미치고 있는 상태
- 형태: 〈② _____ + _____〉
  - 부정형: 〈③ _____ + _____ + _____〉
  - 의문형: 〈Have[Has] + 주어 + v-ed ~?〉

 when이나 특정 과거 시점을 나타내는 말은 현재완료와 함께 쓰지 않는다는 것 기억하기!

- 용법
  - 경험: '~한 적이 있다' [before, ever, never, once 등과 사용]
  - ④ _____ : '벌써/이미/막 ~했다', '아직 ~하지 않았다' [already, just, yet 등과 사용]
  - 계속: '(지금까지 계속) ~해 왔다' [for, since, how long 등과 사용]
  - ⑤ _____ : '~해 버렸다 (그래서 지금은 ~하다)'

 현재완료의 각 용법과 같이 쓰는 부사 표현 알아두기!

문제로 개념 다지기

밑줄 친 부분이 어법상 맞으면 O, 틀리면 X 표시하고 바르게 고치시오.

1 Dan <u>has been</u> to the Golden Gate Bridge twice.

2 She <u>has stayed</u> home since last week.

3 Emily <u>has gone</u> to Turkey two days ago.

4 We <u>are seeing</u> a movie tomorrow.

5 Alice <u>is cleaning</u> the desk when Peter entered the room.

6 He has had this doll <u>for he was young</u>.

7 I <u>was learning</u> how to play the drums these days.

8 My sister <u>is liking</u> K-pop music so much.

CHAPTER 06

조동사

Steven **can** play the piano, but he **can't** play the guitar.

You **must** do it right now.

You **had better** stop watching TV.

Jake **used to** be my friend.

조동사

동사 앞에 쓰여 동사의 기본 의미에 능력, 허가, 예정, 추측, 의무 등의 의미를 더해주는 말입니다. 조동사는 주어의 인칭이나 수에 따라 변하지 않는다는 특징이 있고, 조동사 뒤에는 반드시 동사원 형이 온다는 것을 기억해 두세요.

Point 01 can

- can의 의미
  - 능력(~할 수 있다): He **can** lift this heavy stone with one hand.
  - 허가(~해도 좋다): You **can** drive my car, but please be careful.
  - 요청(~해 주시겠어요?): **Can** you get me some bread?
- can의 부정형은 〈cannot[can't]+동사원형〉, 의문형은 〈Can+주어+동사원형 ~?〉이다.

★ **PLUS TIP**
- 능력을 나타내는 can은 be able to로 바꾸어 쓸 수 있다.
- 요청을 나타낼 때 could를 쓰면 can보다 더 정중한 표현이 된다.

A 다음 문장을 지시대로 바꾸어 쓰시오.

1 You can make noise in a library. (부정문으로)

_____

2 You can call me after 5 p.m. (의문문으로)

_____

3 Mark can tie his shoes without help. (부정문으로)

_____

4 Jeremy can make computer programs. (be able to를 사용)

_____

B 다음 문장을 밑줄 친 부분에 유의하여 우리말로 해석하시오.

1 You <u>can't take</u> photos here.

_____

2 Fish <u>cannot live</u> without water.

_____

3 <u>Can</u> you turn off the TV?

_____

C 다음 우리말과 같은 뜻이 되도록 (   ) 안의 말을 이용하여 문장을 완성하시오.

1 너는 일본어를 할 줄 아니? (speak, Japanese)

_____ _____ _____ _____?

2 너는 내 펜을 사용해도 좋아. (use)

_____ _____ _____ _____ .

3 나에게 컵 하나만 가져다주겠니? (bring)

_____ _____ _____ _____ _____?

may

- may의 의미
  - 허가(~해도 좋다): **May** I eat this jelly?
  - 불확실한 추측(~일지도 모른다): He **may** come to school late today.
- may의 부정형은 〈may not+동사원형〉, 의문형은 〈May+주어+동사원형 ~?〉이다.

A ( ) 안의 말을 알맞게 배열하여 대화를 완성하시오.

1 A: Who is that girl with Mike?
  B: I'm not sure. _____ (be, may, his sister, she)

2 A: Why don't you call your mom?
  B: I left my phone at home. _____ (I, use, may, yours)

3 A: Did you hear that Tony is sick?
  B: Yes, but it _____. (true, not, be, may)

4 A: Where is Judy? I can't find her.
  B: _____ in the library. (be, studying, may, she)

5 A: Mom, _____ Becky? (with, I, play, may)
  B: No, you may not. Do your homework first.

6 A: Where are you going for your vacation?
  B: I'm not sure yet. _____ (go, may, Jeju, to, I)

B 다음 우리말과 같은 뜻이 되도록 ( ) 안의 말을 이용하여 문장을 완성하시오.

1 네 우산을 빌려도 되겠니? (borrow)
  _____ _____ _____ your umbrella?

2 오늘 눈이 올지도 모른다. (snow)
  _____ _____ _____ _____.

3 당신 이메일 주소를 알 수 있을까요? (have)
  _____ _____ _____ your email address?

4 Sharon은 너와 이야기하고 싶어 할지도 모른다. (talk)
  Sharon _____ _____ _____ _____ with you.

5 나는 내년에 이집트로 여행을 갈지도 모른다. (travel)
  I _____ _____ _____ Egypt next year.

6 둘러보셔도 좋지만, 어떤 것도 만지지 마세요. (look around)
  You _____ _____ _____, but do not touch anything.

will / be going to

- **will의 의미**
  - 예정(~일 것이다): She **will** be 16 next year.
  - 의지(~할 것이다): I **will** study hard to pass the exam.
  - 요청(~해 주시겠어요?): **Will** you close the door?
  - 부정형은 〈will not[won't]+동사원형〉, 의문형은 〈Will+주어+동사원형 ~?〉이다.
- **be going to의 의미**
  - 가까운 미래의 일 예측(~일 것이다): It **is going to** rain this afternoon.
  - 계획(~할 것이다): I'**m going to** invite John and Carrie.
  - 부정형은 〈be동사+not+going to+동사원형〉, 의문형은 〈be동사+주어+going to+동사원형 ~?〉이다.

★ *PLUS TIP*　요청을 나타낼 때 would를 쓰면 will보다 더 정중한 표현이 된다.

A　다음 문장을 지시대로 바꾸어 쓰시오.

1　I'm going to go there by subway. (부정문으로)

　　_____

2　Jake will be happy to see her. (의문문으로)

　　_____

3　She is going to meet him at the park. (의문문으로)

　　_____

4　The plane will arrive in 30 minutes. (부정문으로)

　　_____

B　다음 (　) 안의 말을 알맞게 배열하여 대화를 완성하시오.

1　A: What are you going to do after school?
　　B: _____ my uncle's house. (visit, I'm, to, going)

2　A: I don't know how to use this smartphone.
　　B: _____ how to use it. (show, you, will, I)

3　A: Can I borrow your comic book?
　　B: No, _____ today. (I'm, it, to, going, read)

4　A: We're going to go to the movies. Can you come?
　　B: Okay, _____ later. (join, will, I, you)

5　A: Oh, I have no money to pay for this meal.
　　B: Don't worry. _____ (lend, will, some, I, you, money)

must

- must의 의미
  - 의무(~해야 한다): You **must** turn off your cell phone in class.
  - 강한 추측(~임이 틀림없다): She is absent today. She **must** be very sick.
- must의 부정형
  - 금지: must not[mustn't]의 형태로, '~해서는 안 된다'라는 의미이다.
  You **must not** talk during the test.
  - 강한 부정적 추측: cannot[can't]의 형태로, '~일 리가 없다'라는 의미이다.
  She **can't** be in China. I met her this morning.

 ★ 내신만점 *TIP* ▶ must의 의미에 따라 부정형의 형태가 다르다는 것을 기억하자.

A 다음 〈보기〉에서 알맞은 말을 골라 문장을 완성하시오. (단, 한 번씩만 사용할 것)

> 〈보기〉　must be tired　　　　　must drive slowly
> 　　　　　can't lose the game　　must n't tell anyone

1 It is a secret. You _____.

2 Kate studied for seven hours today. She _____.

3 There is a school nearby. You _____.

4 They are the better team. They _____.

B 다음 우리말과 같은 뜻이 되도록 (　) 안의 말을 이용하여 문장을 완성하시오.

1 너는 수업에 빠져서는 안 된다. (miss)
You _____ _____ _____ class.

2 도서관 안에서는 조용히 해야 한다. (be quiet)
You _____ _____ _____ in the library.

3 너는 나가기 전에 불을 꺼야 한다. (turn off)
You _____ _____ _____ the light before leaving.

4 George는 아프다. 그가 학교에 있을 리가 없다. (be at school)
George is sick. He _____ _____ _____ _____.

5 Brian은 매우 잘생겼다. 여자아이들이 그를 좋아하는 것이 틀림없다. (like)
Brian is very handsome. Girls _____ _____ _____.

6 Ted는 여기서 20년 동안 살았다. 그는 이곳의 많은 사람들을 알고 있음이 틀림없다. (know)
Ted has lived here for 20 years. He _____ _____ _____
here.

have to

- have to의 의미
  - '~해야 한다'라는 의미로 의무를 나타내며, 같은 의미의 must와 바꾸어 쓸 수 있다.
  You **have to** listen to me. → You **must** listen to me.
- have to의 부정형은 〈don't[doesn't / didn't] have to+동사원형〉으로 '~할 필요가 없다'라는 의미이며,
  의문형은 〈Do[Does / Did]+주어+have to+동사원형 ~?〉이다.
  You **don't have to** leave now.
  Do I **have to** stand in line?
- have to의 과거형은 had to로 '~해야 했다'라는 의미이다.
  I **had to** study hard for a test.

★ **PLUS TIP**
- must는 과거형이 없으므로 had to를 써서 과거를 나타낸다.
- don't have to는 don't need to 또는 need not(=needn't)으로 바꾸어 쓸 수 있다.

A 다음 문장을 지시대로 바꾸어 쓰시오.

1 I have to finish reading this book today. (부정문으로)

_____

2 She had to send the package. (부정문으로)

_____

3 He has to get up early tomorrow. (의문문으로)

_____

4 We have to take a test now. (의문문으로)

_____

B 다음 우리말과 같은 뜻이 되도록 (   ) 안의 말을 이용하여 문장을 완성하시오.

1 너는 그 파티에 가려면 옷을 차려입어야 했다. (dress up)

_____ _____ _____ _____ to go to the party.

2 내가 그것을 부모님과 상의해야 할까? (discuss)

_____ _____ _____ _____ it with my parents?

3 저희는 언제 진찰을 받아야 하나요? (see)
When _____ we _____ _____ _____ a doctor?

4 그는 전화를 받을 필요가 없다. (pick up)

_____ _____ _____ _____ _____ the

phone.

should

- should의 의미
  - '~해야 한다'라는 의미로, 의무나 충고·조언을 나타낸다.

  You **should** come to my birthday party.

- should의 부정형은 〈should not[shouldn't]+동사원형〉으로 '~하면 안 된다'라는 금지를 나타내며, 의문형은 〈Should+주어+동사원형 ~?〉이다.

  You **should not[shouldn't]** throw stones at animals.

  Should we tell Jack about Diane?

★ *PLUS TIP* should는 must와 의미가 유사하나 must보다 의무의 정도가 약하며, 주로 충고나 권유를 할 때 쓴다.

A 다음 빈칸에 should와 shouldn't 중 알맞은 말을 쓰시오.

1 You _____ visit the Eiffel Tower in Paris.

2 Be quiet. You _____ make noise in the classroom.

3 You _____ eat anything in the concert hall.

4 You _____ touch paintings in the gallery.

5 It's cold outside. You _____ wear a hat and gloves.

6 It is not yours. You _____ take it back to him.

7 It's already dark outside. You _____ stay out so late.

B 다음 우리말과 같은 뜻이 되도록 ( ) 안의 말을 배열하여 문장을 완성하시오.

1 이 영어 문장들을 다 외워야 하나요? (I, memorize, should)

_____ all these English sentences?

2 그에게 이렇게 늦게 전화하면 안 된다. (call, you, not, him, should)

_____ this late.

3 너는 길에 쓰레기를 버리면 안 된다. (should, you, throw, not, garbage)

_____ on the street.

4 우리는 잠자리에 들기 전에 양치질을 해야 한다. (brush, we, our, should, teeth)

_____ before we go to bed.

5 너는 먹기 전에 손을 씻어야 한다. (your, you, hands, wash, should)

_____ before you eat.

6 환경에 도움을 주기 위해 우리는 너무 많은 종이컵을 사용하면 안 된다.
(paper cups, we, too many, use, shouldn't)

To help the environment, _____.

조동사 **85**

would like to / had better

- 〈would like to+동사원형〉은 '~하고 싶다'라는 의미로, want to와 유사하지만 보다 정중한 표현이다.
  I would **like to** try on those shoes.
  - 의문형은 〈Would you like to+동사원형 ~?〉으로 권유를 나타낸다.
  Would you like to dance with me?
- 〈had better+동사원형〉은 '~하는 게 좋겠다'라는 의미로 강한 충고나 권고를 나타내며, 부정형은
  〈had better not+동사원형〉으로 쓴다.
  You **had better** go to school on foot today.
  You **had better not** stay here.

A 다음 밑줄 친 부분을 어법에 맞게 고쳐 쓰시오.

1 She had better to call him right now.

2 You look so sick. You had not better go out tonight.

3 I would like have a hamburger and french fries.

4 Would like you to volunteer for the festival?

B 다음 우리말과 같은 뜻이 되도록 would like to나 had better와 ( ) 안의 말을 이용하여 문장을 완성하시오.

1 나는 월드컵 경기장에서 축구 경기를 보고 싶다. (watch)
_____ a soccer game in World Cup Stadium.

2 이번 주말에 나들이 갈래? (go on a picnic)
_____ this weekend?

3 Tony는 집에서 쉬는 게 좋겠다. (rest)
Tony _____ at home.

4 너는 유럽의 어떤 나라들을 방문하고 싶니? (country, visit)
_____ in Europe?

5 너는 쓸모없는 것에 돈을 쓰지 않는 게 좋겠다. (spend)
_____ on useless things.

6 밖에 비가 오고 있다. 우리는 우리의 계획을 변경하는 게 좋겠다. (change)
It's raining outside. _____ our plans.

7 나는 피곤해. 지금 자러 가고 싶어. (go to sleep)
I'm tired. _____ now.

8 너는 그것에 관해 이야기하지 않는 게 좋겠다. (talk about)
_____ it.

used to / would

- 〈used to+동사원형〉은 과거의 습관이나 상태를 나타낸다.
  - 과거의 습관(~하곤 했다): He **used to** play tennis every morning.
  - 과거의 상태((전에는) ~이었다): There **used to** be a photo studio here.
- 〈would+동사원형〉은 과거의 습관을 나타낸다.

  When I was a child, I **would** go camping with my friends.

★ 내신만점 *TIP* 과거의 상태를 나타낼 때는 would를 쓸 수 없다는 점에 유의하자.
There **used to**[would] be a bookstore near my house.

A 다음 ( ) 안의 말을 배열하여 문장을 완성하시오.

1 Dan _____ a small town. (in, to, live, used)

2 I _____ in summer. (go, would, swimming)

3 He _____ when he was young. (shy, used, be, to, very)

4 I _____ when I was a child. (onions, to, hate, used)

5 Bobby _____ , but now he is a musician.
(be, to, a car designer, used)

6 Olivia _____ , but now she wants to be a teacher.
(a writer, to, being, dream of, used)

B 다음 문장을 밑줄 친 부분에 유의하여 우리말로 해석하시오.

1 This town used to be very peaceful.

_____

2 The house used to be white, but now it looks gray.

_____

3 My dog would often run fast when it snowed.

_____

4 Mary used to read a lot, but now she doesn't.

_____

5 My father would go fishing on weekends.

_____

6 There used to be a big apple tree here.

_____

7 Mike used to like cheese, but now he doesn't.

_____

내신대비 TEST

[01-03] 다음 빈칸에 알맞은 말을 고르시오.

01

A: Can you move this chair?
B: Sure. I _____ do it.

① could   ② will
③ used to   ④ should
⑤ have to

02

A: May I use this washing machine now?
B: No, you _____.

① may not   ② wouldn't
③ need to   ④ won't
⑤ don't have to

03

A: Oh, I left my wallet in the shop.
B: You had better _____ there now!

① go   ② went   ③ to go
④ going   ⑤ be go

[04-06] 다음 우리말과 뜻이 같도록 빈칸에 알맞은 말을 고르시오.

04

그는 지금 그녀와 함께 있을지도 모른다.
He _____ be with her now.

① will   ② may   ③ had better
④ must   ⑤ would

05

너는 점심을 가져올 필요가 없다.
You _____ bring your lunch.

① may not   ② must not
③ cannot   ④ don't have to
⑤ will not

06

그녀는 지금 당장 일을 시작하는 게 좋겠다.
She _____ start working right now.

① used to   ② would
③ had better   ④ should not
⑤ would like to

기출응용
[07-08] 다음 〈보기〉와 의미가 가장 가까운 것을 고르시오.

07

〈보기〉 She need not come here at seven.

① She must not come here at seven.
② She may not come here at seven.
③ She should not come here at seven.
④ She had better not come here at seven.
⑤ She doesn't have to come here at seven.

08

〈보기〉 They went skating in winter, but they
        don't anymore.

① They can't go skating in winter.
② They won't go skating in winter.
③ They used to go skating in winter.
④ They should go skating in winter.
⑤ They would like to go skating in winter.

09

A: Jason _____ be very close to Ann.
B: Yes, they _____ take violin lessons
together.

① should – can
② must – used to
③ can – have to
④ would – must
⑤ may – can't

10

A: _____ I go there right now?
B: No, you don't _____ .

① Can – have to
② Could – used to
③ Should – have to
④ Must – need not
⑤ Should – used to

11

A: I _____ be a professor someday.
B: Then you _____ study harder.

① may – should
② must – used to
③ can – may
④ used to – can
⑤ would like to – should

12

• We're late. We _____ hurry.
• He _____ be rich. He's wearing
expensive clothes.

① must
② could
③ used to
④ must not
⑤ don't have to

13

• _____ you like to go camping this
weekend?
• I _____ often read comic books when I
was a child.

① May[may]
② Must[must]
③ Could[could]
④ Would[would]
⑤ Should[should]

14

다음 대화 중 자연스럽지 <u>않은</u> 것은?

① A: Should I go to the meeting?
   B: No, you don't have to.
② A: May I take your order?
   B: I would like to have the seafood pasta.
③ A: May I help you?
   B: Yes, I'm looking for a pair of sunglasses.
④ A: Do you have a pet now?
   B: Yes, I used to have one.
⑤ A: Are you going to come to the party
   tonight?
   B: Yes, I am.

[15-16] 다음 밑줄 친 부분의 뜻이 나머지와 <u>다른</u> 것을 고르시오.

15

① George <u>may</u> not pass the exam. He didn't study hard.

② You <u>may</u> visit me on Saturday.

③ You <u>may</u> know my brother. He lives near your house.

④ There <u>may</u> be a lot of people in the park.

⑤ He <u>may</u> not have enough money to buy this camera.

16

① We <u>must</u> get there on time.

② You <u>must</u> be polite to the guests.

③ You <u>must</u> turn off your phone in the movie theater.

④ I <u>must</u> save some money to buy a laptop.

⑤ Somebody knocked on the door. It <u>must</u> be Jerry.

17

다음 우리말을 영어로 옮긴 것 중 <u>잘못된</u> 것은?

① 제가 먼저 가도 될까요?
   May I go first?

② 나는 그녀에게 다시 전화하지 않을 거야.
   I won't call her again.

③ 이곳에는 개를 데리고 들어오실 수 없습니다.
   You can't bring your dog in here.

④ 우리는 그 아이들에 대해 걱정할 필요가 없다.
   We must not worry about the kids.

⑤ 전에는 여기에 오래된 공장이 있었었다.
   There used to be an old factory here.

18

빈칸에 들어갈 말이 나머지와 <u>다른</u> 것은?

① In the UK, you _____ drive on the left.

② We _____ always respect older people.

③ You _____ not yell in the classroom.

④ You _____ wear a seat belt in a car.

⑤ _____ you like to go to the play tonight?

19

다음 중 어법상 <u>틀린</u> 것은?

① I didn't have to pay to download the file.

② David had better to wear a hat.

③ I used to be overweight, but I'm slim now.

④ Everybody would like to be a winner.

⑤ Gary and I are going to have dinner together.

고난도

20

다음 중 어법상 옳은 것끼리 짝지어진 것은?

(a) You are able not to stay here.

(b) This handwriting must be Daniel's.

(c) She must give him a present last night.

(d) He had better not wear those pants.

(e) I used to have long hair, but now I have short hair.

① (a), (b), (d)　　② (a), (c), (e)

③ (b), (c), (d)　　④ (b), (d), (e)

⑤ (c), (d), (e)

서술형 따라잡기

01

다음 두 문장이 같은 뜻이 되도록 빈칸에 알맞은 말을 쓰시오.

(1) Will you take a bus?

→ _____ _____ _____

take a bus?

(2) She cannot move the statue by herself.

→ She _____ _____ _____

_____ move the statue by herself.

02

주어진 말을 알맞게 배열하여 우리말과 뜻이 같도록 문장을 완성하시오.

(1) 나는 스페인어를 공부하고 싶다.

(I, Spanish, like, study, to, would)

→ _____

(2) 그는 그 공원에 가지 않는 게 좋겠다.

(to, had, the, he, park, not, better, go)

→ _____

03

다음 그림을 보고, 조동사와 주어진 말을 이용하여 문장을 완성하시오.

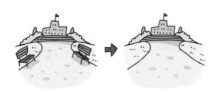

_____ _____ _____ _____ _____,

but now there aren't any. (there, bench)

04

조동사와 주어진 말을 이용하여 대화를 완성하시오.

A: Somebody is ringing the doorbell. Is it Andrew?

B: No. It _____ _____ him. (be)

He's in the kitchen now.

05

각 상자에서 알맞은 말을 골라 문장을 완성하시오.
(단, 한 번씩만 사용할 것)

| may
cannot
must | be the thief
not tell her
be windy tonight |

(1) Why don't you wear a jacket? It _____

_____ _____ _____.

(2) She'll be shocked if she finds out the truth. So you _____ _____ _____

_____.

(3) He was with me when someone stole your wallet. So he _____ _____ _____

_____.

고난도

06

빈칸에 알맞은 조동사를 넣어 대화를 완성하시오.

A: What do you want for dinner?

B: I can't eat anything.

A: Oh, you _____ be sick. You have a fever.

B: Yes, I don't feel well.

A: You _____ _____ go see a doctor now.

B: I _____ _____ _____. I've already taken some medicine.

핵심 포인트 정리하기

- 조동사

can	1) 능력: '~할 수 있다' 2) 허가: '~해도 좋다' 3) 요청: '~해 주시겠어요?'	① _____	1) 허가: '~해도 좋다' 2) 불확실한 추측: '~일지도 모른다'	
② _____	1) 예정: '~일 것이다' 2) 의지: '~할 것이다' 3) 요청: '~해 주시겠어요?'	be going to	1) 가까운 미래의 일 예측: '~일 것이다' 2) 계획: '~할 것이다'	
must	1) 의무: '~해야 한다' 2) 강한 추측: '~임이 틀림없다'		1) 부정형 (금지): '~해서는 안 된다' 　= ③ _____ 2) 부정형 (강한 부정적 추측): '~일 리가 없다' 　= ④ _____	
have to	1) 의무: '~해야 한다' (= must) 2) 부정형: '~할 필요가 없다' 〈⑤ _____ +동사원형〉	should	의무·충고·조언: '~해야 한다'	
would like to	1) '~하고 싶다' 2) 의문형(권유) 〈Would you like to+동사원형 ~?〉	had better	1) 강한 충고나 권고: '~하는 게 좋겠다' 2) 부정형 〈⑥ _____ +동사원형〉	
⑦ _____	1) 과거의 습관: '~하곤 했다' 2) 과거의 상태: '(전에는) ~이었다'	would	과거의 습관	

시험만은 꼭! must와 have to의 부정형과 의미 구분하기!
과거의 상태를 나타내는 used to의 쓰임 기억하기!

문제로 개념 다지기

밑줄 친 부분이 어법상 맞으면 O, 틀리면 X 표시하고 바르게 고치시오.

1 무엇을 마시고 싶으세요?
　What would you like to drink?

2 나는 화가 나면 열까지 세곤 했다.
　When I got angry, I would count up to ten.

3 너는 내게 그 이야기를 할 필요가 없다.
　You have not to tell me the story.

4 Jake는 전에는 나의 가장 친한 친구였었다.
　Jake is used to be my best friend.

5 이 수업에서는 휴대전화를 사용하지 않는 것이 좋겠다.
　You had not better use your cell phone in this class.

CHAPTER 07

비교 표현

My brother is **as tall as** that tree. [원급]

The sun is **brighter than** the moon. [비교급]

These shoes are **the newest** item in the store. [최상급]

비교 표현

둘 이상의 사람이나 사물의 성질·상태를 비교하는 것으로, 형용사나 부사의 형태를 그대로
사용하거나 변형하여 원급, 비교급, 최상급 비교를 표현할 수 있습니다.

원급 비교 – as ~ as 구문

- 〈as+형용사/부사의 원급+as〉는 '~만큼 …한[하게]'라고 해석한다.
  Jason can dance **as well as** Roy.
- 부정형은 〈not+as[so]+형용사/부사의 원급+as〉이며, '~만큼 …하지 않은[않게]'라고 해석한다.
  Jackson is**n't as[so] shy as** his brother.

★ **PLUS TIP** 〈as+원급+as possible〉은 '가능한 한 ~한[하게]'라는 뜻으로, 〈as+원급+as+주어+can[could]〉로 바꾸어 쓸 수 있다.

A 다음 우리말과 같은 뜻이 되도록 ( ) 안의 말을 이용하여 문장을 완성하시오.

1 오늘도 어제만큼 춥다. (cold)
　Today is ＿＿＿＿ ＿＿＿＿ ＿＿＿＿ yesterday.

2 이 휴대전화는 노트북 컴퓨터만큼이나 비싸다. (expensive)
　This cell phone is ＿＿＿＿ ＿＿＿＿ ＿＿＿＿ a laptop.

3 아프리카 코끼리는 대왕고래만큼 무겁지 않다. (heavy)
　African elephants ＿＿＿＿ ＿＿＿＿ ＿＿＿＿ ＿＿＿＿ blue whales.

4 네 오토바이는 내 것만큼 빠르지 않다. (fast)
　Your motorcycle ＿＿＿＿ ＿＿＿＿ ＿＿＿＿ ＿＿＿＿ mine.

5 중국은 캐나다만큼 크지 않다. (large)
　China is ＿＿＿＿ ＿＿＿＿ ＿＿＿＿ Canada.

6 Jamie는 가능한 한 빨리 나에게 전화를 할 것이다. (call, soon)
　Jamie will ＿＿＿＿ ＿＿＿＿ ＿＿＿＿ ＿＿＿＿ ＿＿＿＿ possible.

B 다음 주어진 문장과 같은 뜻이 되도록 as ~ as를 이용하여 문장을 완성하시오.

1 Peter is 180 cm tall. Jack is 180 cm tall, too.
　→ Peter ＿＿＿＿＿＿＿＿＿＿＿＿＿ .

2 My tablet PC is new. Yours is equally new.
　→ My tablet PC ＿＿＿＿＿＿＿＿＿＿＿＿＿ .

3 Nick is 25 years old, and his girlfriend is 22.
　→ Nick's girlfriend ＿＿＿＿＿＿＿＿＿＿＿＿＿ he is.

4 Baseball is popular in Korea. Soccer is equally popular in Korea.
　→ Baseball is ＿＿＿＿＿＿＿＿＿＿＿ soccer in Korea.

5 I tried to run as quickly as possible.
　→ I tried to run ＿＿＿＿＿＿＿＿＿＿＿＿＿ .

비교급＋than / 비교급 만드는 법 – 규칙 변화

- 〈형용사/부사의 비교급＋than〉은 '〜보다 더 …한[하게]'라고 해석한다.
  Ethan is **cuter than** his brother.
- 비교급 만드는 법

대부분의 단어	＋-er	fast – fast**er**
-e로 끝나는 단어	＋-r	large – larg**er**
〈단모음＋단자음〉으로 끝나는 단어	자음을 한 번 더 쓰고＋-er	fat – fat**ter**
-y로 끝나는 단어	y를 i로 바꾸고＋-er	happy – happ**ier**
-ful/-ous/-less/-ing/-ive 등으로 끝나는 단어	단어의 앞에 **more**	beautiful – **more** beautiful
3음절 이상의 단어		

 내신만점 TIP much, even, still, far, a lot 등의 부사는 '훨씬'이라는 의미로 비교급을 강조한다는 것을 알아두자.
Let's take the subway. It's **much** *faster* and *cheaper*.

A 다음 〈보기〉에서 알맞은 말을 골라 비교급 문장을 완성하시오.

〈보기〉 early   important   difficult   clean

1 Your desk is always ＿＿＿＿＿ ＿＿＿＿＿ mine.

2 Health is ＿＿＿＿＿ ＿＿＿＿＿ ＿＿＿＿＿ money.

3 That question was ＿＿＿＿＿ ＿＿＿＿＿ ＿＿＿＿＿ the other ones, so I couldn't answer it.

4 Today, Carol went to bed ＿＿＿＿＿ ＿＿＿＿＿ she did yesterday.

B 다음 ( ) 안에서 알맞은 말을 고르시오.

1 The polar bear is as (tall / taller) as the brown bear.

2 The situation is (very / much) more serious than I thought.

3 This theater has (larger / more large) screens than the other theater.

C 다음 우리말과 같은 뜻이 되도록 ( ) 안의 말을 이용하여 문장을 완성하시오.

1 Jake는 그의 남동생보다 힘이 더 세다. (strong)
Jake is ＿＿＿＿＿ ＿＿＿＿＿ his brother.

2 그의 가방은 내 것보다 더 화려하다. (colorful)
His bag is ＿＿＿＿＿ ＿＿＿＿＿ ＿＿＿＿＿ ＿＿＿＿＿.

3 내 침실은 그녀의 것보다 훨씬 더 크다. (much, big)
My bedroom is ＿＿＿＿＿ ＿＿＿＿＿ ＿＿＿＿＿ ＿＿＿＿＿.

the+최상급/최상급 만드는 법 – 규칙 변화

■ 〈the+형용사/부사의 최상급〉은 '가장 ~한[하게]'이라고 해석하며, 최상급 뒤에 in이나 of를 써서 비교 대상의 범위를 나타내기도 한다.

Which is **the largest** country **in** the world?
(the+최상급+in+장소·범위를 나타내는 단수명사: ~ (안)에서 가장 …한[하게])

Yesterday was **the coldest** day **of** the year.
(the+최상급+of+비교 대상이 되는 명사: ~ 중에서 가장 …한[하게])

■ 최상급 만드는 법

대부분의 단어	+-est	fast – faster – fast**est**
-e로 끝나는 단어	+-st	large – larger – larg**est**
〈단모음+단자음〉으로 끝나는 단어	자음을 한 번 더 쓰고 +-est	fat – fatter – fat**test**
-y로 끝나는 단어	y를 i로 바꾸고 +-est	happy – happier – happ**iest**
-ful/-ous/-less/-ing/-ive 등으로 끝나는 단어	단어의 앞에 **most**	beautiful – more beautiful – **most** beautiful
3음절 이상의 단어		

A 다음 우리말과 같은 뜻이 되도록 ( ) 안의 말을 이용하여 문장을 완성하시오.

1 Jessica는 우리 반에서 가장 똑똑한 학생이다. (smart)
Jessica is _____ _____ student in my class.

2 오늘은 1년 중 가장 더운 날이다. (hot)
Today is _____ _____ day of the year.

3 이것이 알파벳을 가르치는 가장 유용한 방법이다. (useful)
This is _____ _____ _____ way to teach the alphabet.

B 다음 우리말과 같은 뜻이 되도록 ( ) 안의 말을 배열하여 문장을 완성하시오.

1 결혼식 날은 그녀의 인생에서 가장 행복한 날이었다. (happiest, of, day, the, her life)
Her wedding day was _____ .

2 여기가 영화에서 가장 슬픈 부분이다. (part, of, saddest, the, the movie)
This is _____ .

3 Celine은 그녀의 나라에서 가장 유명한 가수이다.
(most, the, her country, famous, in, singer)
Celine is _____ .

4 Alan이 그의 반에서 가장 흥미로운 에세이를 썼다.
(his class, most, in, interesting, essay, the)
Alan wrote _____ .

비교급·최상급 만드는 법 – 불규칙 변화

■ 비교급과 최상급이 불규칙하게 변화하는 경우도 있으므로 주의한다.

원급	비교급	최상급
good / well	better	best
bad / ill / badly	worse	worst
many / much	more	most
little	less	least
far	(거리) farther / (정도) further	(거리) farthest / (정도) furthest

A 다음 밑줄 친 부분을 어법에 맞게 고쳐 쓰시오.

1 The sad song made me feel much badder.

2 You have to go a lot farer to get to the bus stop.

3 Ann got the goodest grade in her class last week.

4 Johnny has the most bad handwriting in his class.

5 Diana's cookies were good, but yours are best than hers.

6 I was tired yesterday, so I went to bed more early than the day before.

7 I thought my mother loved my sister much than me.

8 Who has the little amount of homework to do?

B 다음 우리말과 같은 뜻이 되도록 〈보기〉에서 알맞은 말을 골라 빈칸에 적절한 형태로 써넣으시오.

〈보기〉　bad　　　　far　　　　good　　　　little

1 그것은 내 인생에서 최악의 실수였다.
It was _____ mistake of my life.

2 비가 올 가능성은 10% 미만이다.
The chance of rain is _____ than 10 percent.

3 우리 학교에서 누가 가장 멀리 뛸 수 있니?
Who can jump _____ in our school?

4 오늘의 교통 상황은 어제보다 안 좋다.
Today's traffic is _____ than yesterday's.

5 이 노란색 우산이 저 검은 것보다 훨씬 낫다.
This yellow umbrella is much _____ than that black one.

비교 구문을 이용한 표현 I – 배수사를 이용한 비교

- 〈배수사+as+원급+as〉는 '~의 몇 배 …한[하게]'의 의미로, 〈배수사+비교급+than〉으로 바꾸어 쓸 수 있다.
  배수사란 twice, three times 등과 같이 '~ 배'를 나타내는 말이다.
  This bridge is **three times as long as** that bridge.
  → This bridge is **three times longer than** that bridge.
- twice는 〈배수사+as+원급+as〉의 형태로만 사용하며, 〈배수사+비교급+than〉의 형태로는 쓰지 않는다.

★ **내신만점 TIP** 　배수사를 이용한 비교 구문의 어순에 유의하자.

A 　다음 우리말과 같은 뜻이 되도록 ( ) 안의 말을 배열하여 문장을 완성하시오.

1 이 책은 내 책보다 세 배 더 두껍다. (than, times, thicker, is, three)
This book ＿＿＿＿＿＿＿＿＿＿＿＿＿＿＿ my book.

2 우리 삼촌은 나보다 나이가 두 배 더 많으시다. (as, me, twice, old, as, is)
My uncle ＿＿＿＿＿＿＿＿＿＿＿＿＿＿＿ .

3 우리 누나는 나보다 돈을 열 배 더 썼다. (ten, than, more, times, money, spent)
My sister ＿＿＿＿＿＿＿＿＿＿＿＿＿＿＿ me.

4 그 영화배우의 밴은 내 차보다 세 배 더 컸다. (larger, times, than, three, was)
The movie star's van ＿＿＿＿＿＿＿＿＿＿＿＿＿＿＿ my car.

5 아버지의 시계는 내 것보다 다섯 배 더 비싸다. (expensive, as, times, five, as, is)
My father's watch ＿＿＿＿＿＿＿＿＿＿＿＿＿＿＿ mine.

6 그 가수의 2집은 1집보다 네 배 더 많이 팔렸다. (as, four, as, copies, times, many)
The singer's second album sold ＿＿＿＿＿＿＿＿＿＿＿＿＿＿＿ her first album.

B 　다음 두 문장이 같은 뜻이 되도록 원급이나 비교급을 이용하여 문장을 완성하시오.

1 France is five times bigger than Korea.
→ France is ＿＿＿＿＿＿＿＿＿＿＿＿＿＿＿ Korea.

2 My turtle lived three times longer than my puppy.
→ My turtle lived ＿＿＿＿＿＿＿＿＿＿＿＿＿＿＿ my puppy.

3 David finished the work three times as fast as you.
→ David finished the work ＿＿＿＿＿＿＿＿＿＿＿＿＿＿＿ you.

4 My home is four times as far as yours from the school.
→ My home is ＿＿＿＿＿＿＿＿＿＿＿＿＿＿＿ yours from the school.

Point 06 비교 구문을 이용한 표현 II − the＋비교급, the＋비교급 / 비교급＋and＋비교급

- ⟨the＋비교급, the＋비교급⟩은 '~(하면) 할수록 더 …하다'라고 해석한다.
  The more I thought about him, **the more** I missed him.
- ⟨비교급＋and＋비교급⟩은 '점점 더 ~한[하게]'라고 해석한다.
  Spring is coming. It's getting **warmer and warmer**.

A 다음 밑줄 친 부분을 어법에 맞게 고쳐 쓰시오.

1 It's getting dark and dark outside.

2 The cloudy the weather is, the worse I feel.

3 I got much and much nervous before the game.

4 The blood pressure of giraffes is twice high as that of humans.

5 The later you go to bed, more difficult waking up is.

6 This winter is not cold as last winter.

7 Driving a car at night is much dangerous than during the day.

8 Edwin got three times many gifts than Charles.

B 다음 우리말과 같은 뜻이 되도록 ( ) 안의 말을 이용하여 문장을 완성하시오.

1 점점 더 많은 사람들이 소셜 네트워킹 사이트를 이용하고 있다. (many)
_____ people are using social networking sites.

2 네가 운동을 열심히 할수록, 너의 건강은 더 좋아진다. (hard, good)
_____ you exercise, _____ your health gets.

3 그를 더 오래 기다릴수록, 나는 더 화가 났다. (long, angry)
_____ I waited for him, _____ I got.

4 그녀를 더 알면 알수록, 나는 그녀가 더 좋다. (much, much)
_____ I get to know her, _____ I like her.

5 우리는 직장에서 점점 더 바빠지고 있다. (busy)
We are getting _____ at work.

6 그 소음 때문에, Judy의 목소리는 점점 더 커졌다. (loud)
Because of the noise, Judy's voice got _____.

7 피노키오의 코는 그가 거짓말을 할 때면 점점 더 길어졌다. (long)
Pinocchio's nose got _____ when he told lies.

비교 구문을 이용한 표현 Ⅲ - Which ~ 비교급 / one of the + 최상급 + 복수명사

- 〈Which[Who] ~ 비교급, A or B?〉는 'A와 B 중에 어느 것이[누가] 더 ~한가?'라고 해석한다.
  Which is **more delicious**, strawberry ice cream **or** vanilla ice cream?
- 〈one of the + 최상급 + 복수명사〉는 '가장 ~한 것[사람]들 중 하나'라고 해석한다.
  The *Mona Lisa* is **one of the most famous paintings** in the world.

★ 내신만점 *TIP* 〈one of the + 최상급〉 뒤에 오는 명사가 복수인지 확인하자.

A 다음 문장에서 <u>틀린</u> 부분을 찾아 어법에 맞게 고쳐 쓰시오.

1 Mozart is one of the greatest musician in history.

2 Which planet is biggest, Earth or Mars?

3 Who is more popular, Iron Man and Captain America?

4 Bill Gates is one of the rich men in the world.

5 Which is more convenienter, the bus or the subway?

6 Rome is one of the most famous city in Europe.

B 다음 우리말과 같은 뜻이 되도록 문장을 완성하시오.

1 Sarah와 Chris 중에 누가 더 나이가 많니?
_____ _____ _____, Sarah or Chris?

2 미시시피와 아마존 강 중에 어느 것이 더 길지?
_____ _____ _____, the Mississippi or the Amazon?

3 영어로 쓰는 것과 말하는 것 중에 어느 것이 더 어렵니?
_____ _____ _____ _____, writing in English or speaking
in English?

C 다음 우리말과 같은 뜻이 되도록 (   ) 안의 말을 배열하여 문장을 완성하시오.

1 Mike는 그 팀에서 가장 잘생긴 축구 선수들 중 한 명이다. (the, of, one, handsome, most)
Mike is _____ soccer players on the team.

2 프라이드 치킨은 한국에서 가장 인기 있는 음식들 중 하나이다.
(popular, one, the, foods, most, of)
Fried chicken is _____ in Korea.

3 피지는 세계에서 가장 아름다운 섬들 중 하나이다.
(of, islands, beautiful, the, most, one)
Fiji is _____ in the world.

최상급 표현 – 원급과 비교급 이용

■ 원급과 비교급을 이용하여 최상급을 표현할 수 있다.

No (other)+단수명사 ~ as[so]+원급+as	어떤 ~도 …만큼 ~하지 않은[않게]
No (other)+단수명사 ~ 비교급+than	어떤 ~도 …보다 더 ~하지 않은[않게]
비교급+than any other+단수명사	다른 어떤 ~보다 더 …한[하게]
비교급+than all the other+복수명사	다른 모든 ~보다 더 …한[하게]

Ian is **the sweetest boy** in my school.
→ **No (other) boy** in my school is **as[so] sweet as** Ian.
→ **No (other) boy** in my school is **sweeter than** Ian.
→ Ian is **sweeter than any other boy** in my school.
→ Ian is **sweeter than all the other boys** in my school.

A 다음 문장들이 같은 뜻이 되도록 빈칸에 알맞은 말을 쓰시오.

1 History is the hardest subject.

→ _____ subject is _____ _____ _____ history.

→ _____ subject is _____ _____ history.

→ History is _____ _____ _____ _____ .

→ History is _____ _____ _____ _____ _____ .

2 This is the most expensive book in this bookstore.

→ _____ book in this bookstore is _____ _____ _____ this one.

→ _____ book in this bookstore is _____ _____ _____ this one.

→ This book is _____ _____ _____ _____ _____ in this bookstore.

→ This book is _____ _____ _____ in this bookstore.

B 다음 우리말과 같은 뜻이 되도록 (   ) 안의 말을 배열하여 문장을 완성하시오.

1 이 장미는 이 정원에 있는 다른 어떤 꽃보다 더 아름답다.
(other, any, more, than, flower, beautiful)
This rose is _____ in this garden.

2 요즘 어떤 디자이너도 그녀만큼 유명하지 않다. (famous, as, as, designer, her, no)
_____ is _____ these days.

3 어떤 스포츠도 스피드 스케이팅보다 흥미진진하지 않다. (exciting, more, sport, no, than)
_____ is _____ speed skating.

[01-03] 다음 빈칸에 알맞은 말을 고르시오.

01

A: How's the weather today?
B: It's _____ than yesterday.

① good   ② better   ③ best
④ more   ⑤ most

02

A: Excuse me, I'm looking for a cap.
B: How about this one? It is the _____ one in this shop.

① as popular   ② popularer
③ popularest   ④ more popular
⑤ most popular

03

This travel app is as _____ a guide book.

① useful   ② more useful as
③ the most useful   ④ useful as
⑤ more useful than

기출응용

04

다음 빈칸에 들어갈 수 없는 말은?

A: I'm going to buy a bicycle here.
B: Why don't you buy one at Jack's Bike Shop instead? They're _____ cheaper.

① very   ② a lot   ③ much
④ even   ⑤ far

[05-06] 빈칸에 들어갈 말이 순서대로 알맞게 짝지어진 것을 고르시오.

05

A: Who runs _____, you or Tom?
B: Tom runs twice as _____ as me.

① fast – faster   ② fast – fast
③ faster – fast   ④ fastest – fast
⑤ faster – faster

06

• The younger you are, the _____ it is to learn a foreign language.
• The elephant is the _____ animal in this zoo.

① easy – larger   ② easier – larger
③ easier – largest   ④ easiest – larger
⑤ easiest – largest

07

다음 대화 중 자연스럽지 <u>않은</u> 것은?

① A: Which bag do you want?
   B: A big one. The bigger, the better.
② A: It's getting hotter and hotter.
   B: That's because winter is coming.
③ A: Who is taller, Hal or Adam?
   B: I think Hal is taller than Adam.
④ A: I'm getting fatter and fatter.
   B: You had better exercise.
⑤ A: Do you like your new dishwasher?
   B: No. It takes twice as much time as my old one.

08

Mary is older than I am.

① I'm as old as Mary.
② Mary isn't so old as I am.
③ I'm not as old as Mary.
④ Mary isn't older than I am.
⑤ Mary isn't the oldest.

09

Today is the best day of my life.

① Today is better day of my life.
② Today is better than any other day of my life.
③ Today is the best than any other day of my life.
④ Today is better than any other days of my life.
⑤ Today is the best than all the other days of my life.

10

다음 우리말을 영어로 바르게 옮긴 것은?

너는 이탈리아 음식과 태국 음식 중 어느 것이 더 좋니?

① What is the best, Italian or Thai food?
② What do you like better, Italian food and Thai food?
③ Which do you like the best, Italian food or Thai food?
④ Which do you like better, Italian food or Thai food?
⑤ Which do you like better than Italian food or Thai food?

11

① You don't work <u>as hard as</u> I do.
② His rain boots are <u>nice than</u> mine.
③ I can't speak French <u>as well as</u> you can.
④ I feel <u>much better than</u> I did yesterday.
⑤ He has lived here <u>longer than</u> you have.

12

① Jake is <u>the funniest</u> of my friends.
② He is one of <u>the greatest scientist</u> in the world.
③ Amy is more attractive than <u>any other model</u> in the fashion show.
④ Jupiter is <u>the largest planet</u> in the solar system.
⑤ Who's <u>the richest man</u> in the world?

기출응용

13

다음 빈칸에 high의 비교급 또는 최상급이 들어갈 수 없는 것은?

① David can jump as _____ as Alex.
② Which is _____, Mt. Taebaek or Mt. Jiri?
③ Prices are getting _____ and _____.
④ The _____ I climbed, the more tired I got.
⑤ The _____ building in Korea is in Songpa-gu, Seoul.

14

다음 두 문장이 같은 뜻이 되도록 할 때, 빈칸에 알맞은 말은?

No student in my class is as cheerful as Tasha.
→ Tasha is _____ any other student in my class.

① as cheerful as
② not as cheerful as
③ not cheerful than
④ less cheerful than
⑤ more cheerful than

[15-16] 다음 표의 내용과 일치하는 것을 고르시오.

15

City	Seoul	Daegu	Busan
Temperature	29 °C	31 °C	27 °C

① Busan is as cool as Seoul.
② Seoul isn't cooler than Daegu.
③ Daegu isn't warmer than Seoul.
④ Daegu is warmer than all the other cities.
⑤ Busan is warmer than Daegu.

16

Name	James	Sunmi	Ted
Weight	64 kg	53 kg	72 kg
Height	170 cm	165 cm	181 cm

① James is taller than Ted.
② Ted is lighter than James.
③ Ted isn't heavier than Sunmi.
④ James is shorter than any other person.
⑤ Sunmi is the lightest of the three.

기출응용

17

다음 각 빈칸에 들어갈 말로 알맞지 않은 것은?

• She spoke as ____①____ as possible.
• ____②____ is more spicy, curry or tteok-bokki?
• Asia is ____③____ any other continent in the world.
• This tunnel is ____④____ that tunnel.
• The harder I worked, ____⑤____ the time passed.

① slowly   ② Which
③ larger than   ④ four times as longer as
⑤ the faster

[18-19] 다음 중 어법상 틀린 것을 고르시오.

18

① You look much better in that suit.
② Grace looks younger than she really is.
③ It's getting hard and hard to run.
④ The more I eat, the more weight I'll gain.
⑤ She has three times more books than I have.

19

① He is the most diligent boy in his class.
② The more one has, more one wants.
③ My brother earns more than I do.
④ Who is funnier, Brad or Jacob?
⑤ It was the most exciting game ever.

고난도

20

다음 중 어법상 옳은 것끼리 짝지어진 것은?

(a) No boy in this school is as smart as Peter.
(b) Your eyes are brighter than the stars.
(c) I don't go swimming as often as you do.
(d) Your son's hair is as curlier as yours.
(e) She is one of the most humorous girl in the tennis club.

① (a), (b), (c)   ② (a), (c), (e)
③ (b), (c), (e)   ④ (b), (d), (e)
⑤ (c), (d), (e)

서술형 따라잡기

01

주어진 말을 이용하여 우리말과 뜻이 같도록 문장을 완성하시오.

(1) 저 영화는 원작보다 더 재미있다. (interesting)

→ That movie is _____ _____ the original book.

(2) 그것은 올해 최악의 연설이었다. (bad)

→ It was _____ _____ speech of the year.

02

다음 두 문장이 같은 뜻이 되도록 빈칸에 알맞은 말을 쓰시오.

(1) Their new song is less exciting than their old one.

→ Their new song is _____ _____ _____ _____ their old one.

(2) That building is three times as tall as my apartment building.

→ That building is _____ _____ _____ _____ my apartment building.

03

어법상 틀린 부분을 찾아 바르게 고쳐 쓰시오.

(1) Russia is bigger than all the other country in the world. (1군데)

(2) His painting is the more impressive painting in this gallery. It is as twice big as the other paintings. (2군데)

04

다음 그림을 보고, 주어진 말을 이용하여 비교하는 문장을 완성하시오.

Dress A	Dress B	Dress C
$ 400	$ 100	$ 90

(1) Dress A is _____ _____ dress B. (expensive)

(2) Dress C is _____ _____ of all the dresses. (cheap)

05

다음 표를 보고, 빈칸에 알맞은 말을 쓰시오.

River	Nile	Amazon
길이(km)	6,853 km	6,992 km

(1) The Nile isn't _____ _____ _____ the Amazon.

(2) The Amazon is 139 km _____ _____ the Nile.

기출응용

06

다음 조건에 맞게 우리말을 영어로 옮겨 쓰시오.

> 〈조건〉 1. 비교급 혹은 최상급 표현을 이용할 것
> 2. 어휘 much, healthy, beautiful을 이용할 것

(1) 그는 나보다 훨씬 더 건강하다.

→ He is _____ _____ _____ _____ _____ _____ .

(2) 파리는 세계에서 가장 아름다운 도시들 중 하나이다.

→ Paris is _____ _____ _____ _____ _____ _____ in the world.

핵심 포인트 정리하기

1 비교 표현

원급 비교	〈① _____ + 형용사 / 부사의 원급 + _____ 〉	'~만큼 …한[하게]'
	〈not + as[so] + 형용사 / 부사의 원급 + as〉	'~만큼 …하지 않은[않게]'
	〈② _____ + 원급 + _____ 〉	'가능한 한 ~한[하게]'
	= 〈as + 원급 + as + 주어 + can[could]〉	
비교급	〈형용사 / 부사의 비교급 + ③ _____ 〉	'~보다 더 …한[하게]'
	비교급 강조 부사: much, even, still, far, a lot	'훨씬'
최상급	〈the + 형용사 / 부사의 최상급〉	'가장 ~한[하게]'
	〈the + 최상급 + ④ _____ + 장소 · 범위를 나타내는 단수명사〉	'~ (안)에서 가장 …한[하게]'
	〈the + 최상급 + ⑤ _____ + 비교 대상이 되는 명사〉	'~ 중에서 가장 …한[하게]'

2 비교 구문을 이용한 표현

- 〈배수사 + as + 원급 + as〉 = 〈배수사 + 비교급 + ⑥ _____ 〉: '~의 몇 배 …한[하게]'
- 〈⑦ _____ + _____ , the + 비교급〉: '~(하면) 할수록 더 …하다'
- 〈⑧ _____ + _____ + _____ 〉: '점점 더 ~한[하게]'
- 〈Which[Who] ~ 비교급, A or B?〉: 'A와 B 중에 어느 것이[누가] 더 ~한가?'
- 〈one of the + 최상급 + 복수명사〉: '가장 ~한 것[사람]들 중 하나'

 배수사를 이용한 비교 구문의 어순 기억하기!

3 최상급 주요 표현

- 〈No (other) + 단수명사 ~ as[so] + 원급 + as〉: '어떤 ~도 …만큼 ~하지 않은[않게]'
- 〈No (other) + 단수명사 ~ 비교급 + than〉: '어떤 ~도 …보다 더 ~하지 않은[않게]'
- 〈비교급 + than any other + ⑨ _____ 〉: '다른 어떤 ~보다 더 …한[하게]'
- 〈비교급 + than all the other + 복수명사〉: '다른 모든 ~보다 더 …한[하게]'

 원급이나 비교급으로 나타내는 최상급 표현 익히기!

문제로 개념 다지기

밑줄 친 부분이 어법상 맞으면 O, 틀리면 X 표시하고 바르게 고치시오.

1 James is <u>not so healthier</u> as his sister.

2 Steven looked <u>much more nervous than</u> Julie.

3 The more carefully people drive, <u>fewer</u> accidents there will be.

4 This strawberry is <u>twice as sweet as</u> this peach.

5 No book in the library is <u>the thickest</u> as this novel.

6 That rumor is more shocking than <u>all the other one.</u>

7 Which is <u>most convenient</u> to cook with, a gas oven or an electric oven?

food truck

CHAPTER 08

접속사

I climbed up a tree **and** found a bird's nest.	[등위 접속사]
Not only Gary **but also** Kate likes to travel.	[상관 접속사]
It was surprising **that** Betty didn't go to the concert.	[종속 접속사]

접속사

단어와 단어, 구와 구, 절과 절을 서로 연결해 주는 말로, 접속사의 종류에는 등위 접속사, 상관 접속사, 종속 접속사가 있습니다. 1) 등위 접속사는 문법적으로 대등한 단어, 구, 절을 연결해 주는 역할을 하고, 2) 상관 접속사는 두 개 이상의 단어가 짝을 이루어 하나의 접속사 역할을 합니다. 3) 종속 접속사는 시간, 이유, 결과, 조건, 양보 등의 의미를 나타내며 주절과 종속절을 연결해주는 역할을 합니다.

등위 접속사 and / but / or / so

- 등위 접속사는 문법적으로 대등한 역할을 하는 단어, 구, 절을 연결하는 말이다.
- and: '그리고'의 의미로 앞뒤 내용을 순조롭게 연결하거나 시간적인 순서, 인과관계 등을 나타낼 때 쓴다.
  He bought a sweater, **and** she bought a skirt.
- but: '그러나'의 의미로 서로 상반되는 내용을 연결한다.
  They went to the museum, **but** it was closed.
- or: '또는'의 의미로 선택을 나타낸다.
  Is this a sheep **or** a goat?
- so: '그래서'의 의미로 앞서 나온 내용에 대한 결과를 나타낸다.
  It was dark, **so** I couldn't see anything.

A 다음 우리말과 같은 뜻이 되도록 빈칸에 알맞은 접속사를 쓰시오.

1 나는 뉴욕을 정말 좋아하지만, 그곳에서 살고 싶지는 않다.
I love New York, _____ I don't want to live there.

2 너는 개와 고양이 중에 어느 쪽을 더 좋아하니?
Which do you like better, dogs _____ cats?

3 피아노 수업이 9시에 끝나서, 나는 약간 늦을 거야.
My piano lesson ends at nine, _____ I'll be a little late.

4 그는 문을 두드리고 안으로 들어왔다.
He knocked on the door _____ came in.

5 이것은 비싸지만 매우 유용한 책이다.
This is an expensive _____ very useful book.

B 다음 우리말과 같은 뜻이 되도록 ( ) 안의 말을 배열하여 문장을 완성하시오.

1 나는 안경을 잃어버려서 아무것도 볼 수 없다. (see, I, so, anything, can't)
I have lost my glasses, _____.

2 Amy는 보통 차로 출근하지만, 오늘 아침에는 버스를 탔다.
(took, she, this morning, but, a bus)
Amy usually drives to work, _____.

3 Sue는 창가로 가서 밖을 내다보았다. (looked, outside, and)
Sue went to the window _____.

4 Chris는 Mia에게 전화를 하고 싶었지만, 그녀의 전화번호가 기억나지 않았다.
(her number, he, but, remember, didn't)
Chris wanted to call Mia, _____.

상관 접속사 both A and B/not A but B 등

■ 상관 접속사는 두 개 이상의 단어가 짝을 이루어 하나의 접속사 역할을 하는 말이다.
■ 상관 접속사로 연결되는 어구는 문법적으로 대등해야 한다.

both A and B	A와 B 둘 다	I like **both** oranges **and** apples.
not A but B	A가 아니라 B	**Not** you **but** he has to do it.
either A or B	A와 B 중 하나	**Either** you **or** she should go.
neither A nor B	A도 B도 아닌	The chair is **neither** pretty **nor** comfortable.
not only A but also B	A뿐만 아니라 B도	I like **not only** oranges **but also** apples.

★ PLUS TIP
• 〈both A and B〉는 복수 취급한다.
• 〈not A but B〉, 〈either A or B〉, 〈neither A nor B〉, 〈not only A but also B〉는 B에 동사의 수를 일치시킨다.

A 다음 (   ) 안에서 알맞은 말을 고르시오.

1 I went there not with Tom (and / but) with Max.

2 Either a necklace (or / nor) earrings would be a good present for her.

3 The restaurant has (neither / not only) good food but also great service.

4 Mary can play both the guitar (and / or) the flute.

B 다음 문장에서 <u>틀린</u> 부분을 찾아 어법에 맞게 고쳐 쓰시오.

1 My mother will be either sleeping or to talk on the phone.

2 Both he and his son goes for a walk every day.

3 He is learning not only German also but Russian.

4 Neither Beth and Amanda believes his success story.

5 You should do your best not for your parents or for yourself.

C 다음 우리말과 같은 뜻이 되도록 문장을 완성하시오.

1 내 꿈은 의사뿐만 아니라 연구자도 되는 것이다.
My dream is to become ＿＿＿＿＿ a doctor ＿＿＿＿＿ a researcher.

2 너는 가서 Annie를 찾든지 여기서 그녀를 기다려야 한다.
You should ＿＿＿＿＿ go look for Annie ＿＿＿＿＿ wait for her here.

3 수박과 복숭아 둘 다 인기 있는 여름 과일이다.
＿＿＿＿＿ watermelons ＿＿＿＿＿ peaches are popular summer fruits.

4 Suzie는 아침 식사로 빵도 먹지 않고 우유도 마시지 않았다.
Suzie ＿＿＿＿＿ ate bread ＿＿＿＿＿ drank milk for breakfast.

시간을 나타내는 접속사 I − when / as / while

- 종속 접속사는 시간, 이유, 결과, 조건, 양보 등의 의미를 나타내며 종속절을 주절과 연결해 주는 역할을 한다.
- when: '~할 때'
  I was reading a book **when** he came in.
- as: '~할 때', '~하면서'
  As I walked into the house, I saw a big dog.
- while: '~하는 동안에'
  I fell asleep **while** I was listening to the radio.

★ *PLUS TIP* as는 '~할 때'라는 의미 외에 '~함에 따라', '~대로', '~ 때문에' 등 여러 가지 의미로 쓰이는 접속사이다.

A　다음 〈보기〉에서 알맞은 어구를 골라 문장을 완성하시오.

〈보기〉	they asked for a room	I turned off the TV
	we saw the accident happen	while we were in Paris
	when you're tired	when I was seven years old
	somebody broke into his house	while he was waiting for the bus

1　Don't drive _____.

2　My family moved to Seoul _____.

3　When they got to the hotel, _____.

4　When the program was over, _____.

5　Sam saw a pretty girl _____.

6　We visited a lot of museums _____.

7　While he was on a business trip, _____.

8　As we were crossing the street, _____.

B　다음 우리말과 같은 뜻이 되도록 ( ) 안의 말을 이용하여 문장을 완성하시오.

1　내가 밖에 있는 동안에 누군가 전화했었니? (be out)
　　Did anybody call _____ _____ _____ _____?

2　그곳에 머물고 있는 동안 그는 아무도 만나지 않았다. (stay)
　　He didn't meet anyone _____ _____ _____ _____ there.

3　밖에 나갈 때 창문을 닫아주겠니? (go out)
　　Can you close the window _____ _____ _____ _____?

시간을 나타내는 접속사 II – before / after / until[till]

- before: '~하기 전에'
  Let's go to the beach **before** the sun rises.
- after: '~한 후에'
  I remembered the answer **after** I finished the exam.
- until[till]: '~할 때까지'
  She waited **until[till]** the water boiled.

★ 내신만점 *TIP* ▶ 시간을 나타내는 부사절에서는 미래의 일을 현재시제로 나타낸다는 것을 기억하자.
We will eat dinner **after** the movie *is* over.

A 다음 ( ) 안에서 알맞은 말을 고르시오.

1 She always sets her alarm clock (after / before) she goes to bed.

2 Before I (go / will go) shopping, I will make a list.

3 The Egyptian kings wanted to live (after / before) they died.

4 Jake will save money (until / as) he can buy a new watch.

B 다음 우리말과 같은 뜻이 되도록 빈칸에 알맞은 접속사를 쓰시오.

1 비가 그칠 때까지 우리는 교실 안에 머물렀다.
_____ the rain stopped, we stayed inside the classroom.

2 나는 샤워를 한 후에 잠자리에 들 것이다.
I will go to bed _____ I take a shower.

3 그는 초등학교에 입학하기 전에 이곳에서 4년 동안 살았다.
He lived here for four years _____ he entered elementary school.

C 다음 우리말과 같은 뜻이 되도록 ( ) 안의 말을 이용하여 문장을 완성하시오.

1 내가 돌아올 때까지 여기서 기다려라. (come back)
Wait here _____ _____ _____ _____ .

2 그 광고를 본 후, 그는 그 운동화를 사고 싶었다. (see the ad)
_____ _____ _____ _____ _____ , he wanted to buy the sneakers.

3 그 여자아이는 그녀의 엄마가 그녀를 안아줄 때까지 울었다. (mom, hug)
The girl cried _____ _____ _____ _____ _____ .

4 그 경기가 시작되기 전에 코치는 우리에게 용기를 북돋아 주었다. (game, start)
_____ _____ _____ _____ , the coach encouraged us.

이유를 나타내는 접속사 because/as[since]

- because: '~ 때문에'
  The stores are closed **because** today is a holiday.
- as[since]: '~ 때문에'
  As[Since] they lived near us, we saw them often.

★ 내신만점 *TIP* — because 뒤에는 〈주어+동사〉를 포함하는 절이 오고, because of 뒤에는 (동)명사(구)가 온다는 것을 알아두자.
I don't want to go out **because** *it is raining*.
I don't want to go out **because of** *the rain*.

A 다음 〈보기〉에서 알맞은 말을 골라, because나 because of를 이용하여 문장을 완성하시오.

〈보기〉	the river is very dirty	his English test	the strong sunlight
	she loved children	the heavy clouds	drivers fall asleep

1 The fish will die soon _____.

2 Some car accidents happen _____.

3 I had to wear sunglasses _____.

4 _____, we cannot see the moon.

5 _____, Norah became a kindergarten teacher.

6 My brother studied hard yesterday _____.

B 다음 우리말과 같은 뜻이 되도록 ( ) 안의 말을 배열하여 문장을 완성하시오.

1 Nicole은 배가 아파서 학교에 갈 수 없었다. (Nicole, stomachache, since, had, a)
_____, she couldn't go to school.

2 너는 Chris를 아니까 네가 그에게 전화해야겠다. (know, you, since, Chris)
_____, you should call him.

3 비가 많이 와서 그 경기는 취소되었다. (it, a lot, as, rained)
_____, the game was canceled.

4 Linda가 밖에 나올 수 없으니 우리가 그녀를 찾아가자. (Linda, can't, since, come out)
_____, let's visit her.

5 나는 그 가수의 열혈 팬이어서 그의 새 앨범을 샀다. (the singer, I, am, of, as, a big fan)
_____, I bought his new album.

6 내 남동생이 아파서 내가 그의 숙제를 도와주었다. (sick, my brother, since, was)
_____, I helped him with his homework.

결과를 나타내는 접속사 so~that …

■ so ~ that …: '매우[너무] ~해서 …하다'
– so는 형용사 또는 부사를 수식하며, that 이하는 앞의 내용에 뒤따르는 결과를 나타낸다.
Nancy studied **so** hard **that** she got a perfect score on the exam.

A 다음 두 문장을 〈so ~ that …〉 구문을 이용하여 한 문장으로 만드시오.

1 I was tired. I canceled all my plans.

→ _____

2 He was hungry. He ate all the food.

→ _____

3 It was hot. Children dove into the pool.

→ _____

4 The plane ticket is expensive. I cannot buy it.

→ _____

5 The weather was beautiful. We decided to go out.

→ _____

6 The music was loud. I could hear it from far away.

→ _____

B 다음 우리말과 같은 뜻이 되도록 ( ) 안의 말을 이용하여 문장을 완성하시오.

1 나는 너무 졸려서 버스에서 잠들었다. (sleepy)
I was _____ _____ _____ I fell asleep on the bus.

2 그 상자는 너무 무거워서 나는 그것을 들 수 없다. (heavy, lift)
The box is _____ _____ _____ I _____ _____ it.

3 나는 매우 감명받아서 무슨 말을 해야 할지 몰랐다. (impressed, know)
I was _____ _____ _____ I _____ _____ what to say.

4 우리는 너무 배불러서 후식을 전혀 주문하지 않았다. (full, order)
We were _____ _____ _____ we _____ _____ any dessert.

5 그는 말을 너무 빨리 해서 나는 그의 말을 이해할 수 없었다. (fast, understand)
He spoke _____ _____ _____ _____ _____ _____ him.

조건을 나타내는 접속사 if / unless

- if: '만약 ~라면[하면]'
  If you want to read this magazine, I'll lend it to you.
- unless: '~하지 않으면' (= if ~ not)
  Let's go to a movie **unless** you are busy.
  (→ Let's go to a movie **if** you are **not** busy.)

★ 내신만점 *TIP* 조건을 나타내는 부사절에서는 미래의 일을 현재시제로 나타낸다는 것을 기억하자.
We **won't** be late *if* the bus **comes** soon.

A 다음 두 문장을 if나 unless를 이용하여 한 문장으로 만드시오.

1 You exercise every day. You will be healthy.
→ _____, you will be healthy.

2 You don't go to see a doctor. You will get sicker.
→ _____, you will get sicker.

3 You should say sorry first. It was your fault.
→ You should say sorry first _____.

4 You don't have a library card. You can't borrow books.
→ _____, you can't borrow books.

5 You need my backpack. I'll bring it tomorrow.
→ _____, I'll bring it tomorrow.

B 다음 우리말과 같은 뜻이 되도록 ( ) 안의 말을 이용하여 문장을 완성하시오.

1 배가 고프면, 치즈 케이크 좀 먹으렴. (feel hungry)
_____ _____ _____ _____, have some cheesecake.

2 질문이 있으면, 내게 언제든지 전화해. (have any questions)
_____ _____ _____ _____ _____, call me any time.

3 빨리 걷지 않으면, 너는 버스를 놓칠 것이다. (walk quickly)
_____ _____ _____ _____, you'll miss the bus.

4 네가 크게 말하지 않으면, 사람들은 네 말을 들을 수 없다. (speak loudly)
People can't hear you _____ _____ _____ _____.

5 시간이 있으면, 나와 함께 콘서트에 갈래? (be free)
Will you go to the concert with me _____ _____ _____ _____?

양보를 나타내는 접속사 though[although]

- though[although]: '비록 ～이지만'
  Though[Although] it was cold, we went out.

★ PLUS TIP though와 although는 거의 같은 뜻이지만, 구어체에서는 though가 더 자주 쓰인다.

A 다음 우리말과 같은 뜻이 되도록 ( ) 안의 말을 이용하여 문장을 완성하시오.

1 비록 일요일이었지만, Tim은 출근했다. (Sunday)

_____ _____ _____ _____ , Tim went to work.

2 비록 Monica는 노래를 잘 부르지 못하지만, 최선을 다했다. (sing, well)

_____ _____ _____ _____ _____ , she tried her best.

3 비록 Jack은 키가 크지 않지만, 농구 선수가 되었다. (tall)

_____ _____ _____ , he became a basketball player.

4 비록 Eric은 인기가 많지만, 여자친구가 없다. (popular)

_____ _____ _____ _____ , he doesn't have a girlfriend.

5 비록 내 할머니는 연세가 많으시지만 건강하시다. (old)

_____ _____ _____ _____ _____ , she is healthy.

6 비록 붐비기는 했지만, 나는 자리를 잡을 수 있었다. (be crowded)

_____ _____ _____ _____ , I was able to get a seat.

B 다음 〈보기〉에서 알맞은 말을 골라 though[although]를 이용하여 문장을 완성하시오.

〈보기〉 I don't like Jerry very much.　　　　I understand him.
　　　　The player was injured.　　　　　The skirt was a bit big for me.
　　　　Ellen works really hard.　　　　　The heater was on.
　　　　The traffic was bad.　　　　　　　I have met her before.

1 _____ , he finished playing the game.

2 _____ , the room wasn't warm.

3 _____ , they arrived on time.

4 _____ , I don't remember her.

5 _____ , I don't agree with him.

6 _____ , I invited him to the party.

7 _____ , she doesn't earn a lot of money.

8 _____ , I bought it.

명사절을 이끄는 종속 접속사 that

- 종속 접속사 that: 명사절을 이끄는 접속사로, that절은 문장에서 주어, 목적어, 보어의 역할을 한다.

  1) 주어로 쓰인 that절: '~라는 것은'으로 해석한다. that절이 문장에서 주어 역할을 하는 경우, 보통 그 자리에 가주어 It을 쓰고 that절은 문장 뒤에 쓴다.

  That the player is only 16 years old is amazing.

  → **It** is amazing **that** the player is only 16 years old.
  　　가주어　　　　　　　　　　　진주어

  2) 목적어로 쓰인 that절: '~라는 것을'이라고 해석하며, 이때 that은 생략할 수 있다.

  I think **(that)** we still have a chance.

  3) 보어로 쓰인 that절: '~라는 것(이다)'으로 해석한다.

  The truth is **that** Jessica told you a lie.

A 다음 문장이 어법상 맞으면 O, 틀리면 X 표시하고 바르게 고치시오.

1 I think the exam was too difficult.

2 It surprised me that he still liked me.

3 We learned if Chopin was born in Poland.

4 That was a miracle that he wasn't hurt in the accident.

5 The problem is that I don't know her address.

B 다음 우리말과 같은 뜻이 되도록 (　) 안의 말을 배열하여 문장을 완성하시오.

1 나는 우리 부모님이 나를 사랑하신다는 것을 알고 있다.

(love, I, that, me, parents, my, know)

_____

2 그가 가버렸다는 것이 확실하다. (certain, has, he, gone, that, is, it)

_____

3 나는 그녀가 면접을 통과할 것이라고 믿는다.

(pass, I, the interview, will, believe, that, she)

_____

4 중요한 것은 네가 행복하다는 것이다. (you, important, the, is, are, that, happy, thing)

_____

5 사실은 우리가 숙제를 끝마칠 시간이 충분하지 않다는 것이다.

(the, is, don't, we, that, enough, have, time, fact)

_____ to finish the homework.

명령문+and/or

- 〈명령문+and …〉: '~해라, 그러면 …할 것이다'의 의미로, 접속사 if를 이용해 바꾸어 쓸 수 있다.
  Leave now, **and** you will catch the bus.
  → **If** you leave now, you will catch the bus.
- 〈명령문+or …〉는 '~해라, 그러지 않으면 …할 것이다'의 의미로, if ~ not 또는 unless ~를 이용해 바꾸어 쓸 수 있다.
  Be careful, **or** you will slip on the ice.
  → **If** you are **not** careful, you will slip on the ice.
  → **Unless** you are careful, you will slip on the ice.

A 다음 우리말과 같은 뜻이 되도록 빈칸에 and와 or 중 알맞은 것을 쓰시오.

1 그 버튼을 눌러라, 그러면 그 세탁기는 작동할 것이다.
Push the button, _____ the washing machine will work.

2 앉아주세요, 그러면 제 연설을 시작하겠습니다.
Please sit down, _____ I will begin my speech.

3 나와 가까이 있어라, 그러지 않으면 너는 길을 잃을지도 모른다.
Keep close to me, _____ you may get lost.

B 다음 두 문장이 같은 뜻이 되도록 문장을 완성하시오.

1 Don't make noise, or the baby will wake up.
→ _____, the baby will wake up.

2 Come over here, and you will hear the music.
→ _____, you will hear the music.

3 If you take the subway, you'll get there in time.
→ _____, _____ you'll get there in time.

4 If you don't hurry, you will miss the movie.
→ Hurry, _____.

5 Go straight, and you will see the post office.
→ _____, you will see the post office.

6 Unless you go home now, your mom will be angry.
→ _____, _____.

7 Take your umbrella, or you will get wet.
→ If _____, you will get wet.
→ Unless _____, you will get wet.

Chapter 08

내신대비 TEST

기출응용

01

다음 짝지어진 두 단어의 관계가 나머지와 <u>다른</u> 것은?

① because – as   ② neither – nor

③ both – and   ④ not – but

⑤ not only – but also

[02-04] 다음 빈칸에 알맞은 말을 고르시오.

02

I didn't eat anything today, _____ I'm very hungry now.

① as   ② since

③ or   ④ while

⑤ so

03

Drive carefully, _____ you may get hurt.

① or   ② but

③ so   ④ and

⑤ that

04

The truth is _____ he is honest.

① although   ② that

③ until   ④ since

⑤ when

[05-06] 빈칸에 들어갈 말이 순서대로 알맞게 짝지어진 것을 고르시오.

05

A: What did you do _____ you visited London the other day?

B: I went to the Tower Bridge, _____ it was too crowded.

① if – though   ② when – but

③ while – or   ④ unless – and

⑤ as – since

06

A: Can you wash the dishes _____ you go out?

B: I have to go right now. I'll do it _____ I come back.

① after – until   ② when – so

③ before – when   ④ since – and

⑤ till – that

07

다음 빈칸에 공통으로 들어갈 말로 알맞은 것은?

• _____ the price is high, I can't buy it.

• _____ we walked home, we saw the sunset.

① While   ② Although

③ Since   ④ As

⑤ Unless

08
다음 우리말을 영어로 바르게 옮긴 것은?

그 소파는 너무 무거워서 그녀는 그것을 옮길 수 없었다.

① The sofa was heavy but she couldn't move it.
② The sofa was heavy till she couldn't move it.
③ The sofa was so heavy as she couldn't move it.
④ The sofa was heavy so that she couldn't move it.
⑤ The sofa was so heavy that she couldn't move it.

[09-10] 다음 대화의 빈칸에 알맞은 말을 고르시오.

09

A: Did you clean your room?
B: No. I'll do it _____.

① until I finished reading this book
② before my mom comes back
③ but I have to clean my room
④ so I went shopping to buy some food
⑤ after my friend came here yesterday

10

A: Will you take this train?
B: No. _____, I'll arrive too early.

① If I take this train
② Though the train is coming
③ Unless I want to take a taxi
④ Because I don't have enough money
⑤ When the train comes to the station

11
다음 밑줄 친 부분의 의미가 나머지와 다른 것은?

① Since he is rude, I don't like him.
② We've learned English since we were kids.
③ Since he didn't come, I got upset.
④ I stayed in bed since I didn't feel well.
⑤ I have to take care of them alone since you won't help me.

12
다음 〈보기〉의 밑줄 친 부분과 쓰임이 같은 것은?

〈보기〉 The reason is that I am very tired.

① Frank thinks that science is interesting.
② It is great that you are my best friend.
③ That he was very tall is certain.
④ His problem is that he is too lazy.
⑤ I hope that you are in good health.

[13-14] 다음 밑줄 친 부분의 쓰임이 잘못된 것을 고르시오.

13
① When I saw her, she was crying.
② I'm sorry unless I made you angry.
③ Since I overslept, I was late for school.
④ Although he is smart, he failed the exam.
⑤ The movie was so boring that I stopped watching it.

14
① You can call me if you need help.
② I'll buy it after I save some money.
③ As he lives near us, I can see him often.
④ We decided to go on a picnic because the weather was so nice.
⑤ Although I don't have soccer shoes, I can't play soccer.

15

① Hurry, or you will miss your plane.
② Lynne cooks, and Carl does the dishes.
③ I'll be lonely while you are away.
④ You should do something before it will be too late.
⑤ I'm sad because she will leave tomorrow.

16

① Either Billy or Susan is wrong.
② I will wait here until the rain stops.
③ It is certain that he will arrive soon.
④ I got nervous because of everything was new.
⑤ If you eat too much ice cream, you will have a stomachache.

17

다음 밑줄 친 부분의 우리말 해석이 옳지 <u>않은</u> 것은?

① Don't talk <u>after I turn off the light</u>.
　　　→ 내가 불을 끄고 난 후에
② <u>Since he was young</u>, he couldn't ride the roller coaster.
　　→ 그는 어렸기 때문에
③ <u>Unless you miss the bus</u>, you won't be late for your appointment.
　　→ 네가 버스를 놓친다면
④ She was listening to pop music <u>while her boyfriend was watching the soccer game</u>.
　　→ 그녀의 남자친구가 축구 경기를 보는 동안
⑤ <u>Though he was the youngest student in that class</u>, he got a perfect score.
　　→ 비록 그는 그 수업에서 가장 어린 학생이었지만

18

빈칸에 들어갈 말이 나머지와 <u>다른</u> 것은?

① Be quiet, _____ you will have to leave the room.
② Would you like pie _____ pizza?
③ They wanted to go to either Japan _____ Taiwan.
④ He will bring both a salad _____ a sandwich.
⑤ I'll join the tennis club _____ take private lessons.

기출응용

19

다음 밑줄 친 부분을 바르게 고치지 <u>않은</u> 것은?

① This animal is not a cat <u>and</u> a baby tiger.
　　　　　　　→ but
② Tell your mom the truth, <u>or</u> she will forgive you.
　　　　　　　→ and
③ She made not only a black suit <u>and just</u> a white one.
　　　　　　　→ but also
④ If you want to try this soup, I <u>give</u> some of it to you.
　　　　　　　→ will give
⑤ My dad neither drinks <u>or</u> smokes.
　　　　　　　→ and

고난도

20

다음 중 어법상 옳은 문장의 개수는?

(a) The alarm will ring if there is a fire.
(b) When I will come to see you, I will bring your bag.
(c) Both Jamie and Brad likes camping.
(d) I believe he will get better soon.

① 0개　② 1개　③ 2개　④ 3개　⑤ 4개

01
다음 우리말과 뜻이 같도록 빈칸에 알맞은 말을 쓰시오.

(1) 그 영화는 웃길 뿐만 아니라 감동적이기도 하다.
   → The movie is _____ _____ funny
   _____ _____ moving.

(2) 그녀는 만화책을 읽거나 스마트폰 게임을 할 것이다.
   → She will _____ read a comic book
   _____ play a smartphone game.

02
다음 두 문장이 같은 뜻이 되도록 빈칸에 알맞은 말을 쓰시오.

(1) If you don't call her now, she will be waiting for you all day long.
   → _____ _____ _____, _____
   she will be waiting for you all day long.

(2) If you finish your homework, I'll let you go out and play.
   → _____ _____ _____, _____
   I'll let you go out and play.

03
주어진 접속사를 이용하여 두 문장을 한 문장으로 만드시오.

(1) They went to same school. They don't know each other. (although)
   → _____
   _____

(2) I made noise in class. My teacher gave me a warning. (because)
   → _____
   _____

04
다음 표를 보고, 접속사를 이용하여 문장을 완성하시오.

경기	날짜	비고
Baseball	March 11	Will be canceled if it rains
Soccer	March 12	Won't be canceled
Basketball	March 12	Won't be canceled

(1) There will be a baseball game on March 11
   _____ _____ _____.

(2) There will be _____ a soccer game
   _____ a basketball game on March 12.

05
다음 조건에 맞게 우리말을 영어로 옮겨 쓰시오.

〈조건〉 1. 적절한 접속사를 이용할 것
        2. 주어진 어휘를 이용할 것

(1) 나는 너무 피곤해서 눈을 뜨고 있을 수가 없다.
   (tired, keep my eyes open)
   → _____
   _____ (10단어)

(2) 그 책을 읽어라, 그러면 너는 그 이론을 이해하게 될 것이다. (read the book, understand the theory)
   → _____
   _____ (9단어)

06
다음 대화에서 어법상 틀린 부분을 모두 찾아 바르게 고쳐 쓰시오. (2군데)

A: I'm so bored that I want to leave now.
B: You should stay here until he will come.
   Unless you leave, he will get angry at you.

핵심 포인트 정리하기

1 등위 접속사: 문법적으로 대등한 역할을 하는 단어, 구, 절을 연결

- ① _____ '그리고' / but '그러나' / or '또는' / ② _____ '그래서'

2 상관 접속사: 두 개 이상의 단어가 짝을 이루어 하나의 접속사 역할을 함

③ _____	'A와 B 둘 다'	복수 취급
not A but B	'A가 아니라 B'	
either A or B	'A와 B 중 하나'	주어 B에 동사의 수 일치
④ _____	'A도 B도 아닌'	
⑤ _____	'A뿐만 아니라 B도'	

 각 상관 접속사가 짝을 이루는 형태 기억하기!

3 종속 접속사: 시간, 이유, 결과, 조건, 양보 등을 나타내며 종속절을 주절과 연결

- 시간: when '~할 때' / as '~할 때', '~하면서' / ⑥ _____ '~하는 동안에'
  before '~하기 전에' / after '~한 후에' / until[till] '~할 때까지'
- 이유: because, as[since] '~ 때문에'
- 결과: ⑦ _____ '매우[너무] ~해서 …하다'
- 조건: if '만약 ~라면[하면]' / ⑧ _____ '~하지 않으면' (= if ~ not)
- 양보: though[although] '비록 ~이지만'
- 접속사 that: (1) 주어 '~라는 것은' / 가주어 It ~ that
  (2) ⑨ _____ '~라는 것을' (생략 가능)
  (3) ⑩ _____ '~라는 것(이다)'

 시간이나 조건을 나타내는 부사절에서는 미래의 일을 현재시제로 나타낸다는 것 기억하기!

4 명령문+and/or

- 〈명령문 + ⑪ _____ …〉: '~해라, 그러면 …할 것이다'
- 〈명령문 + ⑫ _____ …〉: '~해라, 그러지 않으면 …할 것이다'

문제로 개념 다지기

다음 ( ) 안에서 알맞은 말을 고르시오.

1 She was sick (and / but) took some medicine.

2 Would you like iced tea (or / so) hot tea?

3 She should take (either / neither) a bus or a taxi to get there.

4 It (was so hot / was hot so) in the room that he took off his jacket.

5 Daniel will answer "Yes" if Mia (asks / will ask) him to join the band.

6 The problem is (because / that) I don't have a ticket.

7 (Because / Though) the car is old, it runs well.

CHAPTER 09

관계사 I

She met $\boxed{\text{the man}}$. $\boxed{\text{He}}$ is the principal of her school.

the man = he

→ She met the man **who** is the principal of her school.

관계사

관계사는 두 문장의 공통된 부분을 하나로 연결해 주는 말입니다. 관계사에는 관계대명사와 관계부사가 있습니다.

관계대명사

두 문장을 이어주는 접속사의 역할과 앞의 명사를 대신하는 대명사의 역할을 하는 말입니다. 관계대명사가 이끄는 절은 앞의 명사(선행사)를 꾸며주는 형용사 역할을 하며, 선행사의 종류에 따라 다른 관계대명사가 쓰인다는 점을 기억해 두세요.

주격 관계대명사 who

- 관계대명사는 접속사와 대명사의 역할을 하며, 앞의 명사(선행사)를 꾸며주는 형용사절을 이끈다.
- 선행사가 사람이고 관계사가 이끄는 절 안에서 주어 역할을 할 때, 주격 관계대명사 who를 쓴다.
  이때, 주격 관계대명사절의 동사는 선행사의 인칭과 수에 일치시킨다.
  I like **a girl**. + **She** has big eyes.
  → I like a girl **who** has big eyes.

★ PLUS TIP 관계사절의 수식을 받는 선행사는 문장에서 주어, 목적어, 보어로 쓰일 수 있다. 이를 '관계대명사의 역할'과 구분해야 한다.
I know the man **who** lives next door. (the man: 문장의 목적어, who: 주격 관계대명사)

A 다음 두 문장을 관계대명사 who를 이용하여 한 문장으로 만드시오.

1 Yesterday I met a boy. He is my classmate.
→ Yesterday I met a boy _____.

2 The woman is a fashion model. She is standing there.
→ The woman _____ is a fashion model.

3 I don't like those men. They are rude to everyone.
→ I don't like those men _____.

4 We like teachers. They care about us a lot.
→ We like teachers _____.

5 My cousin is going to visit me. She lives in Canada.
→ My cousin _____ is going to visit me.

B 다음 우리말과 같은 뜻이 되도록 ( ) 안의 말을 배열하여 문장을 완성하시오.

1 이 가게에서 일하는 사람들은 친절하다. (work, this, who, in, store)
The people _____ are friendly.

2 우리 삼촌은 아프리카에서 아픈 사람들을 도와주는 의사이다.
(in Africa, a doctor, helps, people, who, sick)
My uncle is _____.

3 흰색 셔츠를 입고 있는 소녀가 Stella이다.
(girl, is, who, a white shirt, wearing, the)
_____ is Stella.

4 야구를 하고 있는 몇 명의 아이들이 있다. (playing, a few, who, are, children, baseball)
There are _____.

소유격 관계대명사 whose

- 관계사가 이끄는 절 안에서 소유격 역할을 할 때, 소유격 관계대명사 whose 또는 of which를 쓴다.

I met **a person**. + **His** name is David.

→ I met a person **whose** name is David.

- 선행사가 사람인 경우: whose를 쓴다.
- 선행사가 사물·동물인 경우: whose 또는 of which를 쓴다. 하지만 of which는 보통 잘 쓰지 않는다.

This is the painting **whose** price is very high.

★ **내신만점 TIP** 주격 관계대명사 바로 뒤에는 동사, 소유격 관계대명사 whose 바로 뒤에는 반드시 명사가 온다는 사실을 기억하자.

A 다음 두 문장을 관계대명사 whose를 이용하여 한 문장으로 만드시오.

1 I have a friend. His job is delivering pizzas.

→ I have a friend _____ .

2 There is a woman. Her dream is to become a travel guide.

→ There is a woman _____ .

3 I like the woman. Her voice is beautiful.

→ I like the woman _____ .

4 Mr. Jones is a technician. His son is my best friend.

→ Mr. Jones is a technician _____ .

5 Look at that car. Its windows are open.

→ Look at that car _____ .

6 Britney has a teddy bear. Its fur is very soft.

→ Britney has a teddy bear _____ .

B 다음 우리말과 같은 뜻이 되도록 (   ) 안의 말을 이용하여 문장을 완성하시오.

1 나는 형이 유명한 친구가 한 명 있다. (famous)

I have a friend _____ _____ _____ _____ .

2 우리는 높이가 520m였던 산에 올라갔다. (height)

We climbed a mountain _____ _____ was 520 meters.

3 나는 어머니가 드라마 대본을 쓰시는 소녀를 만났다. (write)

I met a girl _____ _____ _____ drama scripts.

4 그 노인은 다리가 긴 고양이를 길렀다. (leg)

The old man had a cat _____ _____ were long.

목적격 관계대명사 whom

- 선행사가 사람이고 관계사가 이끄는 절 안에서 동사나 전치사의 목적어 역할을 할 때, 목적격 관계대명사 whom을 쓴다. 구어체에서는 목적격 관계대명사로 whom 대신 who를 쓰는 경우가 많다.
  The girl came to my birthday party. + I like **her**.
  → The girl **who(m)** I like came to my birthday party.

★ PLUS TIP 관계대명사가 전치사의 목적어일 때 전치사는 관계사절 맨 뒤나 관계사 앞에 온다. 이때 전치사 바로 뒤에는 who가 올 수 없다.
This is **the woman**. + I studied Chinese **with her**.
→ This is the woman **who(m)** I studied Chinese **with**.
→ This is the woman **with whom** I studied Chinese.

A 다음 두 문장을 관계대명사 who(m)를 이용하여 한 문장으로 만드시오.

1 I don't like the actor. My sister likes him the most.
→ I don't like the actor _____ .

2 I know the girl. Tom is talking to her.
→ I know the girl to _____ .

3 Do you remember the boy? We met him at church.
→ Do you remember the boy _____ ?

4 I have a true friend. I've known her for ten years.
→ I have a true friend _____ .

B 다음 밑줄 친 부분을 어법에 맞게 고쳐 쓰시오.

1 Sam is someone <u>whom</u> trusts me.

2 Alice has a friend with <u>who</u> she will go to the concert.

3 The girl <u>whom</u> hair is long and blond spoke to me.

4 This is a picture of the guy <u>whose</u> you are going to meet on the blind date.

C 다음 우리말과 같은 뜻이 되도록 ( ) 안의 말을 배열하여 문장을 완성하시오.

1 Jenny는 모든 사람이 좋아하는 학생이다. (likes, whom, student, a, everyone)
Jenny is _____ .

2 이 사람은 내가 어제 얘기했던 그 사람이다. (the man, about, I, whom, yesterday, talked)
This is _____ .

3 Sally는 그녀의 여동생이 피아노 교습을 해 준 그 소년을 안다.
(sister, piano lessons, whom, her, gave, to)
Sally knows the boy _____ .

관계대명사 who와 의문사 who의 구별

- 관계대명사 who 앞에는 선행사가 있지만 의문사 who 앞에는 선행사가 없다.
- 관계대명사 who는 보통 '~하는', '~한'으로 해석하며 앞의 선행사를 수식하는 역할을 하지만, 의문사 who는 '누가', '누구'로 해석한다.

Do you know the man **who** works at that bookstore? (관계대명사 who)

I don't remember **who** called me yesterday. (의문사 who)

A 다음 문장에서 who가 관계대명사인지 의문사인지 쓰시오.

1 I'm not sure who asked me the question. 〈　　〉

2 She has a friend who is a great cook. 〈　　〉

3 The mice wondered who moved their cheese. 〈　　〉

4 Most students who took the exam were accepted by the school. 〈　　〉

5 Do you know who invented this machine? 〈　　〉

6 The math teacher asked who could answer the question. 〈　　〉

7 This book is about a man who dreams of being an actor. 〈　　〉

8 What happened to the worker who worked at the information desk? 〈　　〉

B 다음 우리말과 같은 뜻이 되도록 who와 (　) 안의 말을 이용하여 문장을 완성하시오.

1 나는 Bob이 누구인지 모른다. (be)
I don't know ＿＿＿＿＿ ＿＿＿＿＿ ＿＿＿＿＿.

2 그녀는 누가 꽃을 보냈는지 궁금해했다. (send)
She wondered ＿＿＿＿＿ ＿＿＿＿＿ the flowers.

3 나는 항상 불평하는 사람들을 좋아하지 않는다. (complain)
I don't like people ＿＿＿＿＿ ＿＿＿＿＿ ＿＿＿＿＿.

4 선생님은 나에게 누가 책상을 망가뜨렸는지 물어보셨다. (break)
The teacher asked me ＿＿＿＿＿ ＿＿＿＿＿ the desk.

5 나를 가장 지지해 주는 사람들은 나의 부모님이다. (support)
The people ＿＿＿＿＿ ＿＿＿＿＿ the most are my parents.

6 선글라스를 끼고 있는 그 남자는 경호원이다. (wear)
＿＿＿＿＿ ＿＿＿＿＿ ＿＿＿＿＿ ＿＿＿＿＿ sunglasses is a bodyguard.

7 그는 그 병으로 고통받는 아이들을 위해 약간의 돈을 기부할 것이다. (suffer from)
He will donate some money for the kids ＿＿＿＿＿ ＿＿＿＿＿ ＿＿＿＿＿ the disease.

관계대명사 which

- 선행사가 사물이나 동물이고, 관계사가 이끄는 절 안에서 주어 역할을 할 때에는 주격 관계대명사 which를, 동사나 전치사의 목적어 역할을 할 때에는 목적격 관계대명사 which를 쓴다.
  I want a room **which** has a nice view. (주격)
  This is the book **which** I read last week. (목적격: 동사의 목적어)
  Mr. Norris has a dog **which** I'm very afraid of. (목적격: 전치사의 목적어)

★ **PLUS TIP** 관계대명사 which가 전치사의 목적어일 때 전치사는 관계사절 맨 뒤나 관계사 앞에 온다.

A 다음 두 문장을 관계대명사 which를 이용하여 한 문장으로 만드시오.

1 The anchor has a soft voice. Many people like his voice.
→ The anchor has a soft voice _____.

2 A microwave is a machine. It heats food.
→ A microwave is a machine _____.

3 The long coat looks nice. John is wearing the coat.
→ The long coat _____ looks nice.

4 We visited a zoo. The zoo has a polar bear family.
→ We visited a zoo _____.

5 Did you find the ring? Your mother gave it to you.
→ Did you find the ring _____?

6 What's the name of the bird? You told me about it yesterday.
→ What's the name of the bird _____?

B 다음 우리말과 같은 뜻이 되도록 관계대명사 which와 ( ) 안의 말을 이용하여 문장을 완성하시오.

1 이것이 Fred가 자랑스러워하는 정원이다. (be proud of)
This is the garden _____.

2 매운 음식이 나오는 식당으로 가자. (serve, spicy food)
Let's go to a restaurant _____ _____ _____ _____.

3 그 언덕에 서 있는 나무는 매우 크다. (stand on)
The tree _____ the hill is very large.

4 그 극장은 우리가 보고 싶었던 영화들을 하나도 상영하지 않았다. (want, see)
The theater wasn't showing any movies _____ _____
_____ _____.

관계대명사 that

■ 관계대명사 that은 who(m), which를 대신하여 선행사(사람·사물·동물 등)에 관계없이 주격이나 목적격으로 쓸 수 있다. 목적격으로 쓰인 that은 생략할 수 있다.

I cleaned **the gas stove**. + **It** was pretty dirty.

→ I cleaned the gas stove **that** was pretty dirty. (주격)

He is **the singer**. + I like **him** the most.

→ He is the singer **(that)** I like the most. (목적격)

★ *PLUS TIP*   전치사 바로 뒤에는 that을 쓰지 않는다.

A   다음 두 문장을 관계대명사 that을 이용하여 한 문장으로 만드시오.

1   She has a nice watch. It was made in Italy.

→ She has a nice watch _____ .

2   Can you remember the man? You see him at the shop every day.

→ Can you remember the man _____ ?

3   The girl is my friend. She won first prize in the contest.

→ The girl _____ is my friend.

4   Ben and I like to go to a restaurant. It sells Vietnamese food.

→ Ben and I like to go to a restaurant _____ .

5   These are the sandwiches. I made them for my sister.

→ These are the sandwiches _____ .

6   Alex wants to go to a university. The university is located in London.

→ Alex wants to go to _____ in London.

B   다음 우리말과 같은 뜻이 되도록 (   ) 안의 말을 배열하여 문장을 완성하시오.

1   내가 사준 옷을 입는 게 어때? (I, the clothes, that, you, bought)

Why don't you wear _____ ?

2   그는 나의 상황을 이해할 수 있는 사람이다. (situation, that, understand, my, can)

He is a person _____ .

3   나는 그녀에게서 빌린 교과서를 잃어버렸다. (I, from, borrowed, that, her)

I lost the textbook _____ .

4   Ann은 일요일에 교실에 갔었던 유일한 학생이다. (the classroom, went, that, to)

Ann is the only student _____ on Sunday.

Point 07 · 관계대명사 that을 주로 쓰는 경우

- 선행사가 〈사람+동물〉, 〈사람+사물〉일 때:
  What happened to *the girl and the cat* **that** were playing by the tree?
- 선행사에 최상급이나 서수가 있을 때: This is *the first* fan letter **that** I've written.
- 선행사에 the only, the very, the same, the last, all, any, no 등이 포함되어 있을 때:
  You are *the only* person **that** I can trust.
- 선행사가 -thing으로 끝나는 말일 때: I can give you *everything* **that** I have.

★ PLUS TIP 의문대명사 who가 있는 의문문에 선행사가 사람인 관계대명사절이 포함될 경우, 관계대명사 who 대신 that을 쓴다.
Who was the man **that** helped you yesterday?

A 다음 문장에서 <u>틀린</u> 부분을 찾아 어법에 맞게 고쳐 쓰시오.

1 I have the same cell phone which you have.

2 Sam bought the present who I wanted to buy.

3 I remember the first Indian food which I had.

4 Can you see the boy and the dog who are running through the field?

5 I'm looking for a person that last name is "Bae."

6 I don't know the person with that I talked yesterday.

B 다음 우리말과 같은 뜻이 되도록 ( ) 안의 말을 이용하여 문장을 완성하시오.

1 그 피아니스트는 내가 좋아하는 모든 곡을 연주할 수 있다. (like)
The pianist can play all the songs _____ _____ _____.

2 사랑은 Willy에게 중요한 유일한 것이다. (important)
Love is the only thing _____ _____ _____ to Willy.

3 그 가게에는 내가 사고 싶었던 모든 것들이 있었다. (everything, want)
The store had _____ _____ _____ _____ to buy.

4 저기에서 울고 있는 소녀는 누구니? (cry)
Who is the girl _____ _____ _____ over there?

5 테레사 수녀는 가난한 사람들에게 그녀가 가지고 있던 전부를 주었다. (have)
Mother Teresa gave the poor all _____ _____ _____.

6 Larry는 우리 마을에 사는 가장 키가 큰 소년이다. (live)
Larry is _____ _____ _____ _____ in my town.

7 Liz는 Jessica가 어제 입었던 것과 같은 드레스를 입고 있다. (same dress)
Liz is wearing _____ _____ _____ Jessica wore yesterday.

관계대명사 that과 종속 접속사 that의 구별

- 관계대명사 that은 앞에 선행사가 있으며, that이 이끄는 절은 그 선행사를 수식하는 역할을 한다.
- 종속 접속사 that은 문장에서 주어, 목적어, 보어의 역할을 하는 명사절을 이끈다.

The movie **that** I saw last week was terrible. (관계대명사 that)

I heard **that** you are from America. (종속 접속사 that: heard의 목적어 역할을 하는 명사절을 이끎)

A 다음 문장에서 that이 관계대명사인지 종속 접속사인지 쓰시오.

1 My mom told me that I must eat the soup. 〈　　　〉
2 Did you like the hotel that you stayed at in Europe? 〈　　　〉
3 The problem is that we don't have enough time. 〈　　　〉
4 I got chocolate from a friend that sits next to me. 〈　　　〉
5 Dan spent all the money that he had. 〈　　　〉
6 It was surprising that Cathy got a good grade on the test. 〈　　　〉
7 I didn't know that my brother changed his phone number. 〈　　　〉
8 The blue jeans that I used to wear are too small for me now. 〈　　　〉

B 다음 우리말과 같은 뜻이 되도록 that과 (　) 안의 말을 이용하여 문장을 완성하시오.

1 그가 아팠다는 것은 거짓말이다. (be sick)
It is a lie ＿＿＿＿＿ ＿＿＿＿＿ ＿＿＿＿＿ ＿＿＿＿.

2 우리는 그가 추천한 오페라를 보았다. (recommend)
We watched the opera ＿＿＿＿＿ ＿＿＿＿＿ ＿＿＿＿.

3 그는 모든 사람이 존경하는 훌륭한 사람이다. (everyone, admire)
He is a great person ＿＿＿＿＿ ＿＿＿＿＿ ＿＿＿＿.

4 나는 그녀가 잘못한 것이 아무것도 없다고 믿는다. (do nothing wrong)
I believe ＿＿＿＿＿ ＿＿＿＿＿ ＿＿＿＿＿ ＿＿＿＿＿.

5 너는 Mike가 찍은 그 사진들을 봤니? (picture, take)
Did you see ＿＿＿＿＿ ＿＿＿＿＿ ＿＿＿＿＿ ＿＿＿＿?

6 나는 Melina가 일을 그만두기로 결정했다는 것을 들었다. (decide, quit)
I heard ＿＿＿＿＿ ＿＿＿＿＿ ＿＿＿＿＿ ＿＿＿＿＿ her job.

7 내가 들여다본 그 상자는 비어 있었다. (look in, empty)
The box ＿＿＿＿＿ ＿＿＿＿＿ ＿＿＿＿＿ ＿＿＿＿＿.

내신대비 TEST

[01-03] 다음 빈칸에 알맞은 말을 고르시오.

01

My parents know a woman _____ owns a bookstore.

① who   ② whom   ③ whose
④ which   ⑤ of which

02

George is the man _____ house has 10 rooms.

① who   ② whom   ③ whose
④ which   ⑤ that

03

A: Would you like something to eat?
B: The only thing _____ I want is water.

① which   ② whose   ③ that
④ who   ⑤ whom

04
다음 〈보기〉의 밑줄 친 부분과 쓰임이 같은 것은?

〈보기〉 I know the man that is on TV.

① He told me that Laura was sick.
② I'm sure that my son will succeed.
③ We're glad that our team won.
④ We agreed that it was an easy exam.
⑤ He tried on glasses that were popular.

[05-06] 빈칸에 들어갈 말이 순서대로 알맞게 짝지어진 것을 고르시오.

05

• It's the book _____ Harry borrowed from the library.
• Have you seen the guy to _____ I was talking?

① whose – that   ② which – that
③ whose – whom   ④ whom – that
⑤ which – whom

06

• This is the very sweater _____ my mom made for me.
• He is the man _____ car is parked over there.

① that – whose   ② that – which
③ whose – which   ④ that – who
⑤ whose – that

[07-09] 다음 빈칸에 공통으로 들어갈 말을 고르시오.

07

• I don't know _____ our homeroom teacher is.
• The man _____ gave the lecture was very smart.

① who   ② whom
③ that   ④ which
⑤ whose

08

- It is true _____ she is alive.
- Arnold was the only person _____ called me to say "Happy birthday!"

① who   ② whom
③ that   ④ which
⑤ whose

09

- Do you know that basketball player _____ uniform number is twenty?
- He likes the backpack _____ color is navy.

① who   ② which
③ that   ④ whose
⑤ whom

[10-11] 다음 우리말을 영어로 바르게 옮긴 것을 고르시오.

10

여기서 본 어떤 것에 대해서도 말하지 말아라.

① Don't talk about anything to you saw here.
② Don't talk about anything that you saw here.
③ Don't talk about anything who you saw here.
④ Don't talk about anything which you saw here.
⑤ Don't talk about anything whose you saw here.

11

나는 지붕이 파란 저 집이 좋다.

① I like that house that roof is blue.
② I like that house the roof which is blue.
③ I like that house whose roof is blue.
④ I like the roof of that house is blue.
⑤ I like the roof whose house is blue.

12
다음 빈칸에 that이 들어갈 수 없는 것은?

① He didn't know the girl _____ John likes.
② Where is the shop _____ sells medicine?
③ I met the man _____ brother is a painter.
④ I forgot to bring the books _____ I bought.
⑤ Do you remember the guy _____ wore a black jacket?

기출응용

[13-14] 다음 중 어법상 틀린 것을 고르시오.

13

Joe saw the girl who smile was bright.
　　① 　 ② 　 ③ 　 ④ 　 ⑤

14

The necklace that you lost are under the
　　　① 　　 ② 　 ③ 　 ④ 　 ⑤
desk.

15

다음 밑줄 친 부분의 쓰임이 나머지와 다른 것은?

① The man who is standing on that hill is my uncle.

② Please tell me who spilled water on the floor.

③ She is the girl who I usually walk to school with.

④ The teacher praised the boy who cleaned the classroom himself.

⑤ We are big fans of the writer who wrote this touching story.

[16-18] 다음 밑줄 친 부분이 어법상 틀린 것을 고르시오.

16

① This is a hit song that he sang.

② I like women who have long hair.

③ My brother works with people who make movies.

④ We saw a TV show which was about water sports.

⑤ Do you see the man and his dog which are walking on the path?

17

① It's the best diamond which we have.

② Look at the mess that you've made.

③ This is a board game which you can play with your friends.

④ Martin is the only man that believes my story.

⑤ Mike walked with a friend that was funnier than he is.

18

① Tom is the man whose wife is a vet.

② This is the dog that saved his owner's life.

③ Greg is the player who hit a home run.

④ I met a guy whose job is selling clothes.

⑤ He is the boy whom watch went missing.

19

다음 중 어법상 옳은 것을 모두 고르면? (3개)

① I helped the kid that leg is broken.

② He's an actor who was in *Star Wars*.

③ Julie is the girl whom scored the final goal.

④ I saw a boy and a cat that were sleeping under a tree.

⑤ This is the same issue that we discussed before.

20

다음 두 문장을 관계대명사를 이용하여 한 문장으로 만들 때, 잘못된 것은?

① There is a pink sweater. The sweater is popular.
   → There is a pink sweater which is popular.

② I had apple pies. My mom made them for me.
   → I had apple pies that my mom made for me.

③ I am going to meet the man. I used to study with him.
   → I am going to meet the man with who I used to study.

④ The man made many inventions. I've always respected him.
   → The man who I've always respected made many inventions.

⑤ The boy is the tallest student in the class. He is my best friend.
   → The boy who is my best friend is the tallest student in the class.

 서술형 따라잡기

01
다음 두 문장을 관계대명사를 이용하여 한 문장으로 바꾸어 쓰시오.

(1) He invented a robot.
The robot was very useful.

→ _____

(2) I like the notebook.
The notebook's cover is red.

→ _____

02
다음 우리말과 뜻이 같도록 주어진 말을 배열하여 문장을 완성하시오.

서울로 가는 기차는 15분 후에 출발한다.
(to, that, the train, Seoul, goes)

→ _____ leaves in
15 minutes.

03
다음 영화 감상평을 보고, 관계대명사를 이용하여 문장을 완성하시오.

Movie review: *Coco*
(1) zenny1234: Viewers will love it.
(2) moviegoer: It has a moving story.
(3) tbd2018: Its title song is beautiful!

(1) *Coco* is a movie _____.

(2) *Coco* is a movie _____.

(3) *Coco* is a movie _____.

04
다음 그림을 보고, 사람들을 묘사하는 문장을 완성하시오. (단, 현재시제 혹은 현재진행형으로 쓸 것)

(1) There is a girl _____ _____ _____
a skirt.

(2) There are two boys and a dog _____
_____ _____ _____ a ball.

(3) There is an old lady _____ _____
_____ long.

05
다음 우리말을 주어진 말과 관계대명사를 이용하여 영어로 옮겨 쓰시오. (단, 각각 9단어로 쓸 것)

(1) 그는 그 산을 등반한 첫 번째 사람이었다.
(first person, climb the mountain)
→ _____

(2) 내가 만났던 그 남자는 안과 의사였다.
(meet, eye doctor)
→ _____

고난도
06
다음 대화에서 어법상 틀린 부분을 모두 찾아 바르게 고쳐 쓰시오. (2군데)

A: Wow, it's a beautiful vase. Where did
you get it?
B: I received it from the man whom lives
next door.
A: Really? It is the very vase which I've
wanted!

핵심 포인트 정리하기

1 관계대명사
- 두 문장을 연결하는 접속사의 역할과 앞의 명사를 대신하는 대명사의 역할을 하며, 앞의 명사를 꾸며주는 형용사절을 이끎

2 관계대명사의 종류

격 \ 선행사	사람	사물이나 동물	사람+사물[동물]
주격	① _____, that	④ _____, that	⑦ _____
소유격	② _____	⑤ _____, of which	—
목적격	③ _____, that	⑥ _____, that	⑧ _____

- 관계대명사 ⑨ _____을 주로 쓰는 경우
  - 선행사가 〈사람 + 동물〉, 〈사람 + 사물〉일 때
  - 선행사에 최상급이나 서수가 있을 때
  - 선행사에 the only, the very, the same, the last, all, any, no 등이 포함되어 있을 때
  - 선행사가 -thing으로 끝나는 말일 때

 주격 관계대명사 뒤에는 동사, 소유격 관계대명사 뒤에는 명사가 온다는 것 기억하기!
전치사 뒤에는 목적격 관계대명사로 who나 that이 올 수 없다는 것 잊지 말기!
관계대명사 who와 의문사 who, 관계대명사 that과 종속 접속사 that의 쓰임 구분하기!
관계대명사 that을 주로 쓰는 경우 알아두기!

문제로 개념 다지기

밑줄 친 부분이 어법상 맞으면 O, 틀리면 X 표시하고 바르게 고치시오.

1 David is the brave boy <u>that</u> caught the thief.

2 The cafeteria at <u>that</u> I ate is next to my school.

3 This is the only Olympic event <u>which</u> I enjoy watching.

4 I made some egg sandwiches <u>that</u> she liked.

5 Nobody knows who owns the dog <u>which</u> tail is striped.

6 The old lady <u>which</u> is carrying a bag is my grandmother.

7 Is there any specific food <u>that</u> you would like to eat?

food truck

CHAPTER 10

관계사 II

개념 쏙쏙

I want to visit a house . I grew up in that house .

→ I want to visit the house in which I grew up.

→ I want to visit the house **where** I grew up.

관계부사

관계부사는 두 문장을 이어 주는 접속사 역할을 하는 동시에 부사의 역할을 하는 말로, 관계부사가 이끄는 절은 선행사를 수식합니다. 선행사의 종류에 따라 각기 다른 관계부사가 쓰인다는 점을 기억해 두세요.

관계대명사 what

- 관계대명사 what은 선행사를 포함한 관계대명사로 '~하는 것'으로 해석한다. 이때 what은 the thing(s) which[that]로 바꾸어 쓸 수 있으며, what이 이끄는 명사절은 단수 취급한다.
- 관계대명사 what이 이끄는 명사절은 문장에서 주어, 목적어, 보어의 역할을 한다.
  Show me **what** you bought.
  → Show me **the thing which[that]** you bought.

A 다음 ( ) 안에서 알맞은 말을 고르시오.

1 My parents don't let me do (which / what) I want to do.

2 (That / What) I'm saying is that we should protect wildlife.

3 Is she the girl (who / what) you're looking for?

B 다음 문장에서 관계대명사 what이 들어가야 할 곳에 V 표시하시오.

1 Let me see you're hiding behind your back.

2 I don't believe you told me.

3 Do you understand we learned today?

4 My teacher loved we made for her.

5 I brought is your favorite snack.

6 He didn't finish he had to do.

7 Those trees are I planted when I was five.

C 다음 우리말과 같은 뜻이 되도록 ( ) 안의 말을 이용하여 문장을 완성하시오.

1 나는 Jason이 내게 사준 것이 마음에 들었다. (buy)
I liked _____ _____ _____.

2 네가 들은 것을 아무한테도 얘기하지 마. (hear)
Don't tell anybody _____ _____.

3 그가 한 말은 그녀에게 상처를 주었다. (say)
_____ _____ hurt her.

4 죄송하지만 이것은 제가 주문한 것이 아닙니다. (order)
Sorry, but this isn't _____ _____.

5 그가 필요로 했던 것은 단지 약간의 음식과 물이었다. (need)
_____ _____ _____ was just some food and water.

6 대부분의 학생들이 그 교사가 설명한 것을 이해했다. (explain)
Most of the students understood _____ _____ _____.

관계대명사 what과 의문사 what의 구별

■ 관계대명사 what은 '~하는 것', 의문사 what은 '무엇'으로 해석한다.
Here is **what** you should know about Ted. (관계대명사 what)
I can't imagine **what** Mom will say about it. (의문사 what)

A 다음 우리말과 같은 뜻이 되도록 ( ) 안의 말을 배열하여 문장을 완성하시오.

1 나는 저녁 메뉴가 무엇인지 궁금하다. (is, dinner, what, for)
I wonder _____.

2 Ethan에게 일어난 일은 비극이었다. (happened, Ethan, to, what)
_____ was a tragedy.

3 그 파티에서 나를 놀라게 한 것은 그의 선물이었다. (me, what, surprised, at the party)
_____ was his present.

4 당신이 나를 위해 해 준 것에 감사합니다. (you, for, did, what, me)
I'm thankful for _____.

5 나는 네가 방금 말한 것을 이해할 수 없다. (just, you, what, said)
I can't understand _____.

6 그가 부모님에게 말하고 싶었던 것은 그가 그들을 그리워했다는 것이었다.
(wanted, he, tell, what, to, his parents)
_____ was that he missed them.

B 다음 문장에서 what이 관계대명사인지 의문사인지 쓰고, 우리말로 해석하시오.

1 Can you guess <u>what</u> that sound is? 〈   〉
_____

2 <u>What</u> I really need is your love. 〈   〉
_____

3 <u>What</u> we want now is time. 〈   〉
_____

4 I will ask him <u>what</u> I should eat first. 〈   〉
_____

5 Susan didn't like <u>what</u> her husband was wearing. 〈   〉
_____

Point 03 관계대명사의 생략 I

- 동사의 목적어로 쓰인 목적격 관계대명사 who(m), which, that은 생략이 가능하다.
  They are the friends **(who(m)[that])** I met in New York.
- 전치사의 목적어로 쓰인 목적격 관계대명사 who(m), which, that 역시 생략이 가능하다. 단, 전치사가 관계대명사 앞에 오는 경우에는 관계대명사 who나 that을 쓸 수 없고 목적격 관계대명사를 생략할 수 없다.
  This is the building **(which)** I used to live **in**. (which 생략 가능)
  This is the building **in which** I used to live. (which 생략 불가)

★ 내신만점 *TIP*
- 관계대명사가 전치사의 목적어로 쓰이는 경우, 관계사절 끝이나 관계대명사 앞에 전치사가 빠지지 않았는지 확인하자.
- 전치사가 관계대명사 앞에 오는 경우에 목적격 관계대명사를 생략할 수 없다는 것을 기억하자.

A 다음 문장에서 생략할 수 있는 부분을 찾아 ( ) 표시 하시오. (없으면 X 표시할 것)

1 I read the message which Emily sent me.

2 I looked at the pictures which Picasso painted.

3 That's the cell phone that I want to buy.

4 I like the people that I'm working with.

5 Tony is somebody to whom I can talk.

6 Everyone who saw the movie liked it a lot.

7 The boy that your sister is sitting next to looks kind.

8 The teacher who taught me last year was very nice.

9 A girl whom I know is a good swimmer.

10 The hotel which you told me about isn't there anymore.

11 The man with whom I studied music came from Canada.

12 Jack looked at the girl whom Jerry came with.

B 다음 우리말과 같은 뜻이 되도록 ( ) 안의 말을 배열하여 문장을 완성하시오.

1 역사는 Vicky가 관심 있어 하는 과목이다. (is, in, interested, Vicky)
History is a subject _____.

2 Ron은 내가 듣는 음악을 좋아하지 않는다. (the, to, music, listen, I)
Ron doesn't like _____.

3 Ann이 다니는 학교에는 큰 운동장이 있다. (goes, Ann, to, that)
The school _____ has a large playground.

4 Ed가 함께 여행했던 사람들은 재미가 없었다. (Ed, people, with, traveled, the)
_____ were boring.

관계대명사의 생략 II

- 〈주격 관계대명사+be동사〉는 뒤에 형용사구나 분사구가 올 때 생략할 수 있다.
Look at the boy **(who[that] is)** waving at us.
- 〈주격 관계대명사+be동사〉가 생략될 때, be동사 뒤의 형용사구(분사구)는 앞에 있는 명사를 수식하는 관계가 된다.
The girl **(who is)** wearing the red cap is Jenny.

A 다음 문장에서 생략할 수 있는 부분을 찾아 ( ) 표시하시오.

1 The TV that is in my bedroom is broken.

2 Don't call the students who are studying in the library.

3 A friend who is interested in rock music went to the rock festival.

4 I would like to go to the soccer stadium which is in Suwon.

5 Dogs which are left alone all day are unhappy.

6 The vegetables that are sold at this market are very fresh.

7 The woman who is teaching yoga to people is my cousin.

8 The English that is written on this paper is easy to read.

9 I have many friends who are from different countries.

10 People who are trying to lose weight eat low-calorie food.

B 다음 우리말과 같은 뜻이 되도록 ( ) 안의 말을 배열하여 문장을 완성하시오.

1 Ashley에게 이야기하고 있는 저 남자를 아니? (man, talking, the, to)
Do you know _____ Ashley?

2 글자 X로 시작하는 단어를 생각해 볼 수 있니? (with, a, beginning, word)
Can you think of _____ the letter X?

3 Nick을 공항으로 태워다 주던 택시가 고장 났다. (taking, which, Nick, was)
The taxi _____ to the airport broke down.

4 나는 나무로 만든 탁자를 인터넷으로 주문했다. (table, wood, a, made of)
I ordered _____ on the Internet.

5 식당에 올림픽 경기를 함께 보는 사람들이 많았다.
(the, watching, Olympic games, together)
There were a lot of people _____ in the restaurant.

관계부사 when / where

- 관계부사: 〈접속사+부사(구)〉의 역할을 하며, 관계부사가 이끄는 절은 선행사를 수식한다.
  관계부사는 〈전치사+관계대명사〉로 바꾸어 쓸 수 있다.
- when: 선행사가 시간이나 때를 나타내는 경우(the time, the day, the year 등)에 쓴다.
  I remember **the day**. + We first met **on that day**.
  → I remember *the day* **when(= on which)** we first met.
- where: 선행사가 장소를 나타내는 경우(the place, the house, the city 등)에 쓴다.
  This is **the park**. + I met the boy **at the park**.
  → This is *the park* **where(= at which)** I met the boy.

★ **PLUS TIP** 관계부사의 선행사가 the time, the place, the reason 등 일반적인 명사이면 선행사와 관계부사 중 하나를 생략할 수 있다.

A   다음 두 문장을 관계부사를 이용하여 한 문장으로 만드시오.

1   The city has a lot of trees. I was born in the city.
→ The city _____ has a lot of trees.

2   Kelly missed the town. She used to live in the town.
→ Kelly missed the town _____.

3   This is the place. The film festival will be held at the place.
→ This is the place _____.

4   Sunday is the only day. My family has dinner together on that day.
→ Sunday is the only day _____.

5   She remembers the days. She was lonely during those days.
→ She remembers the days _____.

6   He can't forget the day. He became a World Cup champion on that day.
→ He can't forget the day _____.

B   다음 우리말과 같은 뜻이 되도록 (   ) 안의 말을 이용하여 문장을 완성하시오.

1   월요일은 내가 피아노 교습을 받는 날이다. (take piano lessons)
Monday is the day _____ _____ _____ _____.

2   그녀는 그녀의 개를 산책시키는 그 공원을 좋아한다. (walk one's dog)
She likes the park _____ _____ _____.

3   내가 어제 책을 샀던 그 서점이 오늘 할인판매를 하고 있다. (buy books)
The bookstore _____ _____ _____ _____ yesterday is having a sale today.

관계부사 why / how

- why: 선행사가 이유를 나타내는 경우(the reason)에 쓴다.
  I know **the reason**. + My teacher was angry with me **for that reason**.
  → I know *the reason* **why(= for which)** my teacher was angry with me.
- how: 선행사가 방법을 나타내는 경우(the way)에 쓴다. 이때, 선행사 the way와 관계부사 how는 함께 쓰지 않는다.
  He showed me **the way**. + He fixed the machine **in that way**.
  → He showed me **how** he fixed the machine.
  → He showed me **the way** he fixed the machine.

★ 내신만점 *TIP*   관계부사 how는 선행사 the way와 함께 쓰지 않는다는 것을 기억하자.

A   다음 주어진 문장과 같은 뜻이 되도록 문장을 완성하시오.

1   Everyone knows the reason. She met Tim for that reason.
  → Everyone knows _____ _____ _____ she met Tim.
  → Everyone knows _____ she met Tim.

2   I don't like the way. My sister speaks in that way.
  → I don't like _____ _____ my sister speaks.

3   Please tell me the way. You downloaded the program in that way.
  → Please tell me _____ you downloaded the program.

4   My boyfriend doesn't know the reason for which I was nervous.
  → My boyfriend doesn't know _____ I was nervous.

5   She wants to know the reason why she failed the exam.
  → She wants to know the reason _____ _____ she failed the exam.

B   다음 우리말과 같은 뜻이 되도록 (   ) 안의 말을 이용하여 문장을 완성하시오.

1   네가 체중을 줄인 방법 좀 알려줘. (lose weight)
  Let me know _____ _____ _____ _____.

2   숙제를 안 한 이유를 내게 설명해 보아라. (do one's homework)
  Explain to me _____ _____ _____ _____ _____
  _____.

3   그녀가 나에게 사과해야 할 이유는 없다. (should, apologize)
  There is no reason _____ _____ _____ _____ to me.

4   우리가 글을 쓰는 방식은 말하는 방식과 다르다. (write)
  _____ _____ _____ is different from how we speak.

내신대비 TEST

[01-03] 다음 빈칸에 알맞은 말을 고르시오.

01

A: Did you understand _____ I said?
B: Yes, I got it.

① what   ② who   ③ where
④ whom   ⑤ whose

02

The reason _____ I'm contacting you is that I'm interested in your job offer.

① what   ② who   ③ when
④ where   ⑤ why

03

A: Did you solve the math question?
B: No, it's very difficult. I want to know
_____ Barry solved it.

① what   ② when   ③ where
④ who   ⑤ how

04
다음 중 관계대명사가 생략된 부분은?

The man ① I met ② in the gym ③ is ④ my homeroom teacher ⑤.

[05-06] 다음 빈칸에 공통으로 들어갈 말을 고르시오.

05

• This is the building _____ Ian works.
• The bakery _____ I used to buy cookies is closed on Sundays.

① who   ② that   ③ how
④ where   ⑤ why

06

• Can you tell me _____ to turn it on?
• That's _____ Joe saved money.

① who   ② how   ③ that
④ where   ⑤ why

[07-08] 빈칸에 들어갈 말이 순서대로 알맞게 짝지어진 것을 고르시오.

07

A: I don't know _____ I should do.
B: Ask Ted. There's no reason _____ you can't ask him.

① which – that   ② who – why
③ that – why   ④ what – why
⑤ what – which

08

A: The setting of this movie was in a place _____ there is a lot of wildlife.
B: Yes, and the director filmed it at a time _____ there was heavy snow.

① when – where   ② where – when
③ which – when   ④ where – how
⑤ when – what

09
다음 〈보기〉의 밑줄 친 부분과 쓰임이 같은 것은?

〈보기〉 Please let me do what I want to do.

① I can't guess what it is.
② Can you tell me what your name is?
③ I'm not sure what time he left home.
④ She wondered what his secret was.
⑤ Your advice is what makes me confident.

10
다음 중 밑줄 친 부분을 생략할 수 없는 것은?

① Amanda is the girl who has blond hair.
② Let's go to the store which is near here.
③ Jack is the boy who is with his parents.
④ The cat which is lying on the rock looks sick.
⑤ I saw a man who was dancing on the street.

[11-12] 다음 밑줄 친 부분의 쓰임이 잘못된 것을 고르시오.

11
① What he told me was shocking.
② This is the hospital where I was born.
③ The office in that he works is in Seoul.
④ Can you tell me when they met each other?
⑤ That isn't the reason why I left the party early.

12
① She knows the shop that he owns.
② Explain to me why you were late for school.
③ I don't have any friends that I can play with.
④ I asked him the way how he climbed the tree.
⑤ We changed the date when we would meet.

13
빈칸에 들어갈 말이 나머지와 다른 것은?

① That's not _____ I wanted to say.
② I am satisfied with _____ I have done.
③ I have a friend _____ plays the drums.
④ _____ he studied yesterday was math.
⑤ I showed Jeremy _____ I made for him.

14
다음 우리말을 영어로 바르게 옮긴 것은?

Paul이 우리를 데리고 간 방은 붐볐다.

① The room whom Paul took us was crowded.
② The room to that Paul took us was crowded.
③ The room which Paul took us was crowded.
④ The room that Paul took us to was crowded.
⑤ The room what Paul took us to was crowded.

15

다음 중 어느 빈칸에도 들어갈 수 <u>없는</u> 것은?

(a) This is _____ I learned today.
(b) Bill went to the bank _____ is across from the pet shop.
(c) He loves the place _____ he can see animals.
(d) I don't want to know the reason _____ you broke up with her.

① which　　② what　　③ where
④ why　　⑤ who

16

(A), (B), (C)의 괄호 안에서 알맞은 것끼리 바르게 짝지어진 것은?

(A) McDonald's is a fast-food restaurant [which / where] a lot of teenagers like.
(B) 2018 is the year [which / when] I entered middle school.
(C) George is the person with [that / whom] I studied in science class.

	(A)		(B)		(C)
①	which	·····	when	·····	whom
②	which	·····	when	·····	that
③	which	·····	which	·····	that
④	where	·····	which	·····	whom
⑤	where	·····	when	·····	whom

[17-18] 다음 중 어법상 <u>틀린</u> 것을 고르시오.

17

① The city I was born in has many lakes.
② Susan said something I couldn't hear.
③ The singer had the flu canceled the concert.
④ I have two friends I love very much.
⑤ Look at the girl kissing her mom.

18

① The building that I entered was hot.
② Could you tell me the way you save much money?
③ This grammar book we are using now has a lot of exercises.
④ There was a patient of that the nurse had to take care.
⑤ Five students were absent on the day when there was a listening test.

19

다음 빈칸에 들어갈 말이 같은 것끼리 바르게 짝지어진 것은?

(a) _____ I gave Nick was perfume.
(b) The soup _____ he made was awful.
(c) That's exactly _____ I'm saying!
(d) May 30 is the day _____ my parents married.

① (a), (b)　　② (a), (c)　　③ (a), (d)
④ (b), (c)　　⑤ (c), (d)

20

다음 중 어법상 옳은 문장의 개수는?

(a) Dean has a dog that has short legs.
(b) I lost a purse I had all my money in.
(c) Look at the little boy playing the guitar!
(d) Show me the pants what you bought.

① 0개　　② 1개　　③ 2개　　④ 3개　　⑤ 4개

서술형 따라잡기

01

다음 우리말과 뜻이 같도록 관계사와 주어진 말을 이용하여 문장을 완성하시오.

(1) 내가 지금 하고 싶은 것은 쉬는 것이다. (want)

→ _____ _____ _____ _____
_____ now is rest.

(2) 그것이 내가 그를 싫어하는 이유이다.
(the reason, hate)
→ That is _____ _____

_____ _____ _____.

02

주어진 말을 알맞게 배열하여 대화를 완성하시오.

(1) A: What's your plan for the vacation?
B: I'll visit a place _____.
(can, I, surf, where)

(2) A: You speak Japanese really well!
B: Yes, but there were days _____
_____ in Japanese.
(couldn't, when, speak, I, a word)

03

어법상 틀린 부분을 1군데 찾아 바르게 고쳐 쓰시오.

(1) Mary didn't do that she had to do.

(2) This is the scarf for that I've been
looking.

04

다음 두 문장을 관계부사를 이용하여 한 문장으로 쓰시오.

(1) That was the day. I fell in love with her then.

→ _____

(2) That is the street. I found the purse on that
street.

→ _____

05

다음 그림을 보고, 관계사와 주어진 말을 이용하여 문장을 완성하시오.

(1) I graduated on a day _____ _____
_____. (snow)

(2) _____ _____ _____ was a bunch of
flowers. (hold)

(3) The woman with _____ _____

_____ _____ _____ was my math
teacher. (take the picture)

기출응용
06

다음 조건에 맞게 우리말을 영어로 옮겨 쓰시오.

〈조건〉　1. 적절한 관계사를 이용할 것
　　　　2. 주어진 어휘를 이용할 것

(1) 요리를 하고 있는 저 여자를 봐. (look at, cook)

→ _____

(2) 이것이 내가 단어를 암기하는 방법이다.
(memorize, words)

→ _____

1 관계대명사 what

- ① _____를 포함한 관계대명사: '~하는 것'
- 명사절로 쓰여 문장에서 주어, 목적어, 보어 역할을 함

*의문사 what: '무엇'

2 관계대명사의 생략

- 동사나 전치사의 목적어로 쓰인 ② _____는 생략 가능

*목적격 관계대명사 앞에 전치사가 오는 경우에는 생략할 수 없음!

- 〈주격 관계대명사 + ③ _____〉도 생략 가능

 관계대명사의 생략이 가능한 경우와 불가한 경우 구분하기!

3 관계부사 = 〈④ _____ + _____〉

when	선행사가 시간이나 때를 나타내는 경우
⑤ _____	선행사가 장소를 나타내는 경우
why	선행사가 이유를 나타내는 경우
⑥ _____	선행사가 방법을 나타내는 경우

* 선행사가 the time, the place, the reason 등 일반적인 명사이면 선행사와 관계부사 중 하나 생략 가능

 각 관계부사와 자주 쓰이는 선행사 알아두기!
선행사 the way와 관계부사 how는 함께 쓰지 않는다는 것 기억하기!

밑줄 친 부분이 어법상 맞으면 O, 틀리면 X 표시하고 바르게 고치시오.

1 I went to the place <u>when</u> my favorite movie was filmed.

2 He passed an audition. That is <u>where</u> he became a dancer.

3 Everything <u>you did</u> was wrong.

4 I agree with <u>that</u> you're saying.

5 My grandparents encourage me to do <u>what</u> I really want.

6 She'll never forget the day <u>on which</u> she won a prize.

7 Please tell me the way <u>how</u> you made this candle.

CHAPTER 11

분사

I heard an **amazing** story from Jacob.　　　　[현재분사]

She visited a palace **built** 200 years ago.　　　[과거분사]

Waving his hands, the man entered the classroom.　　[분사구문]

분사

형용사처럼 명사를 꾸며주거나 보어로 쓰여 주어와 목적어를 보충 설명하는 말입니다. 분사에는 현재분사(동사원형+-ing)와 과거분사(동사원형+-ed)가 있습니다.

분사구문

분사를 이용하여 〈접속사+주어+동사〉 형태의 부사절을 부사구로 줄여 쓴 것을 말합니다.

현재분사

- 분사는 동사 본래의 의미를 가지면서 형용사처럼 명사를 수식하거나 주어·목적어를 보충 설명하는 보어 역할을 한다.
- 현재분사: 〈동사원형+-ing〉의 형태로 능동·진행의 의미를 가진다. 진행형 〈be동사+v-ing〉를 만들거나 명사를 수식하며, 보어로 쓰이기도 한다.

  My mom *is* **cooking** in the kitchen. (진행형)

  This is an **interesting** story. (명사 앞에서 수식)

  Look at the boy **dancing** on the street. (수식어구와 함께 쓰일 때는 뒤에서 명사 수식)

  I watched people **walking** on the beach. (목적격 보어)

A   다음 우리말과 같은 뜻이 되도록 문장을 완성하시오.

1   그 뉴스는 매우 충격적이었다.

The news was very _____ .

2   그녀는 자는 아기를 바라보았다.

She looked at the _____ baby.

3   그 아기는 정원에서 강아지와 함께 놀고 있다.

The baby is _____ with a puppy in the garden.

4   그는 약 한 시간 동안 나를 기다리게 했다.

He kept me _____ for about an hour.

5   그 연못은 헤엄치는 물고기들로 가득 차 있다.

The pond is full of _____ fish.

6   토요일 저녁에 떠나는 비행기가 있습니다.

There is a flight _____ on Saturday evening.

7   Peter는 그의 애완 거북이에 대해 이야기하고 있다.

Peter is _____ about his pet turtle.

B   다음 우리말과 같은 뜻이 되도록 ( ) 안의 말을 배열하여 문장을 완성하시오.

1   나는 떨어지는 빗소리를 좋아한다. (of, rain, the, falling, the sound)

I love _____ .

2   나는 내 심장이 매우 빠르게 뛰는 것을 느꼈다. (beating, fast, my heart, very)

I felt _____ .

3   그의 성공은 우리에게 감동적이었다. (touching, to, was, us)

His success _____ .

과거분사

- 과거분사: 〈동사원형+-ed〉의 형태로 수동·완료의 의미를 가진다. 완료형 〈have[has]+과거분사(v-ed)〉과 수동태 〈be동사+과거분사(v-ed)〉를 만들거나 명사를 수식하며, 보어로 쓰이기도 한다.
  I *have* just **finished** the report. (완료형)
  This car *was* **made** in Japan. (수동태)
  The **broken** window looks dangerous. (명사 앞에서 수식)
  The hat **made** by my girlfriend is warm. (수식어구와 함께 쓰일 때는 뒤에서 명사 수식)
  You should keep the door **locked** when you are alone. (목적격 보어)

★ 내신만점 *TIP* 감정을 나타내는 동사는 분사형으로 종종 쓰인다. 감정을 유발하는 주체(주로 사물)를 설명할 때는 능동의 의미인 현재분사를, 감정을 느끼게 되는 대상(주로 사람)을 설명할 때는 수동의 의미인 과거분사를 사용한다는 것을 알아두자.
The movie is **interesting**. (현재분사)   I'm **interested** in the movie. (과거분사)

A 다음 우리말과 같은 뜻이 되도록 〈보기〉에서 알맞은 말을 골라 빈칸에 적절한 형태로 써넣으시오.

〈보기〉 call   paint   build   fall   surround

1 그 기차역은 몇 년 전에 지어졌다.
  The train station was _____ a few years ago.

2 나는 Navi라고 불리는 고양이가 한 마리 있다.
  I have a cat _____ Navi.

3 그 남자는 떨어진 나뭇잎들 위에 서 있었다.
  The man was standing on _____ leaves.

4 그 나라는 삼면이 바다로 둘러싸여 있다.
  The country is _____ by water on three sides.

5 그 미술관에는 모네에 의해 그려진 그림 몇 점이 있다.
  There are some pictures _____ by Monet in the art museum.

B 다음 문장에서 <u>틀린</u> 부분을 찾아 어법에 맞게 고쳐 쓰시오.

1 I have a book writing in English.

2 You should be careful with the break glass.

3 Susie is exciting about winning a prize.

4 My parents were disappoint with the new refrigerator.

5 The food cooking by my brother is always delicious.

6 People were shocking by the ending of the movie.

7 The boy injured in the accident was taking to the hospital.

분사구문 만드는 법

- 분사구문이란 분사를 이용하여 〈접속사＋주어＋동사〉 형태의 부사절을 부사구로 줄여 쓴 구문을 말한다.
- 분사구문 만드는 법: ① 접속사를 없앤다.
  ② 주어를 없앤다. (주절과 부사절의 주어가 같은 경우)
  ③ 동사를 〈동사원형＋-ing〉의 형태로 바꾼다.

When he heard the news, he smiled. → **Hearing** the news, he smiled.

★ PLUS TIP 분사구문의 의미를 분명히 전달하기 위해 접속사를 남겨 두기도 한다.
While taking a shower, I heard my mom calling me.

A 다음 밑줄 친 부분을 분사구문으로 바꾸어 쓰시오.

1 <u>When he saw the police officer</u>, he ran away.
→ _____, he ran away.

2 <u>If you turn to the left</u>, you will find the café.
→ _____, you will find the café.

3 <u>Because she knew the way</u>, she got here quickly.
→ _____, she got here quickly.

4 <u>After he put down the book</u>, he looked out the window.
→ _____, he looked out the window.

5 <u>Because he wanted to see the Great Wall</u>, he decided to go to China.
→ _____, he decided to go to China.

B 다음 우리말과 같은 뜻이 되도록 분사구문을 이용하여 문장을 완성하시오.

1 음악을 듣느라 나는 초인종이 울리는 것을 듣지 못했다.
_____ _____, I didn't hear the doorbell ring.

2 늦었기 때문에 나는 그 콘서트장에 들어가지 못했다.
_____ _____, I couldn't enter the concert hall.

3 라디오를 꺼서 나는 바깥의 새소리를 들을 수 있었다.
_____ _____ _____ _____, I could hear the birds outside.

4 택시를 탄다면 당신은 정오 전에 그곳에 도착할 것이다.
_____ _____, you will arrive there before noon.

5 나를 쳐다보며 그는 무슨 일이 일어났는지 물었다.
_____ _____ _____, he asked what happened.

때/이유를 나타내는 분사구문

- 때: '~할 때(when / as)', '~한 후에(after)', '~하는 동안(while)'이라는 의미를 나타낼 수 있다.
  Walking along the street, I saw an old friend.
  (→ As I walked along the street, I saw an old friend.)
- 이유: '~ 때문에(because / as / since)'라는 의미를 나타낼 수 있다.
  Feeling tired, I went to bed early.
  (→ Because I felt tired, I went to bed early.)

★ PLUS TIP 분사구문의 부정은 분사 앞에 not이나 never를 써서 나타낸다.
Not knowing his phone number, I sent him an email.

A 다음 우리말과 같은 뜻이 되도록 〈보기〉의 문장을 이용하여 분사구문을 완성하시오.

〈보기〉 I don't know Japanese.　　She arrived at the station.
　　　　 We waited for him.　　　　He didn't have enough money.

1 그를 기다리는 동안 우리는 신문을 읽었다.
_____, we read the newspaper.

2 역에 도착했을 때 그녀는 그녀의 아이들을 만났다.
_____, she met her children.

3 일본어를 모르기 때문에 나는 그 만화를 이해할 수 없다.
_____, I can't understand the cartoon.

4 충분한 돈이 없었기 때문에 그는 그 스마트폰을 살 수 없었다.
_____, he couldn't buy the smartphone.

B 다음 두 문장이 같은 뜻이 되도록 ( ) 안의 접속사를 이용하여 문장을 완성하시오.

1 Seeing me, she started crying. (when)
→ _____, she started crying.

2 Doing his homework, he listened to classical music. (while)
→ _____, he listened to classical music.

3 Lying on the grass, she watched the clouds move past. (while)
→ _____, she watched the clouds move past.

4 Not feeling very well, I decided not to go to the party. (since)
→ _____, I decided not to go to the party.

Point 05 동시동작/연속상황을 나타내는 분사구문

■ 동시동작: '～하면서(while / as)'라는 의미를 나타낼 수 있다.

Calling my name, she came into the room.

(→ While she was calling my name, she came into the room.)

■ 연속상황: '～하고 나서(and)'라는 의미를 나타낼 수 있다.

The plane leaves at five, **arriving** just three hours later.

(→ The plane leaves at five and arrives just three hours later.)

★ PLUS TIP   Being으로 시작되는 진행형이나 수동형의 분사구문에서는 Being을 보통 생략한다.
While she was watching TV, she ate dinner. → **(Being) Watching** TV, she ate dinner.

A 다음 우리말과 같은 뜻이 되도록 〈보기〉의 문장을 이용하여 분사구문을 완성하시오.

〈보기〉	We were walking home together.	We were holding hands.
	I entered the room.	He shook hands with me.
	I was getting off the bus.	

1 나와 악수를 하면서 그는 환하게 미소 지었다.

_____, he smiled brightly.

2 우리는 손을 잡고 별을 바라봤다.

_____, we looked up at the stars.

3 나는 방에 들어가면서 불을 켰다.

_____, I turned on the light.

4 버스에서 내리다가 나는 미끄러져 넘어졌다.

_____, I slipped and fell.

5 함께 집으로 걸어오면서 우리는 우리의 미래에 대해 이야기했다.

_____, we talked about our future.

B 다음 문장을 분사구문으로 바꾸어 쓰시오.

1 While he was standing on the hill, he watched the ship leaving.

→ _____

2 The shuttle bus leaves at seven and arrives 15 minutes later.

→ _____

3 As we danced together, we laughed and smiled.

→ _____

- 조건: '~하면(if)'이라는 의미를 나타낼 수 있다.
  Going downstairs, you will see a tall woman.
  (→ If you go downstairs, you will see a tall woman.)
- 양보: '~일지라도(though / although)'라는 의미를 나타낼 수 있다.
  Though living near his house, she never saw him.
  (→ Though she lived near his house, she never saw him.)

★ **PLUS TIP** 양보의 의미를 나타내는 분사구문은 실제로는 잘 쓰지 않으며, 주로 분사구문 앞에 접속사 though(although)를 남겨
두거나 〈Despite+동명사〉의 형태로 그 의미를 표현하는 경우가 많다.

A 다음 문장을 〈접속사(If나 Though)+주어+동사〉의 형태로 바꾸어 쓰시오.

1 Though living near the beach, he cannot swim.

→ _____, he cannot swim.

2 Though exercising regularly, the man isn't losing any weight.

→ _____, he isn't losing any weight.

3 Buying this chocolate, you'll get another one for free.

→ _____, you'll get another one for free.

4 Taking this pill, you'll feel much better.

→ _____, you'll feel much better.

B 다음 우리말과 같은 뜻이 되도록 ( ) 안의 말과 분사구문을 이용하여 문장을 완성하시오.

1 많이 먹지는 않지만 그 환자는 잘 지내고 있다. (eat much)
Though _____ _____ _____, the patient is doing fine.

2 그것이 사실인 줄 알았으면서도 나는 여전히 그것을 믿을 수 없었다. (true)
Though _____ _____ _____ _____, I still couldn't believe it.

3 내 조언을 따른다면 너는 시험에 합격할 것이다. (follow, advice)
_____ _____ _____, you will pass the exam.

4 젓가락을 사용하면 너는 그것을 쉽게 집을 수 있다. (chopsticks)
_____ _____, you can pick it up easily.

5 부상을 당했는데도 그 축구 선수는 계속 경기를 했다. (be injured)
Though _____ _____, the soccer player kept playing the game.

6 그와 얘기해보면 너는 그가 좋은 남자라는 것을 알게 될 것이다. (talk with)
_____ _____ _____, you will realize he is a nice man.

내신대비 TEST

[01-03] 다음 빈칸에 알맞은 말을 고르시오.

01

A woman is looking at her _____ child.

① play   ② played   ③ playing
④ to play   ⑤ is playing

02

The computer program is _____ in Korea.

① make   ② made   ③ making
④ to make   ⑤ makes

03

I want that teddy bear _____ flowers in its hand.

① hold   ② holds   ③ held
④ to holding   ⑤ holding

기출응용

04

다음 〈보기〉의 두 단어의 관계와 같도록 빈칸에 들어갈 말이 순서대로 알맞게 짝지어진 것은?

〈보기〉 knowing – known

• eating – _____ • _____ – forgotten

① eaten – forgot   ② eaten – forgetting
③ eaten – forget   ④ ate – forgetting
⑤ ate – forgot

[05-07] 빈칸에 들어갈 말이 순서대로 알맞게 짝지어진 것을 고르시오.

05

A: Did you see any _____ TV programs yesterday?
B: No. _____, I went to bed early.

① interested – Tiring
② interested – Tired
③ interesting – Tiring
④ interesting – Being tired
⑤ interesting – Be tired

06

A: Who is the man _____ there?
B: I'm not sure. _____ my glasses, I can't recognize him from here.

① stand – Not wearing
② stand – Wearing not
③ standing – Wearing
④ standing – Being worn
⑤ standing – Not wearing

07

• I heard my name _____ by someone.
• _____ young, she has little experience.

① call – Being   ② called – Being
③ calling – Been   ④ calling – Being
⑤ called – Been

08

Crossing the street, she saw the traffic light.

① If she crossed the street
② Because she crosses the street
③ While she was crossing the street
④ Though she was crossing the street
⑤ When she is crossing the street

09

Surprised at the news, he turned pale.

① As he was surprised at the news
② If he was surprised at the news
③ When he is surprised at the news
④ Before he was surprised at the news
⑤ Though he was surprised at the news

10

다음 밑줄 친 부분을 분사구문으로 바르게 바꾸지 <u>않은</u> 것은?

① Because I have no car, I have to walk home.
　→ Having no car
② When he arrived in Italy, he took some pictures.
　→ Arriving in Italy
③ While she was talking on the phone, my mother was taking some notes.
　→ Talking on the phone
④ If you read this book once more, you'll understand it.
　→ Reading this book once more
⑤ Though Jake studied very hard, he failed to pass the math exam.
　→ Though studied very hard

11

〈보기〉 Taking a shower, he sang a song.

① Being thirsty, I drank water.
② Lying on the bed, I read a book.
③ Not knowing the way, I got lost.
④ Getting a good night's sleep, people can work better.
⑤ Running into her there, I was really happy.

12

〈보기〉 Having nothing to do, I was bored.

① Being sweet, he is popular.
② Coming up to me, she said hello.
③ Eating snacks, she watched a movie.
④ Smiling happily, the baby watched me.
⑤ Looking out the window, I saw my father coming.

13

다음 대화 중 자연스럽지 <u>않은</u> 것은?

① A: What do you think about his voice?
　B: I think it is amazing.
② A: What happened to your finger?
　B: I cut it on a broken glass.
③ A: Why are you standing here?
　B: I am waiting for my sister.
④ A: Laughing and talking, we had a great time.
　B: Wow, you were very exciting.
⑤ A: Where is the tourist information center?
　B: Turning to your right, you will see it.

14

① The lecture was very satisfying.

② He sat reading a magazine.

③ I saw her singing on the stage.

④ The man danced with the little child is my husband.

⑤ The work should be done as soon as possible.

15

① Disappointed, he couldn't say a word.

② Having no money, I can't go shopping.

③ Knowing not his address, I can't write to him.

④ He picked up a stone, throwing it into a pond.

⑤ Going up the tower, you can see the whole view of the city.

16

① Being late, I took a taxi to the station.

② Being angry, she didn't even look at me.

③ Being on a corner, the shop is hard to find.

④ Being sick makes it hard for me to work.

⑤ Being moved by the movie, she started to cry.

17

① Her hobby is flying drones.

② Look at those people running in a marathon!

③ The player kicking the ball is Korean.

④ This is a really embarrassing question.

⑤ Noticing a person, the cat ran away.

18

다음 우리말을 영어로 바르게 옮긴 것은?

Jason은 그녀의 손을 잡고 걸었다.

① Jason walked held her hand.

② Jason walked holding her hand.

③ Jason was walking held her hand.

④ Jason has walked hold her hand.

⑤ Jason was walked holding her hand.

19

다음 중 어법상 틀린 문장의 개수는?

(a) This is a famous robot invented by college students.

(b) The man fixed the TV needs tools.

(c) She looked disappointing at his attitude.

(d) He opened the window, shouting to his friends.

① 0개 ② 1개 ③ 2개 ④ 3개 ⑤ 4개

고난도
20

(A), (B), (C)의 괄호 안에서 알맞은 것끼리 바르게 짝지어진 것은?

(A) [Leaving / Left] alone, the child fell asleep.

(B) Did you see the book [writing / written] by Kyle?

(C) They walked along the street, [talking / talked] loudly.

	(A)	(B)	(C)
①	Leaving	writing	talking
②	Leaving	writing	talked
③	Leaving	written	talking
④	Left	written	talking
⑤	Left	written	talked

서술형 따라잡기

01

다음 그림을 보고, 〈보기〉에서 알맞은 말을 골라 문장을 완성하시오.

〈보기〉 bark   place   play

(1) A boy is holding a _____ dog.

(2) There is a girl _____ with a doll.

(3) There is a flowerpot _____ on the table.

02

다음 밑줄 친 부분을 분사구문으로 바꾸어 쓰시오.

(1) <u>When I entered the room</u>, I saw her shopping on the Internet.

→ _____, I saw her shopping on the Internet.

(2) <u>As I was not interested in skiing</u>, I stayed home.

→ _____, I stayed home.

03

어법상 틀린 부분을 모두 찾아 바르게 고쳐 쓰시오. (2군데)

Be busy, he couldn't go out for lunch. So he ate all the food leaving on the kitchen table.

04

주어진 말을 알맞게 배열하여 우리말과 뜻이 같도록 문장을 완성하시오.

(1) 그가 그린 그림을 봐라.

(drawn, at, look, by him, the picture)

→ _____

(2) 이 마을에 살지 않아서 나는 그를 모른다.

(town, not, know, I, living, in, don't, him, this)

→ _____

05

주어진 말을 이용하여 대화를 완성하시오.

A: Why didn't you come to the party?

B: _____ _____, I stayed in bed. (sick)

A: What happened to you?

B: _____ _____ a coat, I caught a cold. (wear) So how was the party?

A: It was great. We talked a lot, _____ many delicious desserts. (enjoy)

06

다음 일정표를 보고, 분사구문을 이용하여 문장을 완성하시오.

Mon.	Study at the library because I have an exam on Friday
Tue.	Listen to the radio & Write Christmas cards
Wed.	Play tennis if I am free

(1) _____, I will study at the library on Monday.

(2) _____, I will write Christmas cards on Tuesday.

(3) _____, I will play tennis on Wednesday.

핵심 포인트 정리하기

1 **분사**: 동사 본래의 의미를 가지면서, 형용사처럼 명사를 수식하거나 주어·목적어를 보충 설명하는 보어 역할을 하는 말
- 현재분사(능동·진행의 의미)
  - 형태: 〈① _____ + _____〉
- 과거분사(② _____의 의미)
  - 형태: 〈③ _____ + _____〉

 감정을 유발하는 주체에는 현재분사, 감정을 느끼게 되는 대상에는 과거분사를 쓴다는 것 잊지 말기!

2 **분사구문**: 분사를 이용하여 〈접속사+주어+동사〉 형태의 부사절을 부사구로 줄여 쓴 구문

분사구문 만드는 법		
접속사 생략 →	주어 생략 (주절과 부사절의 주어가 같은 경우) →	동사 변형 (동사원형+-ing) *Being은 보통 생략

- 때: '~할 때(when / as)' / '~한 후에(after)' / '~하는 동안(while)'
- 이유: '~ 때문에(because / as / since)'
- ④ _____ : '~하면서(while / as)'
- 연속상황: '~하고 나서(and)'
- 조건: ⑤ '_____(if)'
- 양보: '~일지라도(though / although)'

 분사구문 만드는 법 기억하기!
분사구문의 서로 다른 용법 구분하기!

문제로 개념 다지기

다음 ( ) 안에서 알맞은 말을 고르시오.

1 The woman (plays / playing) with a child is my aunt.

2 He couldn't join the game because of his (breaking / broken) leg.

3 It was (surprising news / surprised news).

4 When he crossed the street, the man ran into his old friend.
   → (Crossing / Crossed) the street, the man ran into his old friend.

5 Though she smiled at me, she was angry.
   → Though (she smiling / smiling) at me, she was angry.

6 If we take the subway, you can read a book on your way to work.
   → (We take / Taking) the subway, you can read a book on your way to work.

CHAPTER 12
수동태

A lot of people **love** that drama.　　　　　[능동태]

That drama **is loved** by a lot of people.　　[수동태]
　　　　　　　<be+v-ed>

능동태 vs. 수동태

능동태는 주어가 직접 행위를 하는 것(~가 …하다)을 나타낼 때 사용하고, 수동태는 <be동사+v-ed>의 형태로 주어가 행위의 영향을 받거나 행위를 당하는 것(~가 …되다)을 나타낼 때 사용합니다.

Point 01 수동태의 의미 및 만드는 법

■ 수동태: ⟨be동사+v-ed(+by+행위자)⟩의 형태로 주어가 행위의 영향을 받거나 행위를 당할 때 사용하며, '~가 …되다[받다]'라고 해석한다.

⟨능동태 문장을 수동태 문장으로 바꾸는 방법⟩

Spielberg directed this movie.

① ② ③

This movie **was directed** by Spielberg.

① 능동태의 목적어를 수동태의 주어 자리에 둔다.

② 능동태의 동사를 ⟨be동사+과거분사(v-ed)⟩의 형태로 바꾼다. be동사의 수·인칭은 수동태의 주어에 맞추고, 시제는 능동태의 시제를 유지한다.

③ 능동태의 주어를 ⟨by+행위자⟩로 바꾸어 문장의 뒤로 보낸다.

★ 내신만점 TIP 목적어가 필요 없는 동사(appear, disappear, happen, remain 등)와, 상태나 소유를 나타내는 동사(have, fit, resemble 등)는 수동태로 쓰지 않는다는 것을 알아두자.

A 다음 ( ) 안에서 알맞은 말을 고르시오.

1 Popcorn (sells / is sold) in movie theaters.

2 The character is loved (by / to) a lot of children.

3 I (resemble / am resembled by) my father.

4 The soup (smells / is smelled) good.

5 Cristiano (be trusted / is trusted) by his coach.

B 다음 문장을 수동태 문장으로 바꾸어 쓰시오.

1 That woman reads this fashion magazine.
→ This fashion magazine _____.

2 Thousands of people visit this website.
→ This website _____.

3 Teenage girls followed the singer.
→ The singer _____.

4 My uncle designed those nice blue jeans.
→ Those nice blue jeans _____.

5 The director wrote this story.
→ _____.

6 Viewers choose the best actor of the year.
→ _____.

■ 과거시제의 능동태 문장을 수동태로 바꾸면 〈be동사의 과거형+v-ed(+by+행위자)〉의 형태가 된다.
Egyptians first grew watermelons.
→ Watermelons **were** first **grown** by Egyptians.

A 다음 문장을 수동태 문장으로 바꾸어 쓰시오.

1 Polly made this cute doll.
→ This cute doll _____.

2 A thief stole my wallet.
→ My wallet _____.

3 My mom baked this cheesecake.
→ This cheesecake _____.

4 My grandfather built this high school.
→ This high school _____.

5 Beethoven wrote the *Pastoral Symphony*.
→ The *Pastoral Symphony* _____.

6 A university student developed that social networking site.
→ That social networking site _____.

B 다음 우리말과 같은 뜻이 되도록 ( ) 안의 말을 이용하여 문장을 완성하시오.

1 그 쇼에서 새로운 그림들이 그에 의해 소개되었다. (introduce)
New paintings _____ _____ _____ him at the show.

2 달 사진들이 그 우주비행사들에 의해 찍혔다. (take)
The photos of the moon _____ _____ _____ the astronauts.

3 「밤의 카페 테라스」는 빈센트 반 고흐에 의해 그려졌다. (paint)
Café Terrace at Night _____ _____ _____ Vincent van Gogh.

4 좋지 않은 날씨 때문에 모든 비행이 취소되었다. (cancel)
All the flights _____ _____ due to the bad weather.

5 이 드레스는 한 유명 모델에 의해 착용되었다. (dress, wear)
_____ _____ _____ _____ a famous model.

6 그 다큐멘터리는 한국의 한 영화사에 의해 제작되었다. (documentary, produce)
_____ _____ _____ _____ a Korean film company.

미래시제의 수동태

■ 미래시제의 능동태 문장을 수동태로 바꾸면 〈will+be+v-ed(+by+행위자)〉의 형태가 된다.
The next Winter Olympics **will be held** in Beijing.
This art project **will be finished** by Jim next week.

A 다음 문장을 수동태 문장으로 바꾸어 쓰시오.

1 Peter will explain the details.
→ The details _____.

2 My father will make dinner tonight.
→ Dinner _____ tonight.

3 The manager will guide you to the room.
→ You _____ by the manager.

4 My mom will drive me to the birthday party.
→ I _____ by my mom.

5 Your math teacher will check your homework around 9 a.m.
→ Your homework _____ by your math teacher.

6 The teddy bear company will produce 100,000 dolls next year.
→ 100,000 dolls _____ next year.

7 A lot of people will watch the final match tomorrow.
→ _____ tomorrow.

B 다음 우리말과 같은 뜻이 되도록 ( ) 안의 말을 배열하여 문장을 완성하시오.

1 당신의 전화는 자동으로 응답될 것입니다.
(will, answered, your, be, call, automatically)
_____

2 내 마지막 시험은 2시간 후에 끝날 것이다.
(my, last exam, finished, will, in two hours, be)
_____

3 우리 동네에 새로운 극장이 지어질 것이다.
(built, my, a, town, new theater, will, in, be)
_____

4 Jason은 그 일에 대해 100달러를 지급받을 것이다.
(100 dollars, Jason, paid, for, be, the, will, work)
_____

수동태의 부정문·의문문 / 조동사의 수동태

- 수동태의 부정문: 〈be동사+not+v-ed(+by+행위자)〉의 형태이다.
  This memo **was not written** by me.
- 수동태의 의문문: be동사가 주어 앞에 오는 〈be동사+주어+v-ed(+by+행위자)?〉의 형태이다.
  Are these rooms **cleaned** every day?
- 조동사의 수동태: 〈조동사+be+v-ed(+by+행위자)〉의 형태로, 수동태 문장에 조동사의 뜻을 더하여 해석한다.
  The criminal **should be caught** by the police.

A 다음 (   ) 안의 말을 이용하여 대화를 완성하시오.

1 A: Who took my scarf?
B: I don't know. It _____ _____ _____ by me. (take)

2 A: Why _____ the flight _____? (delay)
B: Because it was snowing heavily.

3 A: Are you going to their wedding?
B: No, I _____ _____ _____ to the wedding. (invite)

4 A: When _____ the first camera _____? (make)
B: I'm not sure. Let's search for the answer on the Internet.

5 A: _____ the website _____ by hackers? (attack)
B: I guess so.

B 다음 우리말과 같은 뜻이 되도록 (   ) 안의 말을 이용하여 문장을 완성하시오.

1 그 소포는 제시간에 배송되지 않았다. (deliver)
The package _____ _____ _____ on time.

2 이 순간은 영원히 기억될 것이다. (will, remember)
This moment _____ _____ _____ forever.

3 입장료는 카드로 지불될 수 있습니다. (can, pay)
The admission fee _____ _____ _____ by credit card.

4 Henry가 직장을 그만둔 이유가 곧 알려질지도 모른다. (may, know)
The reason Henry quit his job _____ _____ _____ soon.

5 그 보고서는 이번 주까지 완성되어야 한다. (should, complete)
The report _____ _____ _____ by this week.

6 그 다이아몬드는 금고로 옮겨질 것이다. (be going to, move)
The diamond _____ _____ _____ _____ _____
to the safe.

4형식 문장의 수동태

- 4형식 문장은 목적어가 두 개(간접목적어·직접목적어)이므로 두 가지 형태의 수동태를 만들 수 있다.

Tina gave me a birthday present.
　　　　간접목적어　　직접목적어

→ I **was given** a birthday present by Tina. (간접목적어를 주어로 할 때)

→ A birthday present **was given** to me by Tina. (직접목적어를 주어로 할 때)

- 직접목적어를 주어로 하는 수동태 문장을 만들 경우, 간접목적어 앞에 적절한 전치사(to, for 등)를 써야 한다. 이 때, give 류의 수여동사는 간접목적어 앞에 전치사 to를 쓰고, buy, make 류의 수여동사는 for를 쓴다.

★ PLUS TIP　buy, make, write 등의 동사는 간접목적어를 주어로 하는 수동태 문장에 잘 쓰지 않는다.
Celine made **me some French toast**.
→ **Some French toast** was made for me by Celine. (→ ~~I was made some French toast by Celine.~~)

A 다음 문장을 수동태 문장으로 바꾸어 쓰시오.

1 My mom made us some cookies.
→ Some cookies _____ .

2 Somebody sent me spam messages.
→ Spam messages _____ .

3 Kelvin showed the manager the ticket.
→ The ticket _____ .

4 Laurie told me the rumor about Kelly and me.
→ I _____ .

5 My father teaches the students computer coding.
→ The students _____ .

B 다음 우리말과 같은 뜻이 되도록 (　) 안의 말을 배열하여 문장을 완성하시오.

1 관중들은 그 코미디언에게서 재미있는 이야기를 들었다.
(by, a, story, told, was, funny)
The audience _____ the comedian.

2 따뜻한 옷과 맛있는 식사가 그들에게 제공되었다. (given, them, were, to)
Warm clothes and nice meals _____ .

3 부모님은 내게 졸업 선물로 멋진 정장을 사주셨다.
(nice, for, bought, a, was, me, by, suit)
_____ my parents for my graduation.

5형식 문장의 수동태

■ 5형식 문장(주어+동사+목적어+목적격 보어)을 수동태로 전환할 때는 능동태 문장의 목적어를 주어로 하고, 목적격 보어는 〈be동사+v-ed〉 뒤에 그대로 둔다.
We named our dog *Max*. (목적격 보어가 단어일 때)
→ Our dog **was named** *Max* by us.
Ray advised me *to get some rest*. (목적격 보어가 구일 때)
→ I **was advised** *to get some rest* by Ray.

A 다음 문장을 수동태 문장으로 바꾸어 쓰시오.

1 Students keep the library very clean.
→ _____

2 My parents taught me not to lie.
→ _____

3 Steve told Jenny to go to the ice rink.
→ _____

4 They elected him president.
→ _____

5 A tour guide asked the tourists to wait in line.
→ _____

B 다음 우리말과 같은 뜻이 되도록 (   ) 안의 말을 배열하여 문장을 완성하시오.

1 Rosa는 그녀의 친구들에게 천재라고 불린다.
(called, by, is, a, her, genius, friends)
Rosa _____.

2 그는 10시까지 이곳에 도착할 것이라고 예상되었다.
(expected, arrive, was, here, to, by ten)
He _____.

3 나는 Mark에게 상자를 열지 말라고 주의받았다.
(warned, not, was, open, to)
I _____ the box by Mark.

4 우리는 그 호수에서 수영을 하지 말라는 충고를 받았다.
(not, advised, swim, to, were)
We _____ in the lake.

지각동사·사역동사의 수동태

■ 능동태 문장에서 지각동사의 목적격 보어로 쓰인 동사원형은 수동태로 전환할 때 to부정사 형태로 바뀐다.
지각동사의 목적격 보어가 현재분사인 경우에는 그대로 둔다.
I **saw** someone **break[breaking]** a glass.
→ Someone **was seen to break[breaking]** a glass by me.
■ 사역동사 make의 목적격 보어로 쓰인 동사원형은 수동태로 전환할 때 to부정사 형태로 바뀐다.
The teacher **made** me **return** the books.
→ I **was made to return** the books by the teacher.

 수동태로 전환할 때, 지각동사와 사역동사 make의 목적격 보어로 쓰인 동사원형의 형태 변화에 유의하자.

A 다음 ( ) 안에서 알맞은 말을 고르시오.

1 Ethan was heard (play / to play) the violin.

2 I was made (feeling / to feel) nervous by the interviewer.

3 My sister was seen (waited / to wait) outside by her teacher.

4 She was made (go / to go) camping by her parents.

5 The sports car was seen (drive / driving) on the path by the students.

6 He was made (watered / to water) the plants by his grandmother.

B 다음 문장을 수동태 문장으로 바꾸어 쓰시오.

1 Joseph will make Tom apologize.
→ Tom _____.

2 We saw Harry come out of the classroom.
→ Harry _____.

3 My mother made me wash the dishes.
→ I _____.

4 The police officer made the driver stop.
→ The driver _____.

5 Ann heard the children running upstairs.
→ The children _____.

6 Janet made me tell my secret.
→ I _____.

7 They heard her talking to herself.
→ She _____.

동사구의 수동태

■ 동사가 부사 또는 전치사와 결합하여 하나의 동사 역할을 하는 동사구를 수동태로 쓸 경우에는 동사구 전체를 묶어서 써야 한다.

I **took care of** my nephew for two weeks.

→ My nephew **was taken care of** by me for two weeks.

〈여러 가지 동사구〉

- look after[take care of]: ~을 돌보다
- run over: (차가) ~을 치다
- bring up: ~을 기르다[양육하다]
- laugh at: ~을 비웃다

- turn down: (소리 등을) 낮추다
- look down on: ~을 낮춰보다[얕보다]
- put off: ~을 미루다[연기하다]
- pay for: ~을 지불하다

★ 내신만점 *TIP* 　동사구를 수동태로 쓸 때 전치사나 부사를 빠뜨리지 않도록 주의하자.

A 다음 우리말과 같은 뜻이 되도록 위에 제시된 동사구를 이용하여 문장을 완성하시오.

1 오늘 아침 그 고양이는 버스에 치었다.

The cat ＿＿＿＿＿ ＿＿＿＿＿ ＿＿＿＿＿ by a bus this morning.

2 이 개들은 Sarah에 의해 보살핌을 받을 것이다.

These dogs ＿＿＿＿＿ ＿＿＿＿＿ ＿＿＿＿＿ ＿＿＿＿＿ by Sarah.

3 그 경기는 우천으로 연기되었다.

The game ＿＿＿＿＿ ＿＿＿＿＿ ＿＿＿＿＿ because of the rain.

4 그 선수는 관중들에게 비웃음을 받았다.

The player ＿＿＿＿＿ ＿＿＿＿＿ ＿＿＿＿＿ by the crowd.

5 그 소년은 조부모에 의해 양육되었다.

The boy ＿＿＿＿＿ ＿＿＿＿＿ ＿＿＿＿＿ by his grandparents.

B 다음 문장을 수동태 문장으로 바꾸어 쓰시오.

1 His mother turned down the music.

→ The music ＿＿＿＿＿＿＿＿＿＿＿＿＿＿＿＿＿＿＿ .

2 This woman took care of Kelly.

→ Kelly ＿＿＿＿＿＿＿＿＿＿＿＿＿＿＿＿＿＿＿ .

3 My parents paid for the air conditioner.

→ The air conditioner ＿＿＿＿＿＿＿＿＿＿＿＿＿＿＿＿＿＿＿ .

4 He looked down on me because I was young.

→ I ＿＿＿＿＿＿＿＿＿＿＿＿＿＿＿＿＿＿＿ because I was young.

〈by+행위자〉를 생략하는 경우

■ 수동태 문장에서는 행위자가 일반인(you, we, they, people 등)이거나 누구인지 분명하게 알 수 있을 때, 이와 반대로 행위자가 불분명하거나 중요하지 않을 때 〈by+행위자〉를 생략할 수 있다.
Is Spanish **spoken** in Colombia? (행위자가 일반인인 경우)
The Eiffel Tower **was built** in 1889. (행위자가 불분명한 경우)

A   다음 문장을 수동태 문장으로 바꾸어 쓰시오.

1   People don't speak English in Cuba.
→ English _____ .

2   People don't use this road very often.
→ This road _____ .

3   We make chocolate from cacao beans.
→ Chocolate _____ .

4   The woman pushed the cart toward the door.
→ The cart _____ .

5   We chose Ann to be the class captain.
→ Ann _____ .

6   People built Hollywood in the early 1900s.
→ Hollywood _____ .

7   They don't allow people to smoke in this building.
→ People _____ .

B   다음 우리말과 같은 뜻이 되도록 ( ) 안의 말을 이용하여 문장을 완성하시오.

1   그 책은 1595년에 쓰였다. (write)
The book _____ _____ _____ 1595.

2   나는 시험에 대한 어떤 정보도 받지 못했다. (give)
I _____ _____ any information about the test.

3   정답은 이 책의 뒤에 인쇄되어 있다. (print)
The answers _____ _____ in the back of this book.

4   그 영어마을에서는 영어만 말해야 한다. (should, speak)
Only English _____ _____ _____ in the English village.

Point 10 · by 이외의 전치사를 사용하는 경우

■ 수동태의 행위자를 나타낼 때는 전치사 by를 쓰는 것이 일반적이지만 with, at, in 등 다른 전치사를 쓰는 경우도 있다.

〈자주 사용되는 표현들〉

- be interested in: ~에 관심이 있다
- be known to: ~에게 알려지다
- be tired of: ~에 싫증이 나다
- be filled with: ~로 가득 차다
- be surprised at: ~에 놀라다

- be pleased with: ~에 기뻐하다
- be disappointed with[at / in]: ~에 실망하다
- be satisfied with: ~에 만족하다
- be covered with[in]: ~로 덮여 있다
- be made of[from]: ~로 만들어지다(물리[화학]적 변화)

A 다음 밑줄 친 부분을 어법에 맞게 고쳐 쓰시오.

1 Greg was very pleased <u>in</u> his team's success.

2 She is not satisfied <u>in</u> her test score.

3 Her room is filled <u>of</u> pictures of her favorite singer.

4 The road is covered <u>to</u> snow.

5 I was surprised <u>of</u> the news.

6 We're tired <u>with</u> eating the same food every day.

B 다음 우리말과 같은 뜻이 되도록 ( ) 안의 말을 이용하여 문장을 완성하시오.

1 너는 무엇에 관심이 있니? (interest)
What _____ _____ _____ _____?

2 우리 부모님은 내 최종 성적에 기뻐하셨다. (please)
My parents _____ _____ _____ my final grades.

3 그의 선행이 모든 사람들에게 알려졌다. (know)
His good behavior _____ _____ _____ everybody.

4 너는 유리가 모래로 만들어진다는 사실을 알았니? (make)
Did you know glass _____ _____ _____ sand?

5 Judy는 자신의 새로운 머리 스타일에 만족한다. (satisfy)
Judy _____ _____ _____ her new hairstyle.

6 나는 놀이공원에서 줄을 서서 기다리는 데 싫증이 난다. (tire)
I _____ _____ _____ waiting in line at the amusement park.

7 그녀의 방은 장미 향으로 가득 차 있다. (fill)
Her room _____ _____ _____ the scent of roses.

[01-03] 다음 빈칸에 알맞은 말을 고르시오.

01

We can't get into the room because the door is _____.

① lock
② locking
③ locked
④ have lock
⑤ be locked

02

Your report should _____ by next week.

① finish
② finishes
③ finishing
④ to finish
⑤ be finished

03

I'm not interested _____ inline skating.

① of
② to
③ at
④ with
⑤ in

[04-05] 빈칸에 들어갈 말이 순서대로 알맞게 짝지어진 것을 고르시오.

04

A: Do you know who painted this?
B: Yes, it was painted _____ Renoir.
This painting is known _____ everybody.

① in – by
② by – as
③ by – to
④ at – to
⑤ with – as

05

• The thief was seen _____ the necklace.
• They were ordered _____ there on time.

① take – being
② take – to be
③ to take – to be
④ to take – be
⑤ taking – be

[06-07] 다음 중 수동태로 바꿀 수 없는 문장을 고르시오.

06

① Somebody shot President Lincoln.
② Tim bought a ticket for the concert.
③ I thanked my uncle and aunt.
④ A terrible thing happened yesterday.
⑤ Ann made her parents feel proud.

07

① The woman has a secret garden.
② The man repaired my cell phone.
③ My boss paid me two million won.
④ People use the bridge a lot.
⑤ I left a voice message for Kelly.

08

다음 빈칸에 공통으로 들어갈 말은?

- The trees are covered _____ snow.
- I was disappointed _____ the hotel room.

① on　　　　② at　　　　③ to
④ with　　　⑤ from

[09-10] 다음 우리말과 같은 뜻이 되도록 할 때, 밑줄 친 부분 중 어법상 틀린 것을 고르시오.

09

우리 아이들은 때론 우리에 의해 칭찬을 받아야 한다.

→ ① Our children ② should ③ is praised ④ by ⑤ us sometimes.

10

그 남자가 지하철에 올라타는 것이 내 남동생에 의해 목격되었다.

→ The man ① was ② seen ③ got ④ on the subway ⑤ by my brother.

11

다음 문장을 수동태로 바르게 바꾼 것은?

① She took care of Fiona.
　→ Fiona was taken care of her.
② I saw Mike dance with a girl.
　→ Mike was seen dance with a girl by me.
③ The comedy made me laugh.
　→ I was made laughing by the comedy.
④ They are going to put off their trip.
　→ Their trip is going to be put by them.
⑤ She made him some pasta.
　→ Some pasta was made for him by her.

12

다음 밑줄 친 부분 중 생략할 수 있는 것은?

① I was invited to the party by Mary.
② Sandwiches were made by Andy.
③ Mira was hurt by her best friend.
④ The car was driven by his father.
⑤ Mangoes are grown in the Philippines by people.

[13-14] 빈칸에 들어갈 말이 나머지와 다른 것을 고르시오.

13

① The role was played _____ Robin.
② The bus was filled _____ students.
③ The novel is read _____ many people.
④ Star Wars was directed _____ George Lucas.
⑤ The picture of a sunset was taken _____ the photographer.

14

① The boy was brought _____ the hospital.
② This chair is made _____ wood.
③ The hats will be given _____ babies.
④ They were asked _____ introduce themselves.
⑤ All the students are expected _____ join the summer camp.

15

다음 문장을 수동태 문장으로 바르게 바꾼 것을 모두 고르면? (2개)

Mr. Jang taught us social studies.

① We were taught to social studies by Mr. Jang.
② We were taught social studies by Mr. Jang.
③ Social studies was taught Mr. Jang by us.
④ Social studies was taught to us by Mr. Jang.
⑤ Social studies was taught for us by Mr. Jang.

[16-17] 다음 중 어법상 틀린 것을 고르시오.

16

① This salad was made by my mom.
② A skirt was bought for me by him.
③ This chocolate is eaten by a lot of children.
④ Was this show seen by all of your friends?
⑤ Those people were remained silent.

17

① A fan letter wrote to the actor by her.
② This movie wasn't made in the U.S.
③ He was taken to the police station.
④ She was looked after by her grandmother.
⑤ The agreement between you and me was broken.

18

다음 우리말과 같은 뜻이 되도록 주어진 말을 배열할 때, 네 번째에 올 단어는?

나는 엄마에 의해 그 상자들을 옮기게 되었다.
(my mom, the boxes, to, was, by, made, carry, I)

① made   ② to
③ carry   ④ boxes
⑤ was

19

다음 밑줄 친 부분이 어법상 틀린 것은?

① The baby is called Nora.
② Tony was advised to eat vegetables by his friends.
③ He was seen to steal things.
④ My sister was made wash the dishes.
⑤ She was persuaded to accept the offer.

20

(A), (B), (C)의 괄호 안에서 알맞은 것끼리 바르게 짝지어진 것은?

(A) They were all tired [by / of] his lectures.
(B) The plane was heard [pass / to pass] over the village.
(C) We were expected [to be / being] polite to others.

	(A)	(B)	(C)
①	of	pass	to be
②	by	to pass	to be
③	by	pass	being
④	of	to pass	being
⑤	of	to pass	to be

서술형 따라잡기

01

다음 문장을 수동태 문장으로 바꿔 쓰시오.

(1) My grandmother gave me advice.

→ Advice _____.

(2) The doctor told me to exercise.

→ _____

02

주어진 말을 이용하여 우리말과 뜻이 같도록 문장을 완성하시오.

(1) 이 건물은 가우디에 의해 설계되었다. (design)

→ This building _____ _____ _____ Gaudi.

(2) 그는 그의 블로그에 달린 좋은 댓글에 기뻐했다. (please)

→ He _____ _____ _____ the nice comments on his blog.

03

다음 상연 예정인 연극 포스터를 보고, 〈보기〉의 말을 이용하여 문장을 완성하시오.

Our Town
- Time: May 11
- Ticket Price: $70
- Place: Seoul Arts Center in Seocho-gu

〈보기〉　locate　　perform　　sell

(1) The play _____ _____ _____ on May 11.

(2) The tickets _____ _____ _____ for $70.

(3) Seoul Arts Center _____ _____ in Seocho-gu.

04

다음 그림을 보고, 문장을 완성하시오. (단, 과거형으로 쓸 것)

(1) A boy _____ _____ _____ a car. (hit)

(2) The girls _____ _____ _____ the accident. (surprise)

05

주어진 말을 알맞게 배열하여 우리말과 뜻이 같도록 문장을 완성하시오.

(1) Brian은 Cathy에게 조용히 하라는 말을 들었다. (be, by, quiet, to, Cathy, was, told, Brian)

→ _____

(2) 그 질문들은 교사들에 의해 답변이 되었습니까? (the teachers, were, by, the questions, answered)

→ _____

고난도
06

다음 Joe의 일기를 읽고, 틀린 부분을 모두 찾아 바르게 고쳐 쓰시오. (3군데)

November 29, Wednesday
When I was playing soccer, my leg injured. I went to the hospital and was advised rest for a few days by a doctor. So the family picnic postponed until next Sunday.

핵심 포인트 정리하기

1 수동태: 주어가 행위의 영향을 받거나 행위를 당할 때 사용하며 '~가 …되다[받다]'라고 해석함

- 형태: ⟨① _____ + _____ (+ by + 행위자)⟩

  ┌ 과거시제: ⟨② _____ + _____ (+ by + 행위자)⟩
  ├ 미래시제: ⟨③ _____ + _____ + _____ (+ by + 행위자)⟩
  ├ 부정문: ⟨be동사 + ④ _____ + v-ed (+ by + 행위자)⟩
  ├ 의문문: ⟨be동사 + 주어 + v-ed (+ by + 행위자)?⟩
  └ 조동사의 수동태: ⟨⑤ _____ + be + v-ed (+ by + 행위자)⟩

- ⟨by + 행위자⟩를 생략하는 경우

  − 행위자가 일반인이거나 누구인지 분명하게 알 수 있는 경우, 반대로 행위자가 불분명하거나 중요하지 않은 경우

2 다양한 형태의 수동태

4형식 문장의 수동태	• 간접목적어나 직접목적어를 주어로 한 두 가지 형태 가능 • 직접목적어를 주어로 한 수동태는 간접목적어 앞에 전치사를 씀
5형식 문장의 수동태	• 능동태 문장의 목적어 → 수동태의 주어 • 목적격 보어 → ⟨be동사+v-ed⟩ 뒤에 그대로 유지
지각동사·사역동사의 수동태	• 능동태 문장의 목적어 → 수동태의 주어 • 목적격 보어의 변화 1) 지각동사(see, hear) → ⑥ _____ 나 현재분사(v-ing) 2) 사역동사(make) → ⑦ _____
동사구의 수동태	• 동사구 전체를 묶어서 씀 (look after, put off 등)
by 이외의 전치사를 사용하는 수동태	be interested ⑧ _____, be tired ⑨ _____, be filled ⑩ _____, be satisfied ⑪ _____ 등

 수동태로 쓰지 않는 동사 알아두기!
4형식·5형식 문장, 지각동사·사역동사의 수동태 형태 익히기!
by 이외의 전치사를 사용하는 수동태 기억하기!

문제로 개념 다지기

밑줄 친 부분이 어법상 맞으면 O, 틀리면 X 표시하고 바르게 고치시오.

1 This blog <u>is visited by</u> a lot of parents.

2 <u>Will be your work done</u> by tomorrow?

3 The Korean alphabet, Hangeul, <u>was invent</u> in 1443.

4 Linda was made <u>cleaning</u> her room by her mother.

5 A new smartphone was given <u>to Mary</u> by Peter.

6 The girl should be <u>looked by her parents after</u>.

7 The boxes are filled <u>in</u> chocolate for the children.

CHAPTER

13

가정법

If I **had** enough money, I **could buy** a car.　　　　[가정법 과거]

If Ann **had missed** the bus, she **would have been** late.　[가정법 과거완료]

가정법

실제로 일어나지 않았거나 일어나지 않을 것 같은 일을 가정할 때 쓰는 표현입니다. 현재 사실과 반대되는 상황을 가정하여 나타내는 가정법 과거 구문과, 과거 사실과 반대되는 상황을 가정하여 나타내는 가정법 과거완료 구문이 있습니다.

가정법 과거

- 형태: 〈If+주어+동사의 과거형 ~, 주어+조동사의 과거형[would / could / might]+동사원형 …〉
- 의미: '만약 ~하면[라면] …할 텐데.' (현재 …하지 않음)
- 사용: 현재 사실과 반대되거나 실현 가능성이 희박한 상황을 가정할 때
  If you **lived** here, I **could see** you every day.
  → Because you don't live here, I can't see you every day.

★ **PLUS TIP**   가정법 과거에서 if절의 be동사는 주어의 인칭과 수에 관계없이 항상 were를 쓴다.
If I **were** you, I would choose the green pants.

A   다음 우리말과 같은 뜻이 되도록 (   ) 안의 말을 이용하여 문장을 완성하시오.

1   내가 20대라면, 혼자 살 수 있을 텐데. (be, live)
If I _____ in my 20s, I _____ _____ by myself.

2   그건 너무 비싸. 내가 너라면, 나는 그것을 사지 않겠어. (be, buy)
That's too expensive. If I _____ you, I _____ _____ it.

3   내게 자유시간이 더 있다면, 나는 더 많은 책을 읽을 텐데. (have, read)
If I _____ more free time, I _____ _____ more books.

4   내가 영어를 유창하게 말한다면, 이 반에 있지 않을 텐데. (speak, be)
If I _____ English fluently, I _____ _____ in this class.

5   내게 남자친구가 있다면, 그에게 너를 소개해줄 텐데. (have, introduce)
If I _____ a boyfriend, I _____ _____ you to him.

6   그 상을 탄다면 너는 무엇을 할 거니? (do, win)
What _____ you _____ if you _____ the prize?

7   네가 수업에 집중한다면, 그 시험에서 A를 받을 텐데. (focus on, get)
If you _____ _____ the class, you _____ _____ an A
on the test.

B   다음 두 문장이 같은 뜻이 되도록 문장을 완성하시오.

1   Because I don't know the answer, I can't tell you.
→ _____, I could tell you.

2   Because I don't have a car, I can't drive my girlfriend home.
→ _____, I could drive my girlfriend home.

3   Because I am not dressed up, I can't enter the restaurant.
→ _____, I could enter the restaurant.

가정법 과거완료

- 형태: 〈If+주어+had v-ed ~, 주어+조동사의 과거형[would / could / might]+have v-ed …〉
- 의미: '만약 ~했다면[였더라면] …했을 텐데.' (과거에 …하지 않았음)
- 사용: 과거 사실과 반대되는 상황을 가정할 때

  If I **hadn't come** to this city, I **wouldn't have met** you.

  → Because I came to this city, I met you.

★ 내신만점 *TIP* 가정법 과거와 과거완료의 형태에서 if절과 주절의 시제에 유의하자.

A 다음 ( ) 안의 말을 이용하여 가정법 과거완료 문장을 완성하시오.

1 If Ed (meet) Liz, he would (like) her.

2 If you (watch) the movie, you would (enjoy) it very much.

3 If you (not remind) me, I would (forget) his birthday.

4 If we (take) the subway, we could (get) there much quicker.

5 If we (live) 100 years ago, we would (not use) computers.

B 다음 우리말과 같은 뜻이 되도록 〈보기〉에서 알맞은 말을 골라 빈칸에 적절한 형태로 써넣으시오.

| 〈보기〉 | buy | go to sleep | answer | be sick | cancel |
| | get | hear | rain | travel | eat |

1 그녀가 전화벨 소리를 들었다면, 전화를 받았을 텐데.
If she _____ _____ the phone ring, she _____ _____ _____ it.

2 오늘 비가 왔었다면, 그 경기는 취소되었을 텐데.
If it _____ _____ today, the game _____ _____ _____ _____.

3 내가 좋은 성적을 받았더라면, 엄마가 내게 새 휴대전화를 사 주셨을 텐데.
If I _____ _____ good grades, my mom _____ _____ _____ me a new cell phone.

4 그가 아프지 않았더라면, 우리와 함께 여행을 갔었을 텐데.
If he _____ _____ _____ _____, he _____ _____ _____ with us.

5 네가 일찍 자지 않았더라면, 내가 산 피자를 먹을 수 있었을 텐데.
If you _____ _____ _____ _____ _____ early, you _____ _____ _____ the pizza I bought.

I wish+가정법 과거

- 형태: 〈I wish (that)+주어+동사의 과거형〉 *be동사의 경우 were를 사용
- 의미: '~하면[라면] 좋을 텐데'
- 사용: 현재의 이룰 수 없거나 실현 가능성이 희박한 소망을 나타낼 때
  I wish you **were** here with me.
  → I'm sorry (that) you aren't here with me.

A 다음 우리말과 같은 뜻이 되도록 〈보기〉에서 알맞은 말을 골라 빈칸에 적절한 형태로 써넣으시오.

〈보기〉　We are in the same class.　　I am tall like that model.
　　　　I can sing as well as you.　　It is Saturday today.
　　　　I attend that university.

1 오늘이 토요일이라면 좋을 텐데.
　　I wish _____.

2 내가 저 대학에 다닌다면 좋을 텐데.
　　I wish _____.

3 내가 저 모델처럼 키가 크면 좋을 텐데.
　　I wish _____.

4 우리가 같은 반이라면 좋을 텐데.
　　I wish _____.

5 내가 너처럼 노래를 잘하면 좋을 텐데.
　　I wish _____.

B 다음 두 문장이 같은 뜻이 되도록 문장을 완성하시오.

1 I wish I could dance very well.
　　→ I'm sorry that _____.

2 I'm sorry I don't have Julie's phone number.
　　→ I wish that _____.

3 I wish the boy liked me.
　　→ I'm sorry that _____.

4 I'm sorry I am not good at math.
　　→ I wish that _____.

5 I'm sorry I have a lot of work to do.
　　→ I wish that _____.

Point 04 · I wish + 가정법 과거완료

- 형태: 〈I wish (that)+주어+had v-ed〉
- 의미: '~했다면[였더라면] 좋을 텐데'
- 사용: 과거에 이루지 못한 소망이나 과거에 했던 일에 대한 아쉬움을 나타낼 때
  I wish I **had been** nice to my friends.
  → I'm sorry (that) I wasn't nice to my friends.

A 다음 우리말과 같은 뜻이 되도록 ( ) 안의 말을 이용하여 문장을 완성하시오.

1 내가 그를 도와줬더라면 좋을 텐데. (help)
I wish I _____ _____ _____.

2 내가 그렇게 자주 늦지 않았더라면 좋을 텐데. (be late)
I wish I _____ _____ _____ _____ so often.

3 내가 너를 좀 더 일찍 만났더라면 좋을 텐데. (meet)
I wish I _____ _____ _____ earlier.

4 내가 내 반지를 집에 두었더라면 좋을 텐데. (leave)
I wish I _____ _____ my ring at home.

5 내가 그녀에게 그 비밀을 말하지 않았더라면 좋을 텐데. (tell)
I wish I _____ _____ _____ _____ the secret.

6 그 사고가 Paul에게 일어나지 않았더라면 좋을 텐데. (happen)
I wish the accident _____ _____ _____ to Paul.

B 다음 두 문장이 같은 뜻이 되도록 문장을 완성하시오.

1 I wish I had known about the test.
→ I'm sorry that _____.

2 I'm sorry that I had my hair cut short.
→ I wish _____.

3 I'm sorry that I didn't bring my camera today.
→ I wish _____.

4 I'm sorry that I didn't learn to play a musical instrument.
→ I wish _____.

5 I wish I had memorized their names.
→ I'm sorry that _____.

6 I'm sorry that I didn't listen to my parents.
→ I wish _____.

as if + 가정법 과거

- 형태: 〈as if+주어+동사의 과거형〉 *be동사의 경우 were를 사용
- 의미: '마치 ~인 것처럼' (실제로는 아님)
- 사용: 주절의 시제와 같은 때의 상황을 반대로 가정할 때

James talks **as if** he **were** my boyfriend.

→ In fact, James isn't my boyfriend.

A 다음 우리말과 같은 뜻이 되도록 ( ) 안의 말을 배열하여 문장을 완성하시오.

1 Julia는 마치 나보다 나이가 많은 것처럼 행동한다. (as, older, she, if, than, were, me)
Julia acts _____.

2 Cathy는 마치 그 이야기를 알고 있는 것처럼 말한다. (as, knew, if, the story, she)
Cathy speaks _____.

3 그는 마치 Sally를 모르는 것처럼 행동한다. (Sally, know, if, as, he, didn't)
He behaves _____.

4 Jessica는 마치 자기가 그 영화배우의 친구인 것처럼 이야기한다.
(a friend, the movie star, as, she, if, were, of)
Jessica talks _____.

B 다음 우리말과 같은 뜻이 되도록 〈보기〉에서 알맞은 말을 골라 빈칸에 적절한 형태로 써넣으시오.

〈보기〉　He has a lot of money.　　I am his younger sister.
　　　　 I am dreaming.　　　　　 He knows everything about cars.
　　　　 You understand everything.

1 나는 마치 꿈을 꾸고 있는 것처럼 느껴진다.
I feel as if _____.

2 그는 마치 자기가 돈이 많은 것처럼 행동한다.
He acts _____.

3 Brian은 마치 내가 자기의 여동생인 것처럼 나를 대한다.
Brian treats me _____.

4 Gary는 마치 자신이 차에 대한 모든 것을 아는 것처럼 말한다.
Gary talks _____.

5 너는 마치 모든 것을 이해하는 것처럼 항상 고개를 끄덕인다.
You always nod your head _____.

as if + 가정법 과거완료

- 형태: 〈as if+주어+had v-ed〉
- 의미: '마치 ~였던 것처럼' (실제로는 아니었음)
- 사용: 주절의 시제보다 앞선 때의 상황을 반대로 가정할 때
  Bob talks **as if** he **had lived** in Paris.
  → In fact, Bob didn't live in Paris.

A 다음 우리말과 같은 뜻이 되도록 〈보기〉에서 알맞은 말을 골라 빈칸에 적절한 형태로 써넣으시오.

〈보기〉 It was his last game.　　　　She called me.
It was never cleaned.　　　　He won the prize.
I said something shocking.

1 그녀는 마치 나에게 전화했던 것처럼 이야기한다.
She talks _____.

2 그 방은 마치 한 번도 청소되지 않았던 것처럼 보인다.
The room looks _____.

3 Harry는 마치 자신이 상을 탔던 것처럼 보인다.
Harry looks _____.

4 그는 마치 그것이 그의 마지막 경기였던 것처럼 이야기한다.
He talks _____.

5 우리 아빠는 마치 내가 충격적인 것을 말한 것처럼 행동하신다.
My dad acts _____.

B 다음 두 문장이 같은 뜻이 되도록 문장을 완성하시오.

1 In fact, he wasn't there.
→ He talks _____ _____ _____ _____ _____ there.

2 In fact, she heard the news.
→ She talks _____ _____ _____ _____ _____ the news.

3 In fact, Mike was not on time.
→ Mike speaks _____ _____ he _____ on time.

4 In fact, Jack didn't see her yesterday.
→ Jack is looking at her _____ _____ _____
_____ her yesterday.

Chapter 13

내신대비 TEST

[01-03] 다음 빈칸에 알맞은 말을 고르시오.

01

What _____ you do if you were famous?

① be   ② will   ③ were
④ would   ⑤ would be

02

If my parents _____ my grades, they would have been proud of me.

① know   ② knew
③ would know   ④ have known
⑤ had known

03

Eric didn't play baseball. But he talks as if he _____ it.

① play   ② played   ③ has played
④ had played   ⑤ is playing

[04-05] 빈칸에 들어갈 말이 순서대로 알맞게 짝지어진 것을 고르시오.

04

A: I had a fight with Sam.
B: If I _____ you, I _____ say "sorry" first.

① am – have   ② am – would
③ was – could   ④ were – would
⑤ were – have

05

• I wish I _____ be good at drawing.
• If she _____ me, I would have upgraded her computer for her.

① can – ask   ② can – had asked
③ could – asked   ④ could – can ask
⑤ could – had asked

06
다음 빈칸에 공통으로 들어갈 말은?

• I wish I _____ at the mall yesterday.
• If I _____ free, I would have visited you.

① be   ② am   ③ were
④ had been   ⑤ have been

[07-08] 다음 우리말을 영어로 바르게 옮긴 것을 고르시오.

07

내가 거기에 더 일찍 도착했더라면 좋을 텐데.

① I wish I arrived there earlier.
② I wish I had arrived there earlier.
③ I wish I could arrive there earlier.
④ I wished I arrive there earlier.
⑤ I wished I arrived there earlier.

08

Jeff는 마치 모든 것을 아는 것처럼 행동한다.

① Jeff acts as if he will know everything.
② Jeff acts as if he knows everything.
③ Jeff acts as if he knew everything.
④ Jeff acted as if he had known everything.
⑤ Jeff acted as if he could knew everything.

09
다음 대화의 빈칸에 알맞은 말은?

A: I heard she failed the exam!
B: Yes. _____

① If she studied hard, she would pass.
② If she didn't study hard, she would fail.
③ If she studied hard, she wouldn't have failed.
④ If she hadn't studied hard, she would fail.
⑤ If she had studied hard, she would have passed.

고난도

10
다음 대화 중 자연스럽지 <u>않은</u> 것은?

① A: You didn't tell me about the rumor.
   B: If I had known about it, I'd have told you.
② A: Those students are very noisy.
   B: Yes. I wish they would be quiet.
③ A: Am I pale?
   B: Yes. You look as if you had seen a ghost.
④ A: Why are you so late?
   B: I overslept. I wouldn't have been late if I had set my alarm clock.
⑤ A: Why didn't you call me?
   B: Sorry. I wouldn't have called you if my phone hadn't broken.

기출응용

11
다음 우리말과 같은 뜻이 되도록 주어진 말을 배열할 때 <u>뒤에서 세 번째에 올 단어</u>는?

시험이 없다면, 나는 기쁠 텐데.
If (I, no exams, glad, be, there, would, were).

① be   ② exams   ③ would
④ glad   ⑤ were

12
다음 두 문장이 같은 뜻이 되도록 할 때 <u>잘못된</u> 것은?

① I'm sorry that I can't help you.
   → I wish I could help you.
② I'm sorry that I didn't eat lunch.
   → I wish I ate lunch.
③ As I am not slim, I can't wear it.
   → If I were slim, I could wear it.
④ As I'm not 19, I can't drive.
   → If I were 19, I could drive.
⑤ If you were tall, you could reach it.
   → As you aren't tall, you can't reach it.

13
다음 밑줄 친 부분 중 어법상 <u>틀린</u> 것은?

It was rainy yesterday, so I couldn't climb the mountain. ① <u>If it</u> ② <u>did not</u> ③ <u>rained</u> yesterday, I ④ <u>could</u> ⑤ <u>have climbed</u> the mountain.

14
다음 우리말을 영어로 옮긴 것 중 <u>잘못된</u> 것은?

① Justin이 지금 한국에 있다면 좋을 텐데.
   I wish Justin is in Korea now.
② 지난 크리스마스에 눈이 왔었더라면 좋을 텐데.
   I wish it had snowed last Christmas.
③ 그녀는 그 사고를 봤었던 것처럼 말한다.
   She talks as if she had seen the accident.
④ 내가 복권에 당첨된다면 그 돈을 부모님께 드릴 텐데.
   If I won the lottery, I would give the money to my parents.
⑤ 내가 Amy와 싸우지 않았더라면 그녀와 함께 여행을 했을 텐데.
   If I had not fought with Amy, I would have taken a trip with her.

15
빈칸에 들어갈 말이 나머지와 다른 것은?

① I miss you. I wish you _____ here with me.
② He is my brother. But he talks as if he _____ my dad.
③ I would give you medicine if I _____ a doctor.
④ If you _____ there, you would have enjoyed the event.
⑤ They don't have any money. But they act as if they _____ rich.

16
다음 〈보기〉의 문장과 의미가 같은 것은?

〈보기〉 As he was full, he didn't have dinner.

① If he isn't full, he would have dinner.
② If he weren't full, he would have dinner.
③ If he had not been full, he would have dinner.
④ If he had been full, he would have had dinner.
⑤ If he had not been full, he would have had dinner.

17
다음 중 어법상 틀린 문장의 개수는?

(a) I wish I could go to the opera.
(b) If I could cook like Tim, I would open a restaurant.
(c) You didn't come to the party. Don't act as if you came.
(d) If I had had some money, I could have bought that dress.

① 0개　② 1개　③ 2개　④ 3개　⑤ 4개

[18-20] 다음 밑줄 친 부분이 어법상 틀린 것을 고르시오.

18
① If I slept more, I would feel better.
② What would you do if you were Amy?
③ If I found a lot of money, I wouldn't tell anybody.
④ If I took a taxi, I would have gotten there in time.
⑤ If I had remembered his birthday, I would have called him.

19
① I wish I had seen the award-winning movie.
② If you had told me, I could have helped you.
③ I wish my roommate didn't talk on the phone so much.
④ If I didn't have to study math, I would have had more free time.
⑤ If I could change one thing about myself, I would change my skin.

20
① If I had gone to the meeting, I would have met a lot of people.
② If he had had a dance partner, he could have come to the party.
③ I wish it weren't snowing outside.
④ I wish somebody would buy me a car.
⑤ They weren't at the class. But they talk as if they were there.

서술형 따라잡기

01
다음 문장을 가정법 문장으로 바꾸어 쓰시오.

(1) As it is late at night, I can't call her.
　→ If it ＿＿＿＿ ＿＿＿＿ late at night, I
　＿＿＿＿ ＿＿＿＿ her.

(2) I'm sorry that I can't go on a trip.
　→ I wish ＿＿＿＿ ＿＿＿＿ ＿＿＿＿
　＿＿＿＿ ＿＿＿＿ ＿＿＿＿.

02
다음 그림을 보고, 가정법 과거완료와 주어진 말을 이용하여 문장을 완성하시오.

(rain, go)　　　　(be, trip)

(1) If it ＿＿＿＿ ＿＿＿＿ ＿＿＿＿, Ben could
　＿＿＿＿ ＿＿＿＿ on a picnic.

(2) If Ben ＿＿＿＿ ＿＿＿＿ careful, he would
　＿＿＿＿ ＿＿＿＿ ＿＿＿＿ over the stone.

03
주어진 말을 적절한 형태로 바꾸어 대화를 완성하시오.

(1)　A: You were the heaviest boy in your
　　　class when you were in elementary
　　　school.
　　B: Yes. I wish I ＿＿＿＿＿＿＿ then.
　　　(be slim)

(2)　A: Do you think he is depressed because
　　　she broke up with him?
　　B: No. He acts as if nothing
　　　＿＿＿＿＿＿＿. (happen)

04
주어진 말을 이용하여 우리말과 뜻이 같도록 문장을 완성하시오.

네가 그 소식을 들었다면 놀랐을 텐데.
(hear, surprised)

→ If you ＿＿＿＿ ＿＿＿＿ ＿＿＿＿
＿＿＿＿, you would ＿＿＿＿ ＿＿＿＿
＿＿＿＿.

05
다음 나의 소원 목록을 보고, 문장을 완성하시오.

> **My wish**
> (1) be a movie star
> (2) can go to Europe

(1) I wish ＿＿＿＿＿＿＿＿＿＿＿＿＿.

(2) I wish ＿＿＿＿＿＿＿＿＿＿＿＿＿.

고난도
06
다음 대화를 읽고, B의 답변을 〈보기〉와 같이 가정법 문장으로 쓰시오.

〈보기〉
A: Shall we go to the seafood restaurant?
B: No, I won't go there. I don't like seafood.
→ If I liked seafood, I would go to the
　seafood restaurant.

(1) A: Did you go to the art exhibit?
　　B: No, I didn't. I was not interested in the
　　　paintings.
　→ ＿＿＿＿＿＿＿＿＿＿＿＿＿＿＿＿

(2) A: Will you buy a laptop?
　　B: Yes. I don't have one now.
　→ ＿＿＿＿＿＿＿＿＿＿＿＿＿＿＿＿

핵심 포인트 정리하기

1 가정법 과거: 현재 사실과 반대되거나 실현 가능성이 희박한 상황을 가정할 때
- 형태: ⟨① _____ + 주어 + ② _____ ~, 주어 + 조동사의 과거형[would / could / might] + ③ _____ …⟩
- '만약 ~하면[라면] …할 텐데.' (현재 …하지 않음)

2 가정법 과거완료: 과거 사실과 반대되는 상황을 가정할 때
- 형태: ⟨④ _____ + 주어 + ⑤ _____ ~, 주어 + 조동사의 과거형[would / could / might] + ⑥ _____ …⟩
- '만약 ~했다면[였더라면] …했을 텐데.' (과거에 …하지 않았음)

 가정법 과거와 과거완료의 형태에서 if절과 주절의 시제에 유의하기!

3 I wish 가정법

I wish + 가정법 과거	I wish + 가정법 과거완료
현재 이룰 수 없거나 실현 가능성이 희박한 소망을 나타낼 때	과거에 이루지 못한 소망이나 과거에 했던 일에 대한 아쉬움을 나타낼 때
⟨I wish (that) + 주어 + 동사의 과거형⟩ *be동사의 경우 – ⑦ _____	⟨I wish (that) + 주어 + ⑧ _____⟩
'~하면[라면] 좋을 텐데'	'~했다면[였더라면] 좋을 텐데'

4 as if 가정법

as if + 가정법 과거	as if + 가정법 과거완료
주절의 시제와 같은 때의 상황을 반대로 가정할 때	주절의 시제보다 앞선 때의 상황을 반대로 가정할 때
⟨as if + 주어 + 동사의 과거형⟩ * be동사의 경우 – were	⟨as if + 주어 + had v-ed⟩
'마치 ~인 것처럼' (실제로는 아님)	'마치 ~였던 것처럼' (실제로는 아니었음)

 I wish 가정법과 as if 가정법의 시제 구분하기!

문제로 개념 다지기

밑줄 친 부분이 어법상 맞으면 O, 틀리면 X 표시하고 바르게 고치시오.

1 If I <u>see</u> a UFO, I wouldn't tell anybody.

2 If I <u>had</u> more time, I could have finished the work earlier.

3 내가 좀 더 큰 티셔츠를 샀더라면 좋을 텐데.
   I wish I <u>have bought</u> a bigger T-shirt.

4 일주일에 3일만 등교하면 좋을 텐데.
   I wish I <u>went</u> to school just three days a week.

5 Liz는 아이이지만, 그녀는 마치 자신이 어른인 것처럼 행동한다.
   Liz is a child, but she acts as if she <u>is</u> an adult.

CHAPTER 14

일치와 화법

개념 쏙쏙

We **knew** that Jerry **had visited** Paris.	[시제 일치]
Melody **said to** me, "I **need** something to drink."	[직접화법]
Melody **told** me that she **needed** something to drink.	[간접화법]
Do you know **where your sister is**?	[간접의문문]

시제 일치

주절의 시제에 따라 종속절의 시제를 일치시키는 것을 말합니다.

화법

말하는 방법으로, 다른 사람이 한 말을 그대로 전달하는 직접화법과, 전달자의 입장에 맞게 바꿔서 전달하는 간접화법이 있습니다.

간접의문문

의문사나 if[whether]를 포함한 명사절로 문장 내에서 의문을 나타냅니다.

시제 일치

- 주절의 시제가 현재일 때, 종속절에는 모든 시제가 올 수 있다.

  I **think** that he **is** tired now. (현재 – 현재)

  I **think** that he **was** tired last night. (현재 – 과거)

  I **think** that he **will be** tired by 2 a.m. (현재 – 미래)

- 주절의 시제가 과거일 때, 종속절에는 과거시제 또는 과거완료만 올 수 있다.

  We **believed** that Chris **was** honest. (과거 – 과거: 종속절의 때가 주절의 때와 일치)

  Megan **realized** that he **had told** her secret to everyone.

  (과거 – 과거완료: 종속절의 때가 주절의 때보다 앞섬)

★ *PLUS TIP*　주절의 시제가 과거일 때 종속절에 있는 조동사는 과거형(would, could, might, must[had to] 등)으로 쓴다.

A　다음 문장의 시제를 과거로 바꿀 때, 빈칸에 알맞은 말을 쓰시오.

1　I wonder why Jane loves Tom.

→ I _____ why Jane _____ Tom.

2　She realizes that her son is ill.

→ She _____ that her son _____ ill.

3　Jenny finds out that Chris went to China.

→ Jenny _____ that Chris _____ to China.

4　Tim says that he saw the play with Kate on Tuesday.

→ Tim _____ that he _____ the play with Kate on Tuesday.

5　I think that she was a flight attendant before.

→ I _____ that she _____ a flight attendant before.

6　Everyone hopes that his team can win the next game.

→ Everyone _____ that his team _____ the next game.

B　다음 우리말과 같은 뜻이 되도록 (　) 안의 말을 이용하여 문장을 완성하시오.

1　나는 그 남자가 매우 친절하다고 생각했다. (think, very kind)

I _____ that the man _____ _____ _____.

2　나는 엄마가 내 셔츠를 세탁해 놓으셨다는 것을 깨달았다. (realize, wash)

I _____ that my mom _____ _____ my shirt.

3　우리는 함께 있으면 행복할 것이라고 믿었다. (believe, happy)

We _____ that we _____ _____ _____ together.

4　그는 자기가 그 집을 혼자서 지었다고 말했다. (say, build)

He _____ that he _____ _____ the house by himself.

시제 일치의 예외

- 과학적 사실, 변하지 않는 사실, 격언·속담 등은 주절의 시제와 관계없이 현재시제를 쓴다.
  I knew that water **boils** at 100 ℃. (과학적 사실)
- 현재에도 지속되는 습관이나 사실은 주절이 과거시제더라도 종속절에 현재시제를 쓸 수 있다.
  She **said** that she always **goes to bed** at 10 p.m.
- 역사적 사실은 주절의 시제와 관계없이 항상 과거시제를 쓴다.
  The students **learned** that World War II **ended** in 1945.

A 다음 문장의 시제를 과거로 바꿀 때, 빈칸에 알맞은 말을 쓰시오.

1 I know that two and two makes four.
→ I _____ that _____.

2 We learn that oil is lighter than water.
→ We _____ that _____.

3 Even a child knows that the sun rises in the east.
→ Even a child _____ that _____.

4 The book says that William Shakespeare was born in 1564.
→ The book _____ that _____.

5 Whitney says that her school begins at eight.
→ Whitney _____ that _____.

6 She tells me that her family goes to church every Sunday.
→ She _____ me that _____.

7 The teacher says that light moves faster than sound.
→ The teacher _____ that _____.

8 I realize that a friend in need is a friend indeed.
→ I _____ that _____.

B 다음 문장에서 **틀린** 부분을 찾아 어법에 맞게 고쳐 쓰시오.

1 I learned that the earth moved around the sun.

2 She is meeting the person who you talk about before.

3 We learned that Mozart had been born in Austria.

4 Children knew that bears slept all winter.

5 My history teacher said that the American Civil War had begun in 1861.

평서문의 직접화법과 간접화법

■ 다른 사람이 한 말을 그대로 전달하는 것을 직접화법, 전달자의 입장에 맞게 바꿔 전달하는 것을 간접화법이라고 한다.

〈평서문의 직접화법을 간접화법으로 바꾸는 방법〉

① 전달동사가 say[said]인 경우에는 그대로 두고, say to[said to]는 tell[told]로 바꾼다.

② 주절의 콤마(,)와 인용부호(" ")를 없애고 접속사 that을 쓴다. (that은 생략 가능)

③ 인용부호 안의 인칭대명사를 전달자에 맞추고, 동사도 시제 일치 원칙에 맞게 바꾼다.

She **said to** me, "I want you to be happy." (직접화법)

→ She **told** me (that) **she wanted me to be happy**. (간접화법)

A 다음 문장을 간접화법으로 바꾸어 쓰시오.

1 He says, "I want to be a tennis player."

→ He _____ that _____ .

2 David said to me, "I am hungry."

→ David _____ me that _____ .

3 Jina said, "I'll meet you at the park."

→ Jina _____ that _____ .

4 She said to me, "I enjoyed Jane's birthday party."

→ She _____ me that _____ .

5 Mary said to her mother, "I met my teacher at the store."

→ Mary _____ her mother that _____ .

B 다음 문장을 직접화법으로 바꾸어 쓰시오.

1 Paul said that he was doing his homework.

→ Paul _____, " _____ ."

2 He told me that he had seen me at school.

→ He _____ me, " _____ ."

3 She told me that she would leave before noon.

→ She _____ me, " _____ ."

4 Our teacher said that the Korean War began in 1950.

→ Our teacher _____, " _____ ."

5 My mother told me that I had to come home early.

→ My mother _____ me, " _____ ."

의문문의 직접화법과 간접화법 I

- 의문사가 없는 의문문을 간접화법으로 바꾸어 쓸 때는 〈ask(＋목적어)+if[whether]+주어+동사〉의 형태로 쓴다.
- 의문문을 간접화법으로 바꿀 때, 주절의 동사 say[said], say to[said to]는 ask[asked]로 바꾼다.
  She **said to** me, "Is it your scarf?" → She **asked** me **if[whether] it was** my scarf.

A 다음 문장을 간접화법으로 바꾸어 쓰시오.

1 I asked her, "Were you sick?"
→ I ＿＿＿＿＿＿ her ＿＿＿＿＿＿＿＿＿＿＿＿＿＿.

2 Mike said to me, "Will you join us?"
→ Mike ＿＿＿＿＿＿ me ＿＿＿＿＿＿＿＿＿＿＿＿.

3 I asked him, "Can you speak English?"
→ I ＿＿＿＿＿＿ him ＿＿＿＿＿＿＿＿＿＿＿＿.

4 Laura said to me, "Do you have any plans for the vacation?"
→ Laura ＿＿＿＿＿＿ me ＿＿＿＿＿＿＿＿＿＿＿＿.

5 He said to me, "Can I use your cell phone?"
→ He ＿＿＿＿＿＿ me ＿＿＿＿＿＿＿＿＿＿＿＿.

6 She asked me, "Have you ever been to Busan?"
→ She ＿＿＿＿＿＿ me ＿＿＿＿＿＿＿＿＿＿＿＿.

B 다음 문장을 직접화법으로 바꾸어 쓰시오.

1 Jenny asked me if I could help her.
→ Jenny said to me, "＿＿＿＿＿＿＿＿＿＿＿＿＿＿＿"

2 My mother asked my brother if he had had lunch.
→ My mother said to my brother, "＿＿＿＿＿＿＿＿＿＿＿＿＿"

3 My friend asked me if I wanted to get a haircut the next day.
→ My friend said to me, "＿＿＿＿＿＿＿＿＿＿＿＿＿"

4 He asked me if it was the first meeting that day.
→ He said to me, "＿＿＿＿＿＿＿＿＿＿＿＿＿"

5 She asked me if I had heard the sound.
→ She said to me, "＿＿＿＿＿＿＿＿＿＿＿＿＿"

의문문의 직접화법과 간접화법 II

- 의문사가 있는 의문문을 간접화법으로 바꾸어 쓸 때는 〈ask(+목적어)+의문사+주어+동사〉의 형태로 쓴다.
  She **said to** me, "Where do you live?" → She **asked** me **where I lived**.
- 의문사가 의문문에서 주어인 경우에는 〈ask(+목적어)+의문사+동사〉의 어순을 그대로 유지한다.
  I **asked** him, "Who ruined your day?" → I **asked** him **who had ruined** his day.

A 다음 문장을 간접화법으로 바꾸어 쓰시오.

1 Eric said to me, "What are you doing?"
→ Eric _____ me _____.

2 I said to him, "Why didn't you call me today?"
→ I _____ him _____.

3 She said to me, "What can I do for you?
→ She _____ me _____.

4 My mother said, "Who broke the vase?"
→ My mother asked _____.

5 I asked her, "Where are you going?"
→ I _____ her _____.

6 Michelle said to me, "Where did you get your jeans?"
→ Michelle _____ me _____.

7 He asked me, "How long have you been here?"
→ He _____ me _____.

B 다음 문장을 직접화법으로 바꾸어 쓰시오.

1 He asked us what time our flight left.
→ He asked us, "_____"

2 Sean asked me how much money I needed.
→ Sean asked me, "_____"

3 She asked me what I was going to do that day.
→ She asked me, "_____"

4 I asked her what was happening at that time.
→ I asked her, "_____"

5 I asked my brother where he had bought his earphones.
→ I asked my brother, "_____"

Point 06 간접의문문

- 간접의문문은 의문문이 문장 내에서 주어, 보어, 목적어 역할을 하는 것을 말한다.
  - 의문사가 있는 간접의문문: 〈의문사+주어+동사〉의 형태로 쓴다.

  Do you know **when the train leaves**?

  * 단, 의문사가 주어인 경우에는 〈의문사+동사〉의 형태로 쓴다.

  I don't know **who ate my yogurt.**

  - 의문사가 없는 간접의문문: 〈if[whether]+주어+동사〉의 형태로 쓴다.

  Please tell me **if[whether] you will come to the party.**

★ **내신만점 TIP** 　주절의 동사가 think, believe, imagine, guess 등일 경우, 간접의문문의 의문사는 문장의 맨 앞에 온다는 것을 기억하자.

What do you think **he will buy**? (~~Do you think~~ **what he will buy**?)

A　다음 두 문장을 간접의문문으로 만들 때, 빈칸에 알맞은 말을 쓰시오.

1　I don't know. + What is your name?

→ I don't know _____.

2　He wonders. + Do Carrie and her sister study at the library?

→ He wonders _____.

3　The child knows. + What is his father doing?

→ The child knows _____.

4　Do you think? + Why was the hockey game canceled?

→ _____ do you think _____?

5　The reporter wants to know. + Who will arrive at the airport?

→ The reporter wants to know _____.

B　다음 우리말과 같은 뜻이 되도록 (　) 안의 말을 배열하여 문장을 완성하시오.

1　나는 우리가 어느 출구를 이용해야 할지 모르겠다.(should, which exit, use, we)

I'm not sure _____.

2　누가 그 문제에 대답할 수 있다고 생각하니? (the question, who, answer, can)

_____ do you think _____?

3　차로 호텔까지 가는 데 얼마나 걸리는지 내게 말해줄 수 있니?

(it, how long, to, the hotel, takes, get to)

Can you tell me _____ by car?

4　그녀는 날씨가 좋을지 모른다. (the weather, nice, if, will, be)

She doesn't know _____.

내신대비 TEST

[01-03] 다음 빈칸에 알맞은 말을 고르시오.

01

Jessica thought that her mom _____ cooking in the kitchen.

① was ② is ③ be
④ being ⑤ have

02

I learned that Jupiter _____ larger than Earth.

① is ② was ③ has been
④ had been ⑤ will be

03

She asked John _____ he liked me.

① that ② if ③ as
④ while ⑤ which

[04-06] 빈칸에 들어갈 말이 순서대로 알맞게 짝지어진 것을 고르시오.

04

- The teacher said that whales _____ the biggest animals in the sea.
- I learned that the French Revolution _____ in 1789.

① are – began ② were – began
③ are – begins ④ were – had begun
⑤ had been – had begun

05

- My teacher asked me what I _____.
- She told me that she _____ the Christmas tree that morning.

① think – decorates
② think – had decorated
③ was thinking – has decorated
④ was thinking – had decorated
⑤ am thinking – has decorated

06

A: Do you know why Rick _____ in the hospital now?
B: Yes. He told me that he _____ his leg.

① is – breaks ② was – broke
③ is – had broken ④ was – has broken
⑤ is – would break

기출응용

[07-08] 다음 문장을 간접화법으로 알맞게 바꾼 것을 고르시오.

07

Lily said to me, "I will stay home."

① Lily told me that she stayed home.
② Lily told me that I would stay home.
③ Lily told me that she would stay home.
④ Lily told me that I will stay home.
⑤ Lily told me that she stays home.

08

The waiter said to us, "Where do you want to sit?"

① The waiter asked us where do we want to sit.
② The waiter asked us where do you want to sit.
③ The waiter asked us where we want to sit.
④ The waiter asked us where you want to sit.
⑤ The waiter asked us where we wanted to sit.

[09-10] 다음 대화의 빈칸에 알맞은 말을 고르시오.

09

A: What will Danny do this vacation?
B: He told me that he _____ in the mountains with his family.

① goes camping   ② went camping
③ did go camping   ④ had gone camping
⑤ would go camping

10

A: What time does Sarah go to school?
B: She said that she _____ at seven every morning.

① went to school   ② goes to school
③ would go to school   ④ had gone to school
⑤ has gone to school

11

빈칸에 if나 whether가 들어갈 수 없는 것은?

① I asked him _____ he missed Amy.
② I asked her _____ she was late for school.
③ I asked him _____ his hobby was.
④ I asked her _____ she could help me out.
⑤ I asked them _____ they liked pancakes.

12

다음 우리말을 영어로 바르게 옮긴 것은?

Ed는 나에게 어느 도시에 살았었는지 물었다.

① Ed asked me which city I have lived in.
② Ed asked me which city I had lived in.
③ Ed asked me I lived in which city.
④ Ed asked me which city I live in.
⑤ Ed asked me I had lived in which city.

[13-14] 다음 간접화법을 직접화법으로 바꿀 때 잘못된 것을 고르시오.

13

① Jim said that he was proud of Anna.
   → Jim said, "I'm proud of Anna."
② Mom said that Jenny had called me.
   → Mom said, "Jenny called you."
③ Ken said that he didn't think it would rain.
   → Ken said, "I don't think it will rain."
④ Ellen said that he had been late for school.
   → Ellen said, "He is late for school."
⑤ The couple said that they were happy.
   → The couple said, "We are happy."

14

① Lisa asked me where I had bought that.
   → Lisa asked me, "Where did you buy this?"
② I asked Jim if he could fix my car.
   → I asked Jim, "Can you fix my car?"
③ Ann asked her boss if he was busy then.
   → Ann asked her boss, "Are you busy now?"
④ Mom asked us if we wanted to play.
   → Mom asked us, "Do we want to play?"
⑤ My teacher asked me how I was.
   → My teacher asked me, "How are you?"

15

다음 밑줄 친 부분을 바르게 고치지 <u>않은</u> 것은?

① Do you know <u>when did they leave</u> for the airport?   → when they left

② My mom said that every dog <u>had</u> his day.
                    → had had

③ <u>Do you think why</u> the restaurant is closed?
   → Why do you think

④ I wondered why Dan <u>has gone</u> abroad.
               → had gone

⑤ He asked me <u>that</u> I knew Scarlet.
         → if

[16-18] 다음 밑줄 친 부분이 어법상 <u>틀린</u> 것을 고르시오.

16

① He thought his father <u>had left</u> him.

② Yumi said that she <u>wanted</u> to go skiing.

③ I asked Tony <u>if he could</u> lend me some money.

④ My father said that he <u>would come</u> to visit me the next day.

⑤ Dean didn't know America <u>had been discovered</u> by Columbus.

17

① I don't know if <u>it's going to rain</u>.

② I heard that she usually <u>goes to bed</u> at nine.

③ Everybody knows that the Wright brothers <u>invented</u> the airplane.

④ My mom told me that she <u>wanted</u> me to be confident.

⑤ I learned that two-thirds of the earth <u>was covered with</u> water.

18

① Sally asked me <u>what I was reading</u>.

② I asked Alex where <u>did his brother live</u>.

③ Jim asked Ashley <u>if she liked to play golf</u>.

④ He said that he <u>would leave</u> his country.

⑤ Rick told me that he <u>planned to go</u> fishing.

19

다음 우리말을 영어로 옮긴 것 중 <u>잘못된</u> 것은?

① 그가 어느 책을 빌렸는지 말해줘.
   Tell me which book he borrowed.

② 나는 누가 그 공을 던졌는지 모른다.
   I don't know who threw the ball.

③ 너는 누가 춤을 잘 춘다고 생각하니?
   Do you think who dances well?

④ 그는 내게 두통이 있는지 물어보았다.
   He asked me if I had a headache.

⑤ 그녀는 내게 쇼핑하러 갈 건지 물어보았다.
   She asked me whether I would go shopping.

고난도

20

다음 중 어법상 옳은 것끼리 짝지어진 것은?

(a) We believed that he will become a great writer.

(b) I want to know who makes noise every night.

(c) Bill said that he studies economics at university at that time.

(d) I learned that Hermann Hesse wrote *Demian*.

① (a), (b)   ② (a), (c)   ③ (b), (c)
④ (b), (d)   ⑤ (c), (d)

서술형 따라잡기

01

주어진 말을 이용하여 우리말과 뜻이 같도록 문장을 완성하시오.

(1) 너는 누가 이 그림을 그렸는지 아니?
(draw, picture)
→ Do you know _____ _____ _____
_____ ?

(2) 그가 흰색 셔츠를 입고 있는지 알려줘. (wear)
→ Let me know _____ _____ _____
_____ _____ _____ _____ .

02

주어진 말을 알맞게 배열하여 우리말과 뜻이 같도록 문장을 완성하시오.

(1) 그는 그녀의 남동생이 어느 학교에 다니는지 물어보았다. (which, went, asked, to, school, her, he, brother)
→ _____

(2) 그녀는 나에게 내가 메시지를 남겼었는지 물어보았다.
(left, asked, a, had, message, me, I, she, if)
→ _____

03

다음 문장을 직접화법으로 바꾸어 쓰시오.

(1) Emma asked Mason when he would leave for Laos.
(2) Mason told Emma that he was going to leave the next day.

(1) Emma asked Mason, "_____
_____"

(2) Mason said to Emma, "_____
_____"

04

다음 대화를 읽고, 문장을 완성하시오.

(1) Mira: Will you leave on Friday?
Ryan: No, I'll stay here until Sunday.
→ Mira asked Ryan _____ _____
_____ _____ on Friday.

(2) Rosa: Have you seen Jack?
Ian: No, I haven't seen him for a long time.
→ Ian told Rosa that _____ _____
_____ Jack for a long time.

05

다음 문진표를 보고, 〈보기〉와 같이 문장을 완성하시오.

> **Health Check List**
> How old are you?
> (1) Do you exercise?
> (2) What's your favorite food?
> (3) Have you ever been in the hospital?

〈보기〉 The check list asks how old I am.

(1) The check list asks _____ .

(2) The check list asks _____ .

(3) The check list asks _____ .

06

다음 기사를 읽고, 틀린 부분을 찾아 바르게 고쳐 쓰시오. (1군데)

> Today I interviewed a soccer player named Jason Kim. He told me that he has started playing soccer when he was five. I asked what the happiest moment of his career was. He said, "It was winning the championship match in 2017."

핵심 포인트 정리하기

1 시제 일치

- 주절의 시제가 현재 → 종속절은 모든 시제 가능

- 주절의 시제가 과거 → 종속절은 ① _____ 또는 ② _____ 만 가능

*시제 일치의 예외

– 과학적 사실, 변하지 않는 사실, 격언·속담, 현재에도 지속되는 습관이나 사실: ③ _____ 시제를 씀

– 역사적 사실: ④ _____ 시제를 씀

 시제 일치의 원칙과 예외 구분하여 알아두기!

2 간접화법

- 의미: 다른 사람이 말한 내용을 전달자의 입장에 맞게 바꿔 전달하는 것

- 평서문의 간접화법: ① 전달동사 say → 그대로 / say to → ⑤ _____
  　　　　　　　　　② 주절의 콤마와 인용부호를 없애고 접속사 that을 씀
  　　　　　　　　　③ 인용부호 안의 인칭대명사를 전달자에 맞추고, 동사도 시제 일치 원칙에 맞게 바꿈

- 의문문의 간접화법: 의문사가 없는 의문문 → 〈⑥ _____ (+목적어) + _____ + 주어 + 동사〉
  　　　　　　　　　　　의문사가 있는 의문문 → 〈ask(+ 목적어) + ⑦ _____ + _____ + _____〉

 화법을 전환할 때 지시대명사와 때·장소의 부사(구)도 바꾸는 것 잊지 말기!

3 간접의문문

- 의미: 의문문이 문장 내에서 주어, 보어, 목적어 역할을 하는 것

- 의문사가 있는 간접의문문: 〈의문사 + 주어 + 동사〉 *의문사가 주어인 경우: 〈의문사 + 동사〉

- 의문사가 없는 간접의문문: 〈⑧ _____ + 주어 + 동사〉

 주절의 동사가 think, believe, imagine, guess 등일 경우 의문사는 맨 앞에 쓰기!

문제로 개념 다지기

밑줄 친 부분이 어법상 맞으면 O, 틀리면 X 표시하고 바르게 고치시오.

1 It seems that everything has been prepared.

　　→ It seemed that everything <u>had been</u> prepared.

2 My teacher says that the Joseon Dynasty started in 1392.

　　→ My teacher said that the Joseon Dynasty <u>had started</u> in 1392.

3 Please tell me. + Why were you absent yesterday?

　　→ Please tell me <u>why you were</u> absent yesterday.

4 Do you know? + Are they twins?

　　→ Do you know <u>whether are they</u> twins?

MEMO

MEMO

MEMO

MEMO

MEMO

MEMO

MEMO

지은이

NE능률 영어교육연구소

NE능률 영어교육연구소는 혁신적이며 효율적인 영어 교재를 개발하고
영어 학습의 질을 한 단계 높이고자 노력하는 NE능률의 연구조직입니다.

문제로 마스터하는 중학영문법 〈LEVEL 2〉

펴 낸 이	주민홍
펴 낸 곳	서울특별시 마포구 월드컵북로 396(상암동) 누리꿈스퀘어 비즈니스타워 10층
	㈜NE능률 (우편번호 03925)
펴 낸 날	2018년 7월 5일 개정판 제1쇄 발행
	2024년 6월 15일 제21쇄
전 화	02 2014 7114
팩 스	02 3142 0356
홈 페 이 지	www.neungyule.com
등 록 번 호	제1-68호
I S B N	979-11-253-2366-2 53740
정 가	11,000원

NE 능률

고객센터

교재 내용 문의 : contact.nebooks.co.kr (별도의 가입 절차 없이 작성 가능)
제품 구매, 교환, 불량, 반품 문의 : 02-2014-7114
☎ 전화문의는 본사 업무시간 중에만 가능합니다.

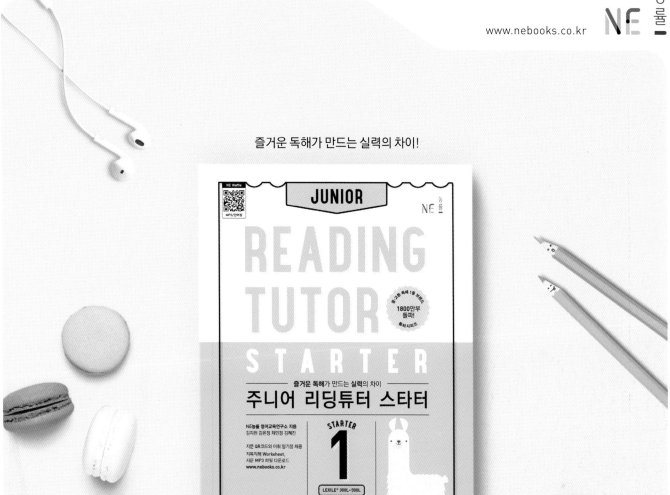

NE능률 교재 MAP

아래 교재 MAP을 참고하여 본인의 현재 혹은 목표 수준에 따라 교재를 선택하세요.
NE능률 교재들과 함께 영어실력을 쑥쑥~ 올려보세요!
MP3 등 교재 부가 학습 서비스 및 자세한 교재 정보는 www.nebooks.co.kr 에서 확인하세요.

문법 구문

초1-2	초3	초3-4	초4-5	초5-6
	그래머버디 1	그래머버디 2	그래머버디 3	Grammar Bean 3
	초등영어 문법이 된다 Starter 1	초등영어 문법이 된다 Starter 2	Grammar Bean 1	Grammar Bean 4
		초등 Grammar Inside 1	Grammar Bean 2	초등영어 문법이 된다 2
		초등 Grammar Inside 2	초등영어 문법이 된다 1	초등 Grammar Inside 5
			초등 Grammar Inside 3	초등 Grammar Inside 6
			초등 Grammar Inside 4	

초6-예비중	중1	중1-2	중2-3	중3
능률중학영어 예비중	능률중학영어 중1	능률중학영어 중2	Grammar Zone 기초편	능률중학영어 중3
Grammar Inside Starter	Grammar Zone 입문편	1316 Grammar 2	Grammar Zone 워크북 기초편	문제로 마스터하는 중학영문법 3
원리를 더한 영문법 STARTER	Grammar Zone 워크북 입문편	문제로 마스터하는 중학영문법 2	1316 Grammar 3	Grammar Inside 3
	1316 Grammar 1	Grammar Inside 2	원리를 더한 영문법 2	열중 16강 문법 3
	문제로 마스터하는 중학영문법 1	열중 16강 문법 2	중학영문법 총정리 모의고사 2	중학영문법 총정리 모의고사 3
	Grammar Inside 1	원리를 더한 영문법 1	쓰기로 마스터하는 중학서술형 2학년	쓰기로 마스터하는 중학서술형 3학년
	열중 16강 문법 1	중학영문법 총정리 모의고사 1	중학 천문장 3	
	쓰기로 마스터하는 중학서술형 1학년	중학 천문장 2		
	중학 천문장 1			

예비고-고1	고1	고1-2	고2-3	고3
문제로 마스터하는 고등영문법	Grammar Zone 기본편 1	필히 통하는 고등 영문법 실력편	Grammar Zone 종합편	
올클 수능 어법 start	Grammar Zone 워크북 기본편 1	필히 통하는 고등 서술형 실전편	Grammar Zone 워크북 종합편	
천문장 입문	Grammar Zone 기본편 2	TEPS BY STEP G+R Basic	올클 수능 어법 완성	
	Grammar Zone 워크북 기본편 2		천문장 완성	
	필히 통하는 고등 영문법 기본편			
	필히 통하는 고등 서술형 기본편			
	천문장 기본			

수능 이상/ 토플 80-89 · 텝스 600-699점	수능 이상/ 토플 90-99 · 텝스 700-799점	수능 이상/ 토플 100 · 텝스 800점 이상		
TEPS BY STEP G+R 1	TEPS BY STEP G+R 2	TEPS BY STEP G+R 3		

LEVEL **2**

문제로
마스터하는
중학영문법

정답 및 해설

NE 능률

문제로 마스터하는 중학영문법

LEVEL 2

정답 및 해설

POINT 01 1형식 / 2형식 문장　　　　　　p.10

A　1　Elizabeth lives in England.
　　　　주어　　　동사

　　2　Many children play on the playground.
　　　　　主어　　　　동사

　　3　These bags are too heavy.
　　　　주어　　동사　　보어

　　4　I will be a famous singer someday.
　　　　주어　동사　　　보어

　　5　The plant will die without water.
　　　　주어　　동사

　　6　The leaves turn red in autumn.
　　　　주어　　동사　보어

B　1　My sister works, 1

　　2　My father smokes, 1

　　3　It snows a lot, 1

　　4　is my boyfriend's birthday, 2

　　5　He can swim, 1

　　6　was very interesting, 2

　　7　will become a doctor, 2

POINT 02 감각동사＋형용사　　　　　　p.11

A　1　looks sad　2　smells nice　3　tastes bitter
　　4　sounds strange　5　feel happy

B　1　sounds like　2　good　3　smooth　4　smells
　　5　looks like

C　1　look cute　2　sounds boring　3　smell sweet
　　4　tastes salty　5　looks like a doll

POINT 03 3형식/4형식 문장　　　　　　p.12

A　1　made us a cake, 4

　　2　reads the English newspaper, 3

　　3　Did you watch TV, 3

　　4　bought her friend a scarf, 4

　　5　sent me a birthday card, 4

B　1　He teaches us history.

　　2　I showed her some photos.

　　3　He lent me 10 dollars.

　　4　I bought her a necklace.

　　5　My parents gave me a laptop.

POINT 04 4형식 문장 → 3형식 문장으로의 전환　　p.13

A　1　to　2　to　3　for　4　to my parents　5　for us

B　1　my life story to you　2　a favor of me
　　3　the movie star letters
　　4　a glass of water for you
　　5　teach me Spanish　6　my son a toy car

POINT 05 5형식 문장의 목적격 보어 I　　　　p.14

A　1　me alone　2　useful　3　nervous
　　4　our pet rabbit "Oreo"
　　5　Edison a great inventor

B　1　made him a famous musician
　　2　keep you safe
　　3　made her a different person
　　4　calls me a genius
　　5　found the online game exciting

POINT 06 5형식 문장의 목적격 보어 II　　　　p.15

A　1　expect him to come
　　2　anybody to know about it
　　3　advised me to drink
　　4　want him to be a scientist

B　1　allowed me to use　2　told her to eat
　　3　expects the package to arrive
　　4　asked me to drive　5　help me to sweep

POINT 07 5형식 문장의 목적격 보어 III　　　　p.16

A　1　keep　2　cry　3　to bring　4　play　5　to close

B　1　makes me clean　2　had her husband buy
　　3　didn't let us talk　4　lets me use
　　5　has them do push-ups　6　make you look tall
　　7　let me go

A 1 sing[singing]   2 take[taking]
     3 play[playing]   4 come[coming]
     5 touch[touching]   6 tell

B 1 We listened to the old man tell
     2 I saw Jenny eating
     3 He felt someone looking at
     4 They heard their daughter playing
     5 People watched the stuntman jump
     6 I could see the light coming

내신대비 TEST   p.18

01 ①   02 ⑤   03 ③   04 ①   05 ⑤   06 ④
07 ③   08 ③   09 ①   10 ①   11 ②   12 ②
13 ⑤   14 ④   15 ②   16 ④   17 ④   18 ①
19 ③, ⑤   20 ④

서술형 따라잡기 - - - - - - - - - - - - - - - - - - p.21

01 look really sad, gave me a low grade
02 free tickets for all of us
03 (1) jumping[jump] rope
     (2) watering[water] flowers
     (3) talking[talk]
04 (1) I found Jack smart and creative
     (2) showed her wedding picture to me
05 (1) clean my room   (2) to read comic books
     (3) play computer games
06 (1) me to cook dinner
     (2) Mary to lend you her notebook

01 5형식 문장에서 사역동사(make)가 사용될 경우, 목적격 보어로 동사원형이 온다.
02 5형식 문장에서 동사 want는 목적격 보어로 to부정사를 쓴다.
03 5형식 문장에서 지각동사(see)가 사용될 경우, 목적격 보어로 동사원형이나 현재분사를 쓴다.
04 ①은 〈주어+동사+목적어+목적격 보어〉 형태의 5형식 문장이고, 나머지는 모두 〈주어+동사+간접목적어+직접목적어〉 형태의 4형식 문장이다.

05 ⑤ 동사 buy는 3형식 문장으로 쓸 때 간접목적어 앞에 전치사 for를 쓴다.
06 감각동사(look) 뒤의 보어 자리에는 형용사가 와야 한다.
07 감각동사(smell) 뒤의 보어 자리에는 형용사를 쓰고, 사역동사(make)의 목적격 보어 자리에는 동사원형을 쓴다.
08 3형식 문장으로 쓸 때 동사 write는 간접목적어 앞에 전치사 to를 쓰고, 5형식 문장에서 동사 ask는 목적격 보어로 to부정사를 쓴다.
09 make+직접목적어+전치사(for)+간접목적어 (3형식)
     make+목적어+목적격 보어(형용사) (5형식)
10 tell+간접목적어+직접목적어 (4형식)
     tell+목적어+목적격 보어(to부정사) (5형식)
11 ② 그녀가 무엇을 만들어 주었는지 묻는 질문에 그녀가 나를 행복하게 해 주었다는 응답은 어색하다.
12 5형식 문장에서 지각동사 hear는 목적격 보어로 동사원형이나 현재분사를 쓴다.
13 수여동사를 3형식 문장으로 쓸 때 동사 make는 간접목적어 앞에 전치사 for를 쓴다. 반면, 동사 tell, give, send, teach는 간접목적어 앞에 전치사 to를 쓴다.
14 bring+직접목적어+전치사(to)+간접목적어 (3형식)
     bring+간접목적어+직접목적어 (4형식)
15 ②의 동사 make는 '만들어주다'라는 의미의 4형식 동사로 쓰였고, 나머지는 '~시키다', '~하게 하다'라는 의미의 5형식 동사로 쓰였다.
16 ④ 5형식 문장에서 동사 expect의 목적격 보어로는 to부정사가 와야 하므로 to lend가 되어야 한다.
17 ④ 〈buy+간접목적어(his parents)+직접목적어(pajamas)〉 혹은 〈buy+직접목적어(pajamas)+전치사(for)+간접목적어(his parents)〉가 되어야 한다.
18 (A) 감각동사(smell)의 보어 자리에는 형용사가 와야 한다.
     (B) 동사 get은 사역의 의미를 지니지만 목적격 보어로 to부정사를 쓴다.
     (C) help는 목적격 보어로 동사원형과 to부정사 둘 다를 쓸 수 있다.
19 ① 감각동사(look)의 보어로는 형용사 wonderful을 쓴다.
     ② 수여동사 give는 3형식 문장에서 간접목적어 앞에 전치사 to를 쓴다.
     ④ 감각동사가 보어로 명사(구)를 취할 때는 〈감각동사+전치사(like)+명사(구)〉의 형태로 쓴다.

3

20 ④는 〈보기〉와 같이 〈주어+동사+목적어+목적격 보어〉 형태의 5형식 문장이다. ①은 〈주어+동사+보어〉 형태의 2형식, ②는 〈주어+동사〉 형태의 1형식, ③은 〈주어+동사+목적어〉 형태의 3형식, ⑤는 〈주어+동사+간접목적어+직접목적어〉 형태의 4형식 문장이다.

서술형 따라잡기

01 2형식 문장에서 감각동사 look은 보어 자리에 형용사를 써야 하고, 4형식 문장에서 수여동사 give는 〈give+간접목적어(me)+직접목적어(a low grade)〉의 어순으로 써야 한다.

02 〈get+간접목적어+직접목적어〉는 〈get+직접목적어+전치사(for)+간접목적어〉로 바꾸어 쓸 수 있다.

03 지각동사인 see와 hear의 목적격 보어로 동사원형이나 현재분사를 쓴다.

04 (1) 동사 find는 5형식 문장에서 〈find+목적어(Jack)+목적격 보어(smart and creative)〉의 형태로 쓴다.
(2) 동사 show는 3형식 문장에서 〈show+직접목적어(her wedding picture)+전치사(to)+간접목적어(me)〉의 형태로 쓴다.

05 (1) 5형식 문장에서 사역동사 make는 목적격 보어로 동사원형을 쓴다.
(2) 5형식 문장에서 동사 allow는 목적격 보어로 to부정사를 쓴다.
(3) 5형식 문장에서 사역동사 let은 목적격 보어로 동사원형을 쓴다.

06 (1) 동사 get은 사역의 의미를 지니지만 목적격 보어로 to부정사를 쓴다.
(2) 5형식 문장에서 동사 tell은 목적격 보어로 to부정사를 쓴다.

SELF NOTE   p.22

A 핵심 포인트 정리하기
① 형용사 ② to ③ for ④ of ⑤ to부정사 ⑥ 동사원형
⑦ 사역동사 ⑧ 현재분사 ⑨ to부정사 ⑩ 과거분사

B 문제로 개념 다지기
1 O 2 X, sweet 3 X, to enter 4 O 5 O
6 X, park 7 X, for me

Chapter 02 to부정사

POINT 01 to부정사의 명사적 용법 I – 주어, 보어   p.24

A 1 is difficult to say sorry
  2 to build a house
  3 is not safe to swim here
  4 To save money now
  5 To exercise every day

B 1 Her hope is to act again.
  2 It is dangerous to walk on the ice.
  3 To solve this problem is not easy.
  4 His dream was to become president.
  5 His goal is to make many friends.

POINT 02 to부정사의 명사적 용법 II – 목적어   p.25

A 1 to play 2 to go 3 to ask 4 to drive
  5 to study 6 to take 7 to meet

B 1 decided to study hard 2 expect to finish
  3 offered to give 4 needs to exercise
  5 refused to eat 6 promise to tell the truth
  7 planned to travel

POINT 03 to부정사의 명사적 용법 III – 의문사+to부정사 p.26

A 1 whom to help 2 when to leave
  3 where to go 4 how to make
  5 what to do

B 1 I don't know where I should start.
  2 She'll let you know how you should dress for the party.
  3 I'm not sure when I should call her.
  4 He asked me what he should try first.

POINT 04 to부정사의 형용사적 용법 I   p.27

A 1 time to rest 2 something sweet
  3 a black pen to use 4 time to have
  5 interesting to watch

B 1 many museums to visit in Paris

2 him a comic book to read

3 to take your medicine

4 some vegetables to cook

5 something to make her happy

6 something exciting to show you

7 anything cold to drink

8 someone to look after her baby

A 1 to live in 2 to drink 3 to listen to

4 to read 5 to talk about 6 to write with

B 1 a roommate to live with

2 few toys to play with 3 a spoon to eat with

4 a chair to sit in 5 a hotel to stay in

6 a partner to dance with

7 any paper to write on

A 1 are to follow 2 is to visit 3 are to lose

B 1 was to become 2 are to come 3 is to wash

4 is to meet 5 are to buy

6 was not[never] to get married to him

A 1 to help 2 to meet you 3 to learn

4 sorry to hear 5 glad[happy] to win

6 to be[become]

B 1 was disappointed to lose

2 came to Korea to meet

3 was very surprised to see him

4 studied hard in order to pass the exam

A 1 to sleep till now 2 to give her a present

3 to be a famous novelist 4 only to fail

5 to be on time every day

B 1 only to find it closed

2 to be on vacation

3 to go abroad by herself

4 to know all of his songs

A 1 To taste this cake 2 To smell that cheese

3 To see him run 4 To look at him

B 1 simple to make 2 difficult to learn

3 To hear her story 4 convenient to use

5 dangerous to travel 6 To hear my cat cry

A 1 for me to watch[see] 2 of me to believe

3 of you to say 4 of him to help

5 for us to climb

B 1 It's brave of Judy to tell the truth.

2 It's easy for Germans to learn English.

3 It's fun for the children to go to the amusement park.

4 It's kind of you to lend me your notebook.

A 1 so difficult that they can't follow it

2 so cold that we couldn't go swimming

3 too salty for her to drink

4 too strange for me to understand

5 too noisy for him to study in

B 1 too young to watch 2 too cold to go

3 too short to be 4 too tired to go

5 too big for me to eat 6 too far for us to walk

A 1 fast enough 2 enough to be

3 rich enough

B 1 so thick that I could walk on

2 so small that I can carry

3 smart enough to go

4 so light that I can lift

C 1 lucky enough to travel

2 sharp enough to cut the potatoes

3 strong enough to move the table

내신대비 TEST

p.36

01 ②	02 ①	03 ①	04 ④	05 ③	06 ②
07 ⑤	08 ③	09 ③	10 ①	11 ⑤	12 ④
13 ④	14 ⑤	15 ④	16 ④	17 ②	18 ④
19 ③	20 ②				

서술형 따라잡기

p.39

01 (1) how to use (2) was never[not] to see

02 (1) It is rude to shout at

(2) is big enough for me to share

03 (1) to live → to live in

(2) too old → old enough / what → how

04 (1) tall enough to reach (2) to sit in[on]

05 (1) It is foolish of Mark to be late for school.

(2) It is easy for Justine to solve math problems.

06 (1) Sarah got up too late to catch the train.

(2) He was too short to ride the roller coaster.

01 동사 decide는 to부정사를 목적어로 취한다.

02 일반적으로 to부정사의 의미상의 주어는 〈for+목적격〉의 형태로 나타낸다.

03 play가 자동사이고 '~와 함께 놀'의 의미가 되어야 하므로 전치사 with를 함께 써야 한다.

04 ④는 목적을 나타내는 부사적 용법이다. ①, ⑤는 문장에서 주어 역할, ②는 목적어 역할, ③은 보어 역할을 하는 명사적 용법으로 쓰였다.

05 첫 번째 빈칸에는 to get 이하를 대신하는 가주어 It이 와야 하고, 두 번째 빈칸에는 조건을 나타내는 부사적 용법의 to부정사가 와야 한다.

06 '어디에 ~할지'라는 의미는 〈where+to-v〉의 형태로, '…하기에는 너무 ~하다'의 의미는 〈too+형용사/부사+to-v〉의 형태로 쓴다.

07 to부정사를 목적어로 취하는 동사는 plan, want, refuse, decide이다. enjoy는 동명사를 목적어로 취한다.

08 '…할 만큼 충분히 ~하다'는 〈형용사/부사+enough+to-v〉의 어순으로 쓴다.

09 talk와 write 같은 자동사가 목적어를 취하려면 반드시 전치사가 있어야 한다. 각각 '~와 말하다', '~을 가지고 쓰다'의 의미가 되어야 하므로 빈칸에는 전치사 with를 쓴다.

10 일반적으로 to부정사의 의미상의 주어는 〈for+목적격〉의 형태로 나타낸다.

11 ⑤〈so+형용사/부사+that+주어+can[could]~〉은 '…할 만큼 충분히 ~하다'라는 의미로, 〈형용사/부사+enough+to-v〉로 바꾸어 쓸 수 있다.

12 〈보기〉의 밑줄 친 부분과 ④는 명사를 수식하는 형용사적 용법으로 쓰였다. ①은 목적을 나타내는 부사적 용법, ②는 주어 역할을 하는 명사적 용법, ③은 목적어 역할을 하는 명사적 용법, ⑤는 감정의 원인을 나타내는 부사적 용법으로 쓰였다.

13 〈보기〉의 밑줄 친 부분과 ④는 주어 역할을 하는 명사적 용법으로 쓰였다. ①은 명사를 수식하는 형용사적 용법, ②는 목적을 나타내는 부사적 용법, ③은 형용사를 수식하는 부사적 용법, ⑤는 조건을 나타내는 부사적 용법으로 쓰였다.

14 ⑤ kind는 사람에 대한 주관적인 평가를 나타내는 형용사이므로 〈of+목적격〉의 형태로 의미상의 주어를 나타낸다.

15 〈의문사+to부정사〉는 〈의문사+주어+should+동사원형〉으로 바꿔 쓸 수 있다.

16 '~에 쓸'이라는 의미로 a piece of paper를 수식하는 to부정사의 동사가 자동사인 write이므로 to write 뒤에 전치사 on을 써야 한다.

17 ② 〈something+형용사(funny)+to부정사〉의 어순이 되어야 한다.

18 ④ to부정사의 의미상의 주어는 〈for/of+목적격〉으로 쓴다.

19 to부정사의 부정형은 〈not[never]+to부정사〉의 형태이므로 주어진 단어들을 배열하면 'Be careful not to make any mistakes.'이며 세 번째에 오는 단어는 not이다.

20 (c) to answer는 an easy question을 수식하는 형용사적 용법의 to부정사로 뒤의 목적어 it은 필요 없다.

(d) 가주어 it에 대한 진주어로 to부정사 형태의 to finish가 와야 한다.

서술형 따라잡기

01 (1) 문맥상 '~하는 방법'이라는 의미의 〈how+to-v〉를 쓴다.

(2) 운명을 나타내는 〈be+to부정사〉를 쓰고, to부정사의 부

정형은 to부정사 앞에 not이나 never를 쓴다.

02 (1) to부정사가 주어로 쓰일 때는, 그 자리에 가주어 It을 쓰고 to부정사는 문장의 뒤로 보낸다.

(2) ⟨so+형용사/부사+that+주어+can ~⟩은 ⟨형용사/부사+enough+to-v⟩로 바꾸어 쓸 수 있다.

03 (1) '~안에 살'이라는 의미의 an apartment를 수식하는 형용사적 용법의 to부정사가 와야 하는데 동사 live가 자동사이므로 to live가 아닌 to live in을 써야 한다.

(2) 문맥상 '…할 만큼 충분히 ~하다'의 의미인 ⟨형용사/부사+enough+to-v⟩가 와야 하므로 too old를 old enough로 고친다. 또, '운전하는 법'이라는 의미가 되어야 하므로 what to drive를 how to drive로 고친다.

04 (1) '…할 만큼 충분히 ~하다'의 의미가 되어야 하므로 ⟨형용사/부사+enough+to-v⟩ 구문을 활용한다.

(2) '~에 앉을'이라는 의미의 a chair를 수식하는 형용사적 용법의 to부정사가 와야 한다. to부정사에 사용된 동사(sit)가 자동사이므로 to sit 뒤에 전치사 in[on]을 써야 한다.

05 to부정사가 주어로 쓰일 때는, 그 자리에 가주어 It을 쓰고 to부정사는 문장의 뒤로 보낸다. 일반적으로 의미상의 주어는 ⟨for+목적격⟩의 형태로 나타내지만, 사람에 대한 주관적인 평가를 나타내는 형용사(foolish)가 보어로 쓰일 때는 ⟨of+목적격⟩의 형태로 쓴다.

06 '…하기에는 너무 ~하다'가 되어야 하므로 ⟨too+형용사/부사+to-v⟩로 쓴다.

SELF NOTE
p.40

A 핵심 포인트 정리하기
① 목적어 ② should ③ 형용사 ④ be+to부정사
⑤ 목적 ⑥ for ⑦ so

B 문제로 개념 다지기
1 X, to finish[finishing] 2 O
3 X, when to meet him[when I should meet him]
4 X, to lock 5 X, not to follow
6 X, too big for me to wear 7 O

Chapter 03 동명사

POINT 01 동명사의 역할
p.42

A 1 Taking[To take] 2 climbing
　3 making[to make] 4 writing
　5 hearing 6 saying 7 Riding[To ride]

B 1 When can you start working?
　2 My job is protecting wild animals.
　3 I'm thinking about joining a movie club.
　4 Exercising is good for your health.
　5 I'm sorry for not keeping my promise.

POINT 02 자주 쓰이는 동명사 표현
p.43

A 1 hiking 2 visiting 3 laughing 4 eating
　5 to make 6 hearing

B 1 How[What] about going to a movie?
　2 Laura is busy preparing for the job fair.
　3 I cannot help missing her.[I cannot (help) but miss her.]
　4 The book is worth reading twice.
　5 It is no use worrying about it.
　6 I feel like taking a walk with my dog.
　7 She is used to handling the machine.
　8 He looks forward to meeting you next month.

POINT 03 동명사와 현재분사 I
p.44

A 1 현재분사 2 현재분사 3 동명사 4 동명사
　5 현재분사 6 동명사

B 1 was making robots
　2 is listening to music
　3 is talking on the phone

C 1 그는 그의 차를 세차하고 있다.
　2 그녀의 직업은 옷을 디자인하는 것이다.
　3 한 아기가 침대에서 자고 있었다.

POINT 04 동명사와 현재분사 II
p.45

A 1 현재분사 2 현재분사 3 동명사 4 동명사
　5 현재분사 6 동명사 7 동명사 8 현재분사

9 현재분사　10 동명사　11 현재분사　12 동명사

B 1 (a) 나는 저 수영하고 있는 돌고래가 좋다.

(b) 수영장에 많은 아이들이 있다.

2 (a) 이 자고 있는 아기는 귀엽다.

(b) 침낭을 가져오는 것을 잊지 마라.

3 (a) 우리는 모든 살아 있는 것들을 존중해야 한다.

(b) 그 여자는 우리를 거실로 안내했다.

4 (a) 우리는 그를 '걸어 다니는 사전'이라고 불렀다.

(b) 그 노부인은 지팡이 없이 걸을 수 없다.

POINT 05 동명사와 to부정사 I　　　　　p.46

A 1 to study　2 watching　3 to leave　4 to rent
5 getting　6 walking　7 trying　8 to bring
9 waiting　10 to make

B 1 I didn't expect to see you here.

2 He hates meeting new people.

3 The children started to pick up the trash
around them.

4 Keira began learning Spanish this month.

5 I'll continue to work at this company.

POINT 06 동명사와 to부정사 II　　　　　p.47

A 1 living　2 to give　3 to lock　4 to buy
5 to open　6 eating

B 1 나는 오래전에 이 영화를 본 것을 기억한다.

2 그들은 작년에 그 파티에서 그녀를 본 것을 잊었다.

3 그녀는 그 신발을 시험 삼아 신어 보았다.

4 나는 매우 피곤했기 때문에 공원에서 쉬기 위해 멈췄다.

내신대비 TEST　　　　　p.48

01 ④　02 ②　03 ⑤　04 ④　05 ⑤　06 ③
07 ⑤　08 ②　09 ④　10 ⑤　11 ①　12 ③
13 ③　14 ④　15 ④　16 ①　17 ②　18 ①
19 ①, ③　20 ②

서술형 따라잡기　----------------------　p.51

01 (1) I am used to eating spicy food.

(2) What about joining this club?

02 (1) On[Upon] seeing　(2) cannot help being

03 going, preparing, asking, to bring

04 (1) refused to build　(2) forgot picking

05 losing → to lose / to work → working

06 helping poor people, taking walks, to take
a vacation, going to sleep late

01 문장의 주어 역할을 할 수 있는 것은 동명사 또는 to부정사이다.

02 be busy v-ing: ~하느라 바쁘다

03 agree는 to부정사를 목적어로 취하는 동사이다.

04 ⓐ는 문장의 주어 역할을 하는 동명사가, ⓑ는 뒤에 오는 명사의 용도나 목적을 나타내는 동명사가 되어야 한다.

05 consider는 동명사를 목적어로 취하는 동사이다.

06 promise는 to부정사를 목적어로 취하는 동사이다.

07 mind는 동명사를, want는 to부정사를 목적어로 취하는 동사이다.

08 remember+to-v: ~할 것을 기억하다
forget+to-v: ~할 것을 잊다

09 ④는 진행형 문장의 현재분사이고, 나머지는 모두 보어로 쓰인 동명사이다.

10 ⑤의 sleeping은 명사 students를 수식하는 현재분사이고, 나머지는 모두 목적어로 쓰인 동명사이다.

11 try+v-ing: 시험 삼아 ~해 보다
try+to-v: ~하려고 노력하다

12 ③ B의 대답으로 보아, A의 말은 '게임하는 것을 그만두어라!'의 의미가 되어야 하므로 to play가 아닌 playing을 써야 자연스럽다. (stop+to-v: ~하기 위해 멈추다)

13 ③ 콘서트가 마음에 들었는지 묻는 말에 콘서트 볼 것을 기억하고 있다는 답변은 어색하다.

14 stop+v-ing: ~하는 것을 멈추다

15 ④ agree는 to부정사를 목적어로 취하는 동사이다.

16 ① hope는 to부정사를 목적어로 취하는 동사이다.

17 (A) promise는 to부정사를 목적어로 취하는 동사이다.
(B) 〈It is no use v-ing〉는 '~해도 소용없다'라는 의미이다.
(C) '~할 것을 잊다'의 의미일 때 forget은 to부정사를 목적어로 취한다.

18 〈보기〉와 ①은 수식하는 명사의 진행 및 능동을 나타내는 현재분사, 나머지는 동사 또는 전치사의 목적어 역할을 하는 동명사이다.

19 ① stop+to-v: ~하기 위해 멈추다

stop+v-ing: ~하는 것을 멈추다

③ forget+to-v: ~할 것을 잊다

forget+v-ing: ~한 것을 잊다

20 (a) 전치사의 목적어로 동명사(going)를 써야 한다.

(c) mind는 동명사를 목적어로 취하는 동사이다.

(d) expect는 to부정사를 목적어로 취하는 동사이다.

서술형 따라잡기

01 (1) 〈be used to v-ing〉는 '~하는 데 익숙하다'라는 의미이다.

(2) 〈What about v-ing?〉는 '~하는 것은 어때?'라는 의미이다.

02 (1) 〈as soon as+주어+동사〉는 〈on[upon] v-ing〉로 바꾸어 쓸 수 있고, '~하자마자'라는 의미이다.

(2) 〈cannot but+동사원형〉은 〈cannot help v-ing〉로 바꾸어 쓸 수 있고, '~하지 않을 수 없다'라는 의미이다.

03 〈feel like v-ing〉: ~하고 싶다

〈be busy v-ing〉: ~하느라 바쁘다

〈It is no use v-ing〉: ~해도 소용없다

〈remember to-v〉: ~할 것을 기억하다

04 (1) refuse는 to부정사를 목적어로 취하는 동사이다.

(2) '~한 것을 잊다'의 의미일 때 forget은 동명사를 목적어로 취한다.

05 decide는 to부정사를 목적어로 취하는 동사이다. 전치사 about의 목적어로는 동명사를 쓴다.

06 전치사 in의 목적어로는 동명사를 쓴다. like는 to부정사와 동명사를 모두 목적어로 취하는 동사이지만 빈칸의 개수가 2개이므로 동명사를 쓴다. plan은 to부정사를 목적어로 취하는 동사이다. stop은 '~하는 것을 멈추다'의 의미일 때 동명사를 목적어로 취한다.

SELF NOTE   p.52

A 핵심 포인트 정리하기

① 동사원형, -ing ② 명사 ③ 형용사 ④ 동명사

⑤ to부정사 ⑥ ~한 것을 기억하다 ⑦ ~할 것을 잊다

⑧ (시험 삼아) ~해 보다 ⑨ ~하는 것을 멈추다

⑩ ~하기 위해 멈추다

B 문제로 개념 다지기

1 O 2 X, calling 3 X, talking 4 X, eating

5 X, to buy 6 O

Chapter 04 대명사

POINT 01 부정대명사 one   p.54

A 1 one, one 2 it 3 it 4 ones 5 one

6 one 7 it 8 it 9 One 10 one

B 1 One should 2 bought new ones

3 don't like it 4 one, give it

POINT 02 부정대명사 all/both   p.55

A 1 Both of us 2 Both teams

3 Both of my parents 4 All of his children

B 1 hates → hate 2 Both → All

3 wants → want 4 Both → All

5 likes → like

C 1 I want to thank all of you.

2 Both of us are seventeen years old.

3 All of my money was in my pocket.

POINT 03 부정대명사 some/any/each/every   p.56

A 1 Some 2 any 3 Each 4 every 5 Each

6 some, any

B 1 Any → Some 2 works → work 3 do → does

4 any → some 5 have → has 6 some → any

POINT 04 부정대명사 another/one ~ the other …   p.57

A 1 another 2 another 3 One, the other

4 One, the other 5 One, another, the other

B 1 another cup of coffee

2 another way to get there

3 the other was from Kelly

POINT 05 부정대명사 some ~ others …/each other/ one another   p.58

A 1 each other 2 one another

3 Some, others 4 each other

5 one another 6 Some, others

B 1 call each other 2 know one another

3 Some answered, others

4 Some, the others rested

POINT 06 재귀대명사의 재귀 용법   p.59

A 1 themselves 2 yourself[yourselves]

   3 ourselves 4 me 5 himself

   6 yourself[yourselves]

B 1 introduce yourself 2 killed himself

   3 said to herself 4 angry with myself

   5 believe in ourselves 6 burned herself

   7 looked at himself 8 take care of himself

POINT 07 재귀대명사의 강조 용법   p.60

A 1 cooked, myself 2 himself[herself]

   3 themselves 4 yourself 5 ourselves

   6 teaching itself 7 the movie itself

B 1 speak to the manager himself

   2 me the news herself

   3 us how to throw a ball himself

   4 I hate English itself

   5 this chocolate cake for you myself

POINT 08 재귀대명사의 관용표현   p.61

A 1 of → by 2 itself → yourself 3 In → Between

   4 by → beside 5 oneself → themselves

B 1 in itself 2 helped himself 3 enjoyed ourselves

   4 beside herself 5 by himself

   6 Make yourself[yourselves] at home

내신대비 TEST   p.62

001 ① 02 ④ 03 ④ 04 ① 05 ② 06 ⑤

07 ① 08 ⑤ 09 ⑤ 10 ② 11 ③ 12 ①

13 ③ 14 ③ 15 ④ 16 ③ 17 ② 18 ②

19 ⑤ 20 ②, ③

서술형 따라잡기 - p.65

01 (1) by themselves (2) each other

02 Both of them made themselves at home.

03 (1) Some, the others (2) Some, others

04 (1) were beside ourselves (2) Each one has

05 One, another, the other

06 are → is / left one → left it /

   of you → of yourself

01 앞에 언급된 것과 같은 종류의 것을 나타낼 때 부정대명사 one 을 쓴다.

02 any는 '약간(의)', '조금(의)'의 의미로, 부정문에 쓴다.

03 〈some ~ others …〉는 '어떤 사람들은 ~, 또 어떤 사람들은 …'이라는 의미이다.

04 ① 주어 I가 하는 동작의 대상이 주어 자신일 때 동사의 목적어로 재귀대명사 myself를 쓴다.

05 앞에 언급된 것과 같은 종류의 것을 나타낼 때와 일반인을 총칭할 때는 부정대명사 one을 쓴다.

06 some은 '약간(의)', '몇몇(의)'이라는 의미로 권유문과 긍정문에 쓴다.

07 첫 번째 문장에서는 '마음껏 드세요.'라는 의미로 help yourself 를 쓴다. 두 번째 문장에서는 주어가 하는 동작의 대상이 주어 자신이므로 재귀대명사 yourself를 쓴다.

08 첫 번째 빈칸에는 복수 취급할 수 있는 대명사 Both나 All 이 알맞다. 두 번째 빈칸에는 둘일 때 '서로'의 의미로 쓰이는 each other가 와야 한다.

09 make oneself at home: 편히 지내다
   between ourselves: 우리끼리 얘기지만

10 세 명[개]의 대상을 하나씩 가리킬 때는 차례대로 one, another, the other를 쓴다.

11 ③은 주어를 강조하는 강조 용법이고, 나머지는 모두 동사의 목적어로 쓰인 재귀 용법이다.

12 ① 〈every+명사〉는 단수 취급하므로 has가 되어야 한다.

13 ③ 부정문이므로 any를 써야 한다. some은 긍정문에 쓴다.

14 ③ 두 개를 차례로 가리킬 때는 〈one ~ the other …〉를 쓴다.

15 ④ 강조 용법으로 쓰인 재귀대명사는 생략이 가능하다. 나머지는 모두 동사 혹은 전치사의 목적어로 쓰인 재귀 용법이므로 생략할 수 없다.

16 ③ B의 말에는 앞에 언급된 특정한 대상(a new laptop)을

가리키는 대명사 it을 써야 한다.

17 (A) in itself: 본래, 그 자체가
(B) 〈every+명사〉는 단수 취급하므로 is가 들어가야 한다.
(C) 앞에 언급된 것과 같은 종류의 것을 나타내는 부정대명사 ones가 들어가야 한다.

18 (a) 둘일 때 '서로'의 의미로 each other를 쓴다.
(b) '어떤 사람들은 ~, 또 어떤 사람들은 …'이라는 의미로 쓰이는 표현은 〈some ~ others …〉이다.

19 (a) 상황을 나타낼 때 단수 취급하는 all이 올 수 있다.
(b) '약간(의)', '조금(의)'라는 의미로 부정문에 쓰이는 any가 올 수 있다.
(c), (d) 복수명사와 함께 쓰일 수 있으며 복수 취급하는 all, both, some이 올 수 있다.

20 ① 옷을 입히는 대상이 주어 자신이므로 재귀대명사 myself를 써야 한다.
④ 앞에 언급된 것이 복수명사이므로, 부정대명사 one의 복수형인 ones를 써야 한다.
⑤ 두 개를 차례로 가리킬 때는 〈one ~ the other …〉를 쓴다.

서술형 따라잡기

01 (1) by oneself: 혼자서
(2) each other: (둘일 때) 서로

02 '~ 둘 다'의 의미일 때는 〈both of+목적격 대명사〉를, '편히 지내다'라는 의미를 나타내는 재귀대명사의 관용표현으로는 make oneself at home을 쓴다.

03 (1) A반 20명의 학생 중 11명은 some으로, 나머지 모든 학생은 the others로 쓴다.
(2) B반 22명의 학생 중 9명은 some으로, 나머지 모든 학생 중 또 다른 일부는 others로 쓴다.

04 (1) '제정신이 아닌'은 beside oneself를 쓴다.
(2) '각각(의)'라는 의미인 대명사 each를 쓴다. 〈Each+명사〉는 단수 취급하므로 동사는 has로 써야 한다.

05 세 명[개]의 대상을 하나씩 가리킬 때는 차례대로 one, another, the other를 쓴다.

06 〈every+명사〉는 단수 취급하므로, are wearing은 is wearing이 되어야 한다. 두 번째 B의 답변 중 뒤에 쓰인 one은 앞에 나온 특정한 대상을 지칭하는 it으로 고쳐야 한다. 마지막 A의 말에서 돌봐야 하는 대상이 바로 주어인 '너 자신'이므로 재귀대명사 yourself가 되어야 한다.

SELF NOTE   p.66

A 핵심 포인트 정리하기
① all ② every ③ the other ④ others
⑤ one another ⑥ 목적어

B 문제로 개념 다지기
1 one 2 were 3 are 4 the other 5 others
6 himself 7 themselves

Chapter 05 시제

POINT 01 진행형   p.68

A 1 sit → sitting 2 am → was
   3 burns → was burning

B 1 are drinking 2 was talking 3 is waiting

C 1 are you talking about
   2 We are going fishing
   3 she was cleaning
   4 was choosing a present

POINT 02 과거시제와 현재완료   p.69

A 1 lost 2 read 3 Did you go 4 haven't played
   5 heard

B 1 were 2 changed 3 have known
   4 came 5 had

C 1 the plant has grown
   2 She has gone to borrow a book
   3 He has worked at this restaurant

POINT 03 현재완료의 용법 – 경험   p.70

A 1 Have, eaten 2 have seen
   3 has traveled[travelled] 4 has taken

5 have not[never] missed 6 Have, been

B 1 Have you ever played

2 I have been to the aquarium

3 The team has never lost

4 Sean has never had a pet

5 The singer has held a concert in this city

POINT 04 현재완료의 용법 – 완료　　p.71

A 1 너는 벌써 숙제를 다 했니? 〈완료〉

2 나는 뉴욕에 한 번 가 본 적이 있다. 〈경험〉

3 그들은 막 이 아파트로 이사를 했다. 〈완료〉

B 1 haven't finished eating yet

2 has just come out

3 the store hasn't opened yet

C 1 hasn't worn　2 hasn't told anyone

3 have, gotten[got] a call

4 Have you, brushed your teeth

POINT 05 현재완료의 용법 – 계속　　p.72

A 1 have loved Mina since

2 have had this sofa for

3 has been sick since

4 has lived here[in this house] for

B 1 has studied in Canada for two years

2 I have worn glasses since

3 How long have you known

4 has liked to dance since

5 hasn't seen Sally since

POINT 06 현재완료의 용법 – 결과　　p.73

A 1 has gone　2 has broken　3 has eaten

4 have left　5 have gained

B 1 Steve has lost his key.

2 I have sold my old books.

3 Sarah has left her bag on the bus.

4 My father has gone to Hong Kong on
business.

01 ③　02 ③　03 ②　04 ②　05 ③　06 ⑤

07 ②　08 ④　09 ①　10 ①　11 ②　12 ③

13 ④　14 ⑤　15 ③　16 ④　17 ⑤　18 ⑤

19 ④　20 ⑤

서술형 따라잡기　　p.77

01 (1) has taught　(2) has moved

02 (1) he was eating lunch　(2) hasn't arrived yet

03 (1) How long have you been there?

(2) I have played the piano since I was six.

04 (1) has visited France　(2) has sung on stage

(3) has made a cake

05 (1) had a party　(2) has practiced dancing

06 have you been → were you[did you go] /
have left → are leaving[will leave / are going
to leave]

01 현재완료의 의문형은 〈Have[Has]+주어+v-ed ~?〉의 형
태로 쓴다.

02 과거에 진행 중이었던 일을 나타낼 때는 〈was[were]+v-
ing〉의 형태로 쓴다.

03 과거 특정 시점(last week)에 일어난 일을 나타내므로 과거
시제를 쓴다.

04 ② last night는 과거 특정 시점을 나타내는 부사구로 현재완
료와 함께 쓰지 않는다.

05 '호주에 가 본 적이 있는지'를 묻고 있으므로 〈경험〉을 나타내
는 현재완료 have been to를 쓴다. 이에 대한 부정의 답변
은 No, I haven't.이다.

06 〈완료〉를 나타내는 현재완료와 함께 쓰이는 부사 yet은 '아직',
already는 '벌써, 이미'의 의미를 갖는다.

07 〈계속〉을 나타내는 현재완료에서 for 뒤에는 동작이나 상태가
지속된 기간이 오고, since 뒤에는 동작이나 상태가 시작된 시
점이 온다.

08 '해변에 가서 지금 여기에 없다'고 했으므로 〈결과〉를 나타내는
현재완료 have gone을 쓴다.

09 〈보기〉와 ①은 현재완료의 〈경험〉, ②는 〈결과〉, ③과 ⑤는 〈완
료〉, ④는 〈계속〉을 나타낸다.

10 〈보기〉와 ①은 현재완료의 〈계속〉, ②는 〈경험〉, ③과 ⑤는 〈완료〉, ④는 〈결과〉를 나타낸다.

11 〈보기〉와 ②는 현재완료의 〈완료〉, ①은 〈결과〉, ③은 〈계속〉, ④와 ⑤는 〈경험〉을 나타낸다.

12 ③ 현재완료의 〈경험〉의 의미로 '어디에 다녀왔는지'를 묻는 질문에 〈결과〉의 의미로 '화장실에 가 버렸다'라고 답하는 것은 자연스럽지 않다.

13 ④ 현재완료의 〈계속〉의 의미로 '얼마나 오랫동안 이탈리아에 살았는지'에 대한 질문에 〈경험〉의 의미로 '전에 살았던 적이 있다'라고 답하는 것은 자연스럽지 않다.

14 과거의 어느 시점부터 현재까지 계속되는 일을 나타낼 때는 현재완료를 쓴다. 동작이나 상태가 시작된 시점 앞에는 since를 쓴다.

15 ③ 〈계속〉을 나타내는 현재완료에서 for 뒤에 동작이나 상태가 지속된 기간이 왔으므로 이를 묻는 의문문으로 '얼마나 오랫동안'을 나타내는 'How long'을 쓴다. 의문사를 포함한 현재완료 의문형은 〈의문사+have[has]+주어+v-ed ~?〉의 어순으로 쓴다.

16 (a) 인지를 나타내는 동사 think는 진행형으로 쓸 수 없다.
   (c) 감정을 나타내는 동사 like는 진행형으로 쓸 수 없다.

17 ⑤는 현재완료의 〈계속〉을, 나머지는 모두 현재완료의 〈경험〉을 나타낸다.

18 ⑤ two months ago는 특정 과거 시점을 나타내는 부사이므로 현재완료와 함께 쓰지 않는다.

19 ④ 과거의 특정 시점에 진행 중이던 일을 나타낼 때는 과거진행형을 쓴다.

20 ⑤ when I was young은 특정 과거 시점을 나타내므로 현재완료 have lived와 함께 쓰일 수 없다.

서술형 따라잡기

01 (1) 과거의 어느 시점부터 현재까지 계속되는 일을 나타낼 때는 현재완료를 쓴다.
   (2) 과거에 일어난 일의 결과가 현재까지 영향을 미칠 때 현재완료를 쓴다.

02 (1) 과거의 특정 시점에 진행 중이던 일을 나타내므로 과거진행형으로 쓴다.
   (2) '아직 ~하지 않았다'라는 의미를 나타내기 위해 현재완료의 부정형을 쓴다. 현재완료의 부정형은 〈have[has]+not+v-ed〉로 쓰고, '아직'이란 뜻의 부사 yet은 문장 맨 끝에 쓴다.

03 (1) 의문사를 포함한 현재완료 의문형은 〈의문사+have[has]+주어+v-ed ~?〉의 어순으로 쓴다.
   (2) 과거 어느 시점부터 현재까지 계속되고 있는 일을 나타낼 때는 현재완료를 쓴다. 접속사 since 뒤에는 동작이 시작된 시점인 I was six를 쓴다.

04 과거부터 현재까지의 경험은 현재완료로 나타낸다.

05 (1) 과거 특정 시점에 일어난 일이므로 과거시제를 쓴다.
   (2) 과거의 어느 시점부터 현재까지 계속되는 일을 나타내므로 〈계속〉의 현재완료를 쓴다.

06 last weekend는 과거 특정 시점을 나타내는 부사구로 현재완료와 함께 쓰지 않고, 과거시제와 함께 쓴다. 사촌들이 떠나는 것은 미래의 일이므로 가까운 미래를 나타낼 때 쓰는 현재진행형을 이용해 are leaving으로 쓰거나 미래시제인 will leave 혹은 are going to leave로 쓴다.

SELF NOTE
p.78

A 핵심 포인트 정리하기
① be동사, v-ing ② have[has], v-ed
③ have[has], not, v-ed ④ 완료 ⑤ 결과

B 문제로 개념 다지기
1 O 2 O 3 X, went 4 O 5 X, was cleaning
6 X, since he was young 7 X, am learning
8 X, likes

Chapter 06 조동사

5 used to be a car designer

6 used to dream of being a writer

B 1 이 마을은 (전에는) 매우 평화로웠었다.

2 그 집은 (전에는) 흰색이었는데, 지금은 회색으로 보인다.

3 내 개는 눈이 오면 종종 빠르게 달리곤 했다.

4 Mary는 (전에는) 책을 많이 읽곤 했는데, 지금은 그렇지 않다.

5 우리 아버지는 주말에 낚시를 가시곤 했다.

6 (전에는) 여기에 큰 사과나무 한 그루가 있었었다.

7 Mike는 (전에는) 치즈를 좋아했었는데, 지금은 그렇지 않다.

내신대비 TEST
p.88

01 ②	02 ①	03 ①	04 ②	05 ④	06 ③
07 ⑤	08 ③	09 ②	10 ③	11 ⑤	12 ①
13 ④	14 ④	15 ②	16 ⑤	17 ④	18 ⑤
19 ②	20 ④				

서술형 따라잡기
p.91

01 (1) Are you going to (2) is not able to

02 (1) I would like to study Spanish.

(2) He had better not go to the park.

03 There used to be benches

04 cannot[can't] be

05 (1) may be windy tonight

(2) must not tell her

(3) cannot be the thief

06 must, had better[have to], don't have to

01 요청하는 말에 대한 긍정의 대답에는 의지를 나타내는 조동사 will을 쓰는 것이 적절하다.

02 허가(~해도 좋다)를 나타내는 may의 부정형은 may not이다.

03 '~하는 게 좋겠다'라는 의미로는 〈had better+동사원형〉을 쓴다.

04 '~일지도 모른다'의 의미로 불확실한 추측을 나타낼 때는 조동사 may를 쓴다.

05 '~할 필요가 없다'라는 의미를 나타낼 때는 〈don't have to +동사원형〉을 쓴다.

06 '~하는 게 좋겠다'라는 의미로는 〈had better+동사원형〉을 쓴다.

07 need not은 '~할 필요가 없다'라는 의미로 don't[doesn't] have[need] to로 바꾸어 쓸 수 있다.

08 '~하곤 했다'라는 의미로 과거의 습관을 나타낼 때는 used to 를 쓴다.

09 첫 번째 빈칸에는 '~임이 틀림없다'의 의미로 강한 추측을 나타 내는 조동사 must가, 두 번째 빈칸에는 '~하곤 했다'라는 의미 로 과거의 습관을 나타내는 used to가 와야 한다.

10 첫 번째 빈칸에는 '~해야 한다'라는 의미로 의무를 나타내는 조 동사 Should가, 두 번째 빈칸에는 '~할 필요가 없다'라는 의 미의 don't have to가 와야 하는데 앞에 don't가 있으므로 have to가 오면 된다.

11 첫 번째 빈칸에는 '~하고 싶다'라는 의미의 would like to가, 두 번째 빈칸에는 '~해야 한다'라는 의미의 조동사 should가 와야 한다.

12 조동사 must는 의무를 나타내는 '~해야 한다'와 강한 추측을 나타내는 '~임이 틀림없다'라는 의미가 있다.

13 첫 번째 빈칸에는 would like to(~하고 싶다)의 would가, 두 번째 빈칸에는 '~하곤 했다'라는 의미로 과거의 습관을 나타 내는 would가 와야 한다.

14 ④ used to는 과거의 상태를 나타내므로 현재의 상태를 묻는 A의 질문에 대한 대답으로 적절하지 않다.

15 ②는 허가를 나타내는 may이고, 나머지는 모두 불확실한 추 측을 나타내는 may이다.

16 ⑤는 강한 추측을 나타내는 must이고, 나머지는 모두 의무를 나타내는 must이다.

17 ④ '~할 필요가 없다'라는 의미로는 don't have[need] to를 쓴다. must not은 '~해서는 안 된다'라는 의미이다.

18 ⑤에는 Would가, 나머지에는 모두 '~해야 한다'라는 의미의 must가 와야 한다.

19 ② had better 다음에는 동사원형을 쓴다.

20 (a) be able to의 부정형은 〈be+not able to〉로 쓴다.

(c) must는 과거형이 없으므로 had to를 써서 과거를 나 타낸다.

서술형 따라잡기

01 (1) 가까운 미래를 나타낼 때 be going to를 쓰는데, 이때의 의문형은 〈be동사+주어+going to+동사원형 ~?〉의 어순

으로 쓴다.

(2) 능력을 나타내는 can[cannot]은 be able to[be not able to]로 바꾸어 쓸 수 있다.

02 (1) '~하고 싶다'라는 의미로 〈would like to+동사원형〉을 쓴다.

(2) had better의 부정형은 〈had better not+동사원형〉으로 쓴다.

03 과거의 상태를 나타낼 때는 〈used to+동사원형〉을 쓴다.

04 강한 부정적 추측을 나타내는 '~일 리가 없다'라는 의미의 조동사 cannot[can't]를 쓴다.

05 (1) 불확실한 추측을 나타낼 때는 조동사 may을 쓴다.

(2) 금지를 나타낼 때는 must not을 쓴다.

(3) '~일 리가 없다'라는 의미로 조동사 cannot을 쓴다.

06 '~임이 틀림없다'라는 의미로 조동사 must를, '~하는 게 좋겠다'라는 의미로 had better 또는 '~해야 한다'라는 의미로 have to를, '~할 필요가 없다'라는 의미로 don't have to를 쓴다.

SELF NOTE p.92

A 핵심 포인트 정리하기
① may ② will ③ must not[mustn't]
④ cannot[can't]
⑤ don't[doesn't/didn't] have to
⑥ had better not ⑦ used to

B 문제로 개념 다지기
1 O 2 O 3 X, don't have to
4 X, used to 5 X, had better not

Chapter 07 비교 표현

POINT 01 원급 비교 – as ~ as 구문 p.94

A 1 as cold as 2 as expensive as
3 aren't as[so] heavy as 4 isn't as[so] fast as
5 not as[so] large as 6 call me as soon as

B 1 is as tall as Jack 2 is as new as yours
3 isn't as old as 4 as popular as
5 as quickly as I could

POINT 02 비교급+than / 비교급 만드는 법 – 규칙 변화 p.95

A 1 cleaner than 2 more important than
3 more difficult than 4 earlier than

B 1 tall 2 much 3 larger

C 1 stronger than
2 more colorful than mine
3 much bigger than hers

POINT 03 the+최상급 / 최상급 만드는 법 – 규칙 변화 p.96

A 1 the smartest 2 the hottest
3 the most useful

B 1 the happiest day of her life
2 the saddest part of the movie
3 the most famous singer in her country
4 the most interesting essay in his class

POINT 04 비교급 · 최상급 만드는 법 – 불규칙 변화 p.97

A 1 worse 2 a lot farther 3 best 4 worst
5 better 6 earlier 7 more 8 least

B 1 the worst 2 less 3 the farthest 4 worse
5 better

POINT 05 비교 구문을 이용한 표현 I – 배수사를 이용한 비교 p.98

A 1 is three times thicker than
2 is twice as old as me
3 spent ten times more money than

4 was three times larger than

5 is five times as expensive as

6 four times as many copies as

B 1 five times as big as

  2 three times as long as

  3 three times faster than

  4 four times farther than

POINT 06 비교 구문을 이용한 표현 II – the+비교급, the+비교급 / 비교급+and+비교급   p.99

A 1 darker and darker   2 The cloudier

  3 more and more nervous   4 twice as high as

  5 the more difficult   6 not as cold as

  7 (much) more dangerous than

  8 three times more gifts than

B 1 More and more   2 The harder, the better

  3 The longer, the angrier   4 The more, the more

  5 busier and busier   6 louder and louder

  7 longer and longer

POINT 07 비교 구문을 이용한 표현 III – Which ~ 비교급 / one of the+최상급+복수명사   p.100

A 1 musician → musicians   2 biggest → bigger

  3 and → or   4 rich → richest

  5 more convenienter → more convenient

  6 city → cities

B 1 Who is older   2 Which is longer

  3 Which is more difficult

C 1 one of the most handsome

  2 one of the most popular foods

  3 one of the most beautiful islands

POINT 08 최상급 표현 – 원급과 비교급 이용   p.101

A 1 · No, as[so] hard as

  · No, harder than

  · harder than any other subject

  · harder than all the other subjects

  2 · No, as[so] expensive as

  · No, more expensive than

· more expensive than any other book

· more expensive than all the other books

B 1 more beautiful than any other flower

  2 No designer, as famous as her

  3 No sport, more exciting than

내신대비 TEST   p.102

01 ②   02 ⑤   03 ④   04 ①   05 ③   06 ③

07 ②   08 ③   09 ②   10 ④   11 ②   12 ②

13 ①   14 ⑤   15 ④   16 ⑤   17 ④   18 ③

19 ②   20 ①

서술형 따라잡기 ---------- p.105

01 (1) more interesting than (2) the worst

02 (1) not as[so] exciting as

  (2) three times taller than

03 (1) country → countries

  (2) more → most / as twice → twice as

04 (1) four times more expensive than[four times as expensive as]

  (2) the cheapest

05 (1) as[so] long as (2) longer than

06 (1) much healthier than I am

  (2) one of the most beautiful cities

01 빈칸 뒤에 than이 있으므로 비교급이 들어가야 한다. good의 비교급은 better이다.

02 popular와 같은 3음절 이상의 단어는 앞에 most를 붙여 최상급을 만든다.

03 〈as+형용사 / 부사의 원급+as〉는 '~만큼 …한[하게]'라는 의미이다.

04 비교급을 강조하는 부사는 much, even, still, far, a lot이다. very는 비교급 앞에 쓸 수 없다.

05 〈Who ~ 비교급, A or B?〉: A와 B 중에 누가 더 ~한가? 〈배수사+as+원급+as〉: ~의 몇 배 …한[하게]

06 〈the+비교급, the+비교급〉: ~(하면) 할수록 더 …하다 앞의 the를 보아 최상급 표현이 와야 하므로 largest가 적절하다.

17

07 ② 〈비교급+and+비교급〉은 '점점 더 ~한[하게]'의 뜻이다. 점점 더 더워지고 있다는 말에 겨울이 오고 있기 때문이라는 응답은 자연스럽지 않다.

08 주어진 문장은 Mary가 나보다 나이가 많다는 뜻이므로, 나는 Mary만큼 나이가 많지 않다는 ③이 주어진 문장과 같은 의미이다.

09 〈비교급+than any other+단수명사〉는 '다른 어떤 ~보다 더 …한[하게]'의 의미로 비교급을 이용한 최상급 표현이다.

10 〈Which ~ 비교급, A or B?〉: A와 B 중에 어느 것이 더 ~한가?

11 ② 형용사의 원급과 than은 함께 쓸 수 없다. nicer than 혹은 as nice as로 써야 한다.

12 ② 〈one of the+최상급+복수명사〉가 되어야 하므로 scientist는 scientists가 되어야 한다.

13 ① 〈as+형용사 / 부사의 원급+as〉: '~만큼 …한[하게]'

14 〈No (other)+단수명사 ~ as[so]+원급+as〉는 '어떤 ~도 …만큼 ~하지 않은[않게]'의 의미로 원급을 이용한 최상급 표현이다. 〈비교급+than any other+단수명사〉는 '다른 어떤 ~보다 더 …한'의 의미로 비교급을 이용한 최상급 표현이다.

15 대구의 기온이 가장 높으므로 ④가 맞는 문장이다. 〈비교급+than all the other+복수명사〉는 최상급의 의미이다.

16 선미가 세 명 중 몸무게가 가장 적게 나가므로 ⑤가 맞는 문장이다.

17 ④ '~의 몇 배 …한[하게]'는 〈배수사+as+원급+as〉 혹은 〈배수사+비교급+than〉이다. 따라서 four times as long as 혹은 four times longer than이 되어야 한다.

18 ③ '점점 더 ~한[하게]'는 〈비교급+and+비교급〉이다. 따라서 getting harder and harder가 되어야 한다.

19 ② '~(하면) 할수록 더 …하다'는 〈the+비교급, the+비교급〉이다. 따라서 the more one wants가 되어야 한다.

20 (d) 〈as+원급+as〉 혹은 〈비교급+than〉의 형태가 되어야 하므로, as curly as 혹은 curlier than이 와야 한다.
(e) 〈one of the+최상급+복수명사〉이므로, girls가 되어야 한다.

01 (1) '~보다 더 …한[하게]'의 의미로 〈비교급+than〉을 쓴다. -ing로 끝나는 단어의 비교급은 앞에 more를 붙여 나타낸다.
(2) '~ 중에서 가장 …한[하게]'의 의미로 〈the+최상급+of+

비교 대상이 되는 명사〉를 쓴다. bad의 최상급은 worst이다.

02 (1) '~보다 덜 …한[하게]'의 의미인 비교급 문장은 〈not+as[so]+원급+as〉로 바꾸어 쓸 수 있다.
(2) 〈배수사+as+원급+as〉는 〈배수사+비교급+than〉과 같은 의미이다.

03 (1) 〈비교급+than all the other+복수명사〉는 '다른 모든 ~보다 더 …한[하게]'라는 의미이므로 복수명사인 countries를 써야 한다.
(2) '~ (안)에서 가장 …한[하게]'라는 뜻의 〈the+최상급+in+장소·범위를 나타내는 단수명사〉가 되어야 하므로 most를 써야 하고, '~의 몇 배 …한[하게]'의 의미는 〈배수사+as+원급+as〉가 되어야 하므로, twice as로 써야 한다.

04 (1) 드레스 A는 드레스 B보다 4배 더 비싸므로 〈배수사+비교급+than〉 혹은 〈배수사+as+원급+as〉를 써서 나타낸다.
(2) 드레스 C는 모든 드레스 중에서 가장 저렴하므로 〈the+최상급+of+비교 대상이 되는 명사〉 구문을 이용한다.

05 (1) '나일강은 아마존강만큼 길지 않다.'라는 의미가 되어야 하므로 〈not+as[so]+원급+as〉 구문을 이용한다.
(2) '아마존강이 나일강보다 139km 더 길다.'라는 의미가 되어야 하므로 〈비교급+than〉 구문을 이용한다.

06 (1) '~보다 더 …한[하게]'의 의미이므로 〈비교급+than〉 구문을 쓴다. 비교급을 강조하는 부사 much는 비교급 앞에 쓴다.
(2) '가장 ~한 것들 중 하나'는 〈one of the+최상급+복수명사〉를 쓴다.

SELF NOTE ▶

p.106

A 핵심 포인트 정리하기
① as, as ② as, as possible ③ than ④ in ⑤ of
⑥ than ⑦ the, 비교급 ⑧ 비교급, and, 비교급
⑨ 단수명사

B 문제로 개념 다지기
1 X, not so healthy 2 O 3 X, the fewer
4 O 5 X, as thick 6 X, all the other ones[any other one / all the others]
7 X, more convenient

Chapter 08 접속사

2 If you have any questions

3 Unless you walk quickly

4 unless you speak loudly

5 if you are free

POINT 08 양보를 나타내는 접속사 though[although]　p.115

A 1 Though[Although] it was Sunday

2 Though[Although] Monica can't sing well

3 Though[Although] Jack isn't tall

4 Though[Although] Eric is popular

5 Though[Although] my grandmother is old

6 Though[Although] it was crowded

B 1 Though[Although] the player was injured

2 Though[Although] the heater was on

3 Though[Although] the traffic was bad

4 Though[Although] I have met her before

5 Though[Although] I understand him

6 Though[Although] I don't like Jerry very much

7 Though[Although] Ellen works really hard

8 Though[Although] the skirt was a bit big for me

POINT 09 명사절을 이끄는 종속 접속사 that　p.116

A 1 O　2 O　3 X, if → (that)　4 X, That → It　5 O

B 1 I know that my parents love me.

2 It is certain that he has gone.

3 I believe that she will pass the interview.

4 The important thing is that you are happy.

5 The fact is that we don't have enough time

POINT 10 명령문+and/or　p.117

A 1 and　2 and　3 or

B 1 If you make noise

2 If you come over here

3 Take the subway, and

4 or you will miss the movie

5 If you go straight

6 Go home now, or your mom will be angry

7 you don't take your umbrella, you take your umbrella

내신대비 TEST　p.118

01 ①　02 ⑤　03 ①　04 ②　05 ②　06 ③

07 ④　08 ⑤　09 ②　10 ①　11 ②　12 ④

13 ②　14 ⑤　15 ④　16 ④　17 ③　18 ④

19 ⑤　20 ③

서술형 따라잡기　p.121

01 (1) not only, but also　(2) either, or

02 (1) Call her now, or

(2) Finish your homework, and

03 (1) Although they went to same school, they don't know each other. [They don't know each other, although they went to same school.]

(2) Because I made noise in class, my teacher gave me a warning. [My teacher gave me a warning because I made noise in class.]

04 (1) unless it rains　(2) both, and

05 (1) I'm so tired that I can't keep my eyes open.

(2) Read the book, and you will understand the theory.

06 will come → comes / Unless → If

01 ①은 각각 이유를 나타내는 종속 접속사인 반면, 나머지는 짝을 이루어 상관 접속사를 구성하는 관계이다.

02 '그래서'의 의미로, 앞 내용에 대한 결과를 나타낼 때 쓰는 접속사 so가 적절하다.

03 〈명령문+or …〉는 '~해라, 그러지 않으면 …할 것이다'라는 의미이다.

04 보어절을 이끄는 종속 접속사 that이 와야 한다.

05 첫 번째 빈칸에는 '~할 때'의 의미인 when이, 두 번째 빈칸에는 '그러나'의 의미인 but이 적절하다.

06 첫 번째 빈칸에는 '~하기 전에'의 의미인 before가, 두 번째 빈칸에는 '~할 때'의 의미인 when이 와야 한다.

07 첫 번째 빈칸에는 '~ 때문에'의 의미로 이유를 나타내는 접속사가 와야 하고, 두 번째 빈칸에는 '~하면서'의 의미로 시간을 나타내는 접속사가 와야 하므로 공통으로 들어갈 접속사는 As이다.

08 〈so ~ that …〉은 '매우[너무] ~해서 …하다'라는 의미이다.

09 문맥상 '엄마가 돌아오시기 전에'라고 답하는 접속사 before를 포함한 절이 오는 것이 가장 적절하다.

10 B에서 '너무 일찍 도착하게 될 것'이라고 말하고 있으므로 빈칸에는 문맥상 '이 기차를 탄다면'의 If절이 와야 한다.

11 ②는 '~한 이래로'의 의미이고, 나머지는 모두 '~ 때문에'의 이유를 나타낸다.

12 〈보기〉와 ④의 that은 보어절을 이끄는 종속 접속사이다. ①과 ⑤의 that은 목적어절을 이끄는 종속 접속사이고, ②와 ③은 주어절을 이끄는 종속 접속사이다.

13 ② 문맥상 '만약 ~라면'의 의미인 if가 와야 한다. unless는 '~하지 않으면'의 의미이다.

14 ⑤ 축구를 할 수 없는 이유를 설명하고 있으므로, '~ 때문에'의 의미로 이유를 나타내는 접속사 Because/Since/As가 와야 한다.

15 ④ 시간을 나타내는 부사절에서는 미래의 일을 현재시제로 나타낸다.

16 ④ 뒤에 〈주어+동사〉를 포함한 절이 이어지므로 because를 쓴다. because of 뒤에는 (동)명사(구)가 온다.

17 ③ unless는 '~하지 않으면'의 의미이므로 '네가 버스를 놓치지 않으면'으로 해석하는 것이 적절하다.

18 ④ 'A와 B 둘 다'의 의미인 상관 접속사 〈both A and B〉 구문이므로, 빈칸에는 and가 와야 한다. ①은 '~해라, 그렇지 않으면 …할 것이다'의 〈명령문+or …〉 구문이므로 빈칸에는 or가 와야 한다. ②와 ⑤에는 '또는'의 의미인 or가 와야 한다. ③에는 'A와 B 중 하나'의 의미인 〈either A or B〉의 or가 와야 한다.

19 ⑤ 'A도 B도 아닌'의 의미인 〈neither A nor B〉의 nor로 고쳐야 한다.

20 (b) 시간을 나타내는 부사절에서는 현재시제로 미래의 일을 나타내므로 will come이 아닌 come으로 써야 한다.
(c) 〈both A and B〉는 복수 취급하므로 likes가 아닌 like를 써야 한다.

서술형 따라잡기

01 (1) 〈not only A but also B〉는 'A뿐만 아니라 B도'라는 의미이다.
(2) 〈either A or B〉는 'A와 B 중 하나'라는 의미이다.

02 (1) 〈명령문+or …〉는 '~해라, 그러지 않으면 …할 것이다'라는

의미이다.
(2) 〈명령문+and …〉는 '~해라, 그러면 …할 것이다'라는 의미이다.

03 (1) '비록 같은 학교에 다녔지만 서로를 모른다.'라는 의미가 되어야 하므로 첫 번째 문장 앞에 양보의 접속사 although를 붙여 나타낸다.
(2) 교사가 나에게 경고한 이유는 내가 교실에서 떠들었기 때문이므로 첫 번째 문장 앞에 이유의 접속사 because를 붙여 나타낸다.

04 (1) 야구 경기는 비가 내리면 취소되므로, '비가 내리지 않으면 경기가 열릴 것이다.'의 의미가 될 수 있도록 접속사 unless를 이용한다. 조건을 나타내는 부사절에서는 현재시제로 미래의 일을 나타낸다는 점에 유의한다.
(2) 3월 12일에는 축구 경기와 농구 경기가 무조건 열리므로, 'A와 B 둘 다'의 의미인 상관 접속사 〈both A and B〉 구문을 이용한다.

05 (1) '매우[너무] ~해서 …하다'의 의미인 결과를 나타내는 접속사 〈so ~ that …〉 구문을 이용한다.
(2) '~해라, 그러면 …할 것이다'의 의미인 〈명령문+and …〉를 이용한다.

06 시간을 나타내는 부사절에서는 현재시제로 미래의 일을 나타내므로, will come을 comes로 고쳐야 한다. 문맥상 '만약 ~하면'이 되어야 하므로, Unless는 If가 되어야 한다.

SELF NOTE
p.122

A 핵심 포인트 정리하기
① and ② so ③ both A and B
④ neither A nor B ⑤ not only A but also B
⑥ while ⑦ so ~ that … ⑧ unless
⑨ 목적어 ⑩ 보어 ⑪ and ⑫ or

B 문제로 개념 다지기
1 and 2 or 3 either 4 was so hot 5 asks
6 that 7 Though

Chapter 09 관계사 I

3 everything that I wanted   4 that is crying

5 that she had   6 the tallest boy that lives

7 the same dress that

POINT 08 관계대명사 that과 종속 접속사 that의 구별 p.131

A 1 종속 접속사   2 관계대명사   3 종속 접속사

4 관계대명사   5 관계대명사   6 종속 접속사

7 종속 접속사   8 관계대명사

B 1 that he was sick

2 that he recommended

3 that everyone admires

4 that she did nothing wrong

5 the pictures that Mike took

6 that Melina decided to quit

7 that I looked in was empty

내신대비 TEST   p.132

01 ①	02 ③	03 ③	04 ⑤	05 ⑤	06 ①
07 ①	08 ③	09 ④	10 ②	11 ③	12 ③
13 ③	14 ⑤	15 ②	16 ⑤	17 ①	18 ⑤
19 ②, ④, ⑤	20 ③				

서술형 따라잡기 ----------------------- p.135

01 (1) He invented a robot that[which] was
       very useful.

   (2) I like the notebook whose cover is red.

02 The train that goes to Seoul

03 (1) that[which] viewers will love

   (2) that[which] has a moving story

   (3) whose title song is beautiful

04 (1) who[that] is wearing

   (2) that are playing with (3) whose coat is

05 (1) He was the first person that climbed the
       mountain.

   (2) The man who(m)[that] I met was an eye
       doctor.

06 whom → who[that] / which → that

01 선행사가 사람이고 주어 역할을 하므로 주격 관계대명사 who
   가 적절하다.

02 선행사가 소유격 역할을 하므로 소유격 관계대명사 whose가
   적절하다.

03 선행사가 The only의 수식을 받는 thing이므로, 관계대명사
   that이 적절하다.

04 〈보기〉와 ⑤는 주격 관계대명사이고, 나머지는 모두 종속 접속
   사이다.

05 첫 번째 빈칸의 경우 선행사가 사물이고 목적어 역할을 하므로
   목적격 관계대명사 which가 적절하다. 두 번째 빈칸의 경우
   선행사가 사람이고 전치사 to의 목적어 역할을 하므로 목적격
   관계대명사 whom이 적절하다. that은 전치사 바로 뒤에 쓸
   수 없다.

06 첫 번째 빈칸에는 선행사가 the very의 수식을 받고 있으므로
   관계대명사 that이 적절하다. 두 번째 빈칸에는 선행사가 사람
   이고 소유격 역할을 하므로 소유격 관계대명사 whose가 적
   절하다.

07 첫 번째 빈칸에는 '누구'라는 의미의 의문사가, 두 번째 빈칸에
   는 선행사가 사람이고 주어 역할을 하는 주격 관계대명사가 필
   요하므로 공통으로 들어갈 말은 who이다.

08 첫 번째 문장에는 진주어 역할을 하는 명사절을 이끄는 종속
   접속사 that이 적절하다. 두 번째 문장에서는 선행사가 the
   only의 수식을 받는 person이므로 관계대명사 that이 적절
   하다.

09 선행사가 관계사절에서 소유격 역할을 하므로 첫 번째 빈칸에
   는 소유격 관계대명사가 필요하다. 두 번째 빈칸에도 마찬가
   지로 소유격 관계대명사가 필요하므로 공통으로 들어갈 말은
   whose이다.

10 선행사가 -thing으로 끝나는 경우 관계대명사 that을 쓴다.

11 선행사가 관계사절 안에서 소유격 역할을 할 때, 소유격 관계대
   명사 whose를 쓴다.

12 ③ 선행사가 사람이고 소유격 역할을 하므로 소유격 관계대
   명사 whose가 와야 한다. ①과 ④에는 목적격 관계대명사
   that, ②와 ⑤에는 주격 관계대명사 that이 올 수 있다.

13 ③ 선행사 the girl은 smile과 소유의 관계이므로 소유격 관
   계대명사 whose를 써야 한다.

14 ⑤ 관계사절의 수식을 받는 문장의 주어가 The necklace이
   므로 단수형 동사 is나 was가 와야 한다.

15 ②는 '누가'라는 의미의 의문사로 쓰인 반면 ①, ④, ⑤는 주격

관계대명사로, ③은 목적격 관계대명사로 쓰였다.

16 ⑤ 선행사가 〈사람+동물〉이므로 관계대명사 that을 쓴다.

17 ① 최상급 the best가 선행사를 수식하고 있으므로 관계대명사 that을 쓴다.

18 ⑤ 선행사 the boy는 watch와 소유의 관계이므로 소유격 관계대명사 whose가 와야 한다.

19 ① 선행사 the kid와 leg는 소유의 관계이므로 소유격 관계대명사 whose가 와야 한다.
③ 선행사 the girl이 관계사절 안에서 주어 역할을 하므로 주격 관계대명사 who 또는 that이 와야 한다.

20 ③ 목적격 관계대명사 who는 전치사와 함께 쓸 수 없으므로 whom을 써야 한다.

서술형 따라잡기

01 (1) 두 문장의 공통되는 단어 robot이 두 번째 문장에서 주어로 사용되고 있다. 선행사가 사물이고 주어 역할을 하므로 주격 관계대명사 that 또는 which를 이용한다.
(2) 두 문장의 공통되는 단어 the notebook이 두 번째 문장에서 소유격으로 사용되고 있다. 따라서 소유격 관계대명사 whose를 이용한다.

02 사물을 선행사로 하는 주격 관계대명사 that을 이용한 관계사절이 The train 뒤에 오도록 배열한다.

03 (1) 선행사가 사물이고 관계사절 내에서 목적어 역할을 하므로 관계대명사 that 혹은 which를 이용한다.
(2) 선행사가 사물이고 관계사절 내에서 주어 역할을 하므로 관계대명사 that 혹은 which를 이용한다.
(3) 선행사가 사물이고 관계사절 내에서 소유격 역할을 하므로 소유격 관계대명사 whose를 이용한다.

04 (1) a girl을 선행사로 하고 주어 역할을 하므로 관계대명사 who 혹은 that을 이용한다.
(2) 〈사람+동물〉을 선행사로 하고 주어 역할을 하므로 관계대명사 that을 이용한다.
(3) an old lady를 선행사로 하고 소유격 역할을 하므로 소유격 관계대명사 whose를 이용한다.

05 (1) 선행사에 the first가 포함되어 있고 주어 역할을 하므로 관계대명사 that을 이용한다.
(2) 선행사가 The man이고, 목적어 역할을 하는 관계대명사 who(m)[that]를 이용한다.

06 선행사가 사람(the man)이고 관계사절 내에서 주어의 역할을 하므로 whom 대신 주격 관계대명사 who 또는 that

을 써야 한다. 선행사가 the very의 수식을 받고 있으므로 which 대신 that을 써야 한다.

SELF NOTE
p.136

A 핵심 포인트 정리하기
① who ② whose ③ who(m) ④ which
⑤ whose ⑥ which ⑦ that ⑧ that ⑨ that

B 문제로 개념 다지기
1 O 2 X, which 3 X, that 4 O 5 X, whose
6 X, who[that] 7 O

Chapter 10 관계사 II

POINT 01 관계대명사 what
p.138

A 1 what 2 What 3 who

B 1 see와 you're hiding 사이 2 believe와 you 사이
3 understand와 we learned 사이
4 loved와 we 사이 5 I brought 앞
6 finish와 he 사이 7 are와 I planted 사이

C 1 what Jason bought me 2 what you heard
3 What he said 4 what I ordered
5 What he needed
6 what the teacher explained

POINT 02 관계대명사 what과 의문사 what의 구별
p.139

A 1 what is for dinner 2 What happened to Ethan
3 What surprised me at the party
4 what you did for me 5 what you just said
6 What he wanted to tell his parents

B 1 너는 저 소리가 무엇인지 짐작할 수 있니?, 의문사
2 내가 정말 필요한 것은 너의 사랑이다.., 관계대명사
3 지금 우리가 원하는 것은 시간이다.., 관계대명사
4 나는 내가 무엇을 먼저 먹어야 하는지 그에게 물어볼 것이다.., 의문사

5 Susan은 그녀의 남편이 입고 있던 것이 마음에 들지 않았다.. 관계대명사

POINT 03 관계대명사의 생략 Ⅰ   p.140

A 1 I read the message (which) Emily sent me.

2 I looked at the pictures (which) Picasso painted.

3 That's the cell phone (that) I want to buy.

4 I like the people (that) I'm working with.

5 X   6 X

7 The boy (that) your sister is sitting next to looks kind.

8 X

9 A girl (whom) I know is a good swimmer.

10 The hotel (which) you told me about isn't there anymore.

11 X

12 Jack looked at the girl (whom) Jerry came with.

B 1 Vicky is interested in   2 the music I listen to

3 that Ann goes to

4 The people Ed traveled with

POINT 04 관계대명사의 생략 Ⅱ   p.141

A 1 The TV (that is) in my bedroom is broken.

2 Don't call the students (who are) studying in the library.

3 A friend (who is) interested in rock music went to the rock festival.

4 I'd like to go to the soccer stadium (which is) in Suwon.

5 Dogs (which are) left alone all day are unhappy.

6 The vegetables (that are) sold at this market are very fresh.

7 The woman (who is) teaching yoga to people is my cousin.

8 The English (that is) written on this paper is easy to read.

9 I have many friends (who are) from different countries.

10 People (who are) trying to lose weight eat low-calorie food.

B 1 the man talking to

2 a word beginning with

3 which was taking Nick

4 a table made of wood

5 watching the Olympic games together

POINT 05 관계부사 when / where   p.142

A 1 where I was born

2 where she used to live

3 where the film festival will be held

4 when my family has dinner together

5 when she was lonely

6 when he became a World Cup champion

B 1 when I take piano lessons

2 where she walks her dog

3 where I bought books

POINT 06 관계부사 why / how   p.143

A 1 the reason why, why   2 the way   3 how

4 why   5 for which

B 1 how you lost weight

2 why you didn't do your homework

3 why she should apologize

4 How we write

내신대비 TEST   p.144

01 ①   02 ⑤   03 ⑤   04 ①   05 ④   06 ②
07 ④   08 ②   09 ⑤   10 ①   11 ③   12 ④
13 ③   14 ④   15 ⑤   16 ①   17 ③   18 ④
19 ②   20 ④

서술형 따라잡기   p.147

01 (1) What I want to do

(2) the reason why I hate him

02 (1) where I can surf

(2) when I couldn't speak a word

03 (1) that → what (2) for that → for which

04 (1) That was the day when I fell in love with her.

(2) That is the street where I found the purse.

05 (1) when it snowed (2) What I held

(3) whom I took the picture

06 (1) Look at that woman who[that] is cooking.

(2) This is how I memorize words.

01 선행사를 포함하며 '~하는 것'의 의미인 관계대명사 what을 쓴다.

02 이유를 나타내는 선행사 The reason 다음에는 관계부사 why를 쓴다.

03 문맥상 방법을 나타내는 관계부사 how가 적절하다.

04 The man과 I met 사이에 목적격 관계대명사 who(m) [that]이 생략되었다.

05 선행사 the building과 The bakery가 장소를 나타내며 관계사절 안에서 부사의 역할을 하므로 관계부사 where를 쓴다.

06 문맥상 방법을 나타내는 관계부사 how가 와야 한다.

07 첫 번째 빈칸에는 선행사를 포함하며 '~하는 것'의 의미인 관계대명사 what을, 두 번째 빈칸에는 이유를 나타내는 선행사 reason이 있으므로 관계부사 why를 쓴다.

08 빈칸 앞의 선행사는 모두 관계사절 안에서 부사 역할을 한다. 첫 번째 빈칸에는 장소를 나타내는 선행사 a place가 있으므로 관계부사 where를, 두 번째 빈칸에는 시간을 나타내는 선행사 a time이 있으므로 관계부사 when을 쓴다.

09 〈보기〉와 ⑤의 what은 선행사를 포함하며 '~하는 것'의 의미인 관계대명사인 반면, 나머지는 모두 '무엇'의 의미인 의문사이다.

10 ①은 〈주격 관계대명사+일반동사〉이므로 생략할 수 없는 반면, 나머지는 모두 〈주격 관계대명사+be동사〉이므로 생략할 수 있다.

11 ③ 관계대명사 that 앞에는 전치사를 쓸 수 없으므로 which를 써야 한다.

12 ④ 방법을 나타내는 관계부사 how는 선행사 the way와 같이 쓸 수 없고 둘 중 하나만 쓸 수 있다.

13 ③에는 a friend를 선행사로 하는 주격 관계대명사 who 또

는 that이 적절하다. 나머지는 모두 선행사를 포함하는 관계대명사 what이 와야 한다.

14 ④ '…을 ~로 데려가다'는 take … to ~이므로 장소를 나타내는 선행사 The room 다음에는 관계부사 where 혹은 〈전치사+관계대명사(which)〉가 와야 한다. 관계대명사 which 대신 that이 올 경우 전치사를 앞에 쓸 수 없으므로 전치사 to는 관계사절의 끝에 쓴다.

15 (a) 선행사를 포함하며 '~하는 것'의 의미인 관계대명사 what이 와야 한다.

(b) 선행사는 the bank이고 관계사절 안에서 주어 역할을 하므로 주격 관계대명사 which가 와야 한다.

(c) 선행사 the place가 장소를 나타내며 관계사절 안에서 부사 역할을 하므로 관계부사 where가 와야 한다.

(d) 이유를 나타내는 선행사 the reason이 있으므로 관계부사 why가 와야 한다.

16 (A) 관계사절 안에서 목적어 역할을 하는 관계대명사가 필요하므로 which가 알맞다.

(B) 관계사절 안에서 부사 역할을 하는 관계부사가 필요하고, 시간을 나타내는 선행사 the year가 쓰였으므로 when이 알맞다.

(C) 관계대명사 that 앞에는 전치사를 쓸 수 없고, 선행사가 사람이므로 whom이 알맞다.

17 ③ 주격 관계대명사만을 생략할 수 없으므로, had the flu 앞에 주격 관계대명사 who 혹은 that을 써야 한다.

18 ④ 관계대명사 that 앞에는 전치사를 쓸 수 없으므로 whom을 써야 한다.

19 (a)와 (c)에는 선행사를 포함하며 '~하는 것'의 의미인 관계대명사 what이 와야 한다. (b)에는 The soup를 선행사로 하는 목적격 관계대명사 which[that]가 와야 하며, (d)에는 시간을 나타내는 선행사 the day가 있으므로 관계부사 when이 와야 한다.

20 (d) the pants를 선행사로 하는 목적격 관계대명사 that 혹은 which가 와야 한다. what은 선행사를 포함한 관계대명사이다.

서술형 따라잡기 -

01 (1) 선행사를 포함하며 '~하는 것'의 의미인 관계대명사 what을 사용한다.

(2) the reason을 선행사로 하는 관계부사 why를 사용한다.

02 (1) 선행사가 장소인 관계부사절로 〈관계부사+주어+동사〉 순

으로 배열한다.

(2) 선행사가 시간인 관계부사절로 〈관계부사+주어+동사+목적어〉 순으로 배열한다.

03 (1) 관계사절 앞에 선행사가 없으므로 선행사를 포함하며 '~하는 것'의 의미인 관계대명사 what이 와야 한다.

(2) 관계대명사 that 앞에는 전치사를 쓸 수 없으므로 which를 써야 한다.

04 (1) 선행사가 시간을 나타내는 the day이므로 관계부사 when을 쓴다.

(2) 선행사가 장소를 나타내는 the street이므로 관계부사 where를 쓴다.

05 (1) 시간을 나타내는 선행사 a day가 있으므로 관계부사 when을 사용한다.

(2) 선행사를 포함하며 '~하는 것'의 의미인 관계대명사 What을 사용한다.

(3) 선행사인 The woman이 관계사절 안에서 전치사 with의 목적어 역할을 해야 하므로 whom I took the picture로 쓴다.

06 (1) 선행사는 that woman이고 관계사절 안에서 주어 역할을 하므로 주격 관계대명사 who 혹은 that을 이용한다.

(2) 문맥상 방법을 나타내는 관계부사 how를 이용한다.

SELF NOTE
p.148

A 핵심 포인트 정리하기
① 선행사 ② 목적격 관계대명사 ③ be동사
④ 전치사, 관계대명사 ⑤ where ⑥ how

B 문제로 개념 다지기
1 X, where 2 X, how[the way] 3 O
4 X, what 5 O 6 O 7 X, how 삭제

Chapter 11 분사

POINT 01 현재분사
p.150

A 1 shocking 2 sleeping 3 playing 4 waiting
5 swimming 6 leaving 7 talking

B 1 the sound of the falling rain
2 my heart beating very fast
3 was touching to us

POINT 02 과거분사
p.151

A 1 built 2 called 3 fallen 4 surrounded
5 painted

B 1 writing → written
2 break → broken
3 exciting → excited
4 disappoint → disappointed
5 cooking → cooked
6 shocking → shocked
7 taking → taken

POINT 03 분사구문 만드는 법
p.152

A 1 Seeing the police officer
2 Turning to the left
3 Knowing the way
4 Putting down the book
5 Wanting to see the Great Wall

B 1 Listening to music 2 Being late
3 Turning off the radio 4 Taking a taxi
5 Looking at me

POINT 04 때/이유를 나타내는 분사구문
p.153

A 1 Waiting for him
2 Arriving at the station
3 Not knowing Japanese
4 Not having enough money

B 1 When she saw me
2 While he did his homework

3 While she lay on the grass

4 Since I didn't feel very well

POINT 05 동시동작/연속상황을 나타내는 분사구문   p.154

A 1 Shaking hands with me   2 Holding hands

3 Entering the room   4 Getting off the bus

5 Walking home together

B 1 Standing on the hill, he watched the ship leaving.

2 The shuttle bus leaves at seven, arriving 15 minutes later.

3 Dancing together, we laughed and smiled.

POINT 06 조건/양보를 나타내는 분사구문   p.155

A 1 Though he lives near the beach

2 Though the man exercises regularly

3 If you buy this chocolate

4 If you take this pill

B 1 not eating much   2 knowing it was true

3 Following my advice   4 Using chopsticks

5 being injured   6 Talking with him

내신대비 TEST   p.156

01 ③	02 ②	03 ⑤	04 ②	05 ④	06 ⑤
07 ②	08 ③	09 ①	10 ⑤	11 ②	12 ①
13 ④	14 ④	15 ③	16 ④	17 ①	18 ②
19 ③	20 ④				

서술형 따라잡기 ------------------ p.159

01 (1) barking (2) playing (3) placed

02 (1) Entering the room

(2) Not (being) interested in skiing

03 Be → Being / leaving → left

04 (1) Look at the picture drawn by him.

(2) Not living in this town, I don't know him.

05 Being sick, Not wearing, enjoying

06 (1) Having an exam on Friday

(2) Listening to the radio (3) Being free

01 '놀고 있는'이라는 진행의 뜻으로 뒤의 child를 수식하는 현재분사가 와야 한다.

02 〈be동사+과거분사〉로 '만들어지다'라는 수동의 의미를 나타낼 수 있다.

03 '들고 있는'의 뜻으로 that teddy bear를 수식하는 현재분사가 와야 한다.

04 〈보기〉에서 두 단어의 관계는 '현재분사 – 과거분사'이다. 첫 번째 빈칸에는 eat의 과거분사 eaten, 두 번째 빈칸에는 forget의 현재분사인 forgetting이 와야 한다.

05 첫 번째 빈칸에는 TV programs를 수식하는 분사로, TV 프로그램이 '흥미로운' 것이므로 현재분사 interesting을 쓴다. 두 번째 빈칸에는 이유를 나타내는 분사구문으로, 주절의 주어인 내가 '피곤한' 것이므로 Being tired를 쓴다. 이때 Being은 생략할 수 있다.

06 첫 번째 빈칸에는 the man을 수식하는 분사로, 남자가 '서 있는' 것이므로 현재분사 standing을 쓴다. 두 번째 빈칸에는 이유를 나타내는 분사구문으로, 분사구문의 부정은 분사 앞에 not을 붙인다.

07 첫 번째 빈칸에는 my name을 수식하는 분사로, 이름이 '불리는' 것이므로 수동의 의미인 과거분사 called를 쓴다. 두 번째 빈칸에는 주절의 주어인 그녀가 '어린' 것이므로 현재분사 Being을 쓴다.

08 동시동작을 나타내는 분사구문으로, While she was crossing the street의 의미이다.

09 이유를 나타내는 분사구문으로, As he was surprised at the news의 의미이다.

10 양보 부사절을 분사구문으로 만들 때는 접속사 Though는 남겨두고 주어(Jake)를 생략한 뒤, 동사(studied)를 현재분사로 바꾼다.

11 〈보기〉와 ②는 동시동작을 나타내는 반면, ①과 ③은 이유, ④는 조건, ⑤는 이유나 때를 나타내는 분사구문이다.

12 〈보기〉와 ①은 이유를 나타내는 분사구문이고, ②, ③, ④는 동시동작, ⑤는 때를 나타내는 분사구문이다.

13 ④ 우리가 '신이 난' 것이므로 excited가 되어야 한다. exciting은 '신나는, 흥겹게 하는'이라는 뜻이다.

14 ④ The man을 수식하는 분사로, '춤추고 있는'을 뜻하며 능동의 의미가 있는 현재분사 dancing이 와야 한다.

15 ③ 분사구문의 부정은 분사 앞에 not이나 never를 써서 표현하므로 Not knowing his address가 되어야 한다.

16 ④는 주어로 쓰인 동명사인 반면, 나머지는 모두 분사구문을 만드는 분사이다.

17 ①은 보어로 쓰인 동명사인 반면, ②,③,④는 명사를 수식하는 현재분사, ⑤는 분사구문을 만드는 현재분사이다.

18 '그녀의 손을 잡고'는 동시동작을 나타내는 분사구문 holding her hand로 표현한다.

19 (b) '고치고 있는'의 뜻으로 The man을 수식하는 현재분사 fixing이 와야 한다.
(c) 감정을 느끼게 되는 대상을 설명할 때는 과거분사를 써야 하므로 disappointed가 와야 한다.

20 (A) 아이가 혼자 '남겨진' 것이므로 (Being) Left가 적절하다.
(B) the book을 수식하는 분사로, 책은 '쓰인' 것이므로 수동의 의미를 나타내는 과거분사 written이 알맞다.
(C) '큰 소리로 이야기하면서'의 의미로 동시동작을 나타내는 분사구문이므로 talking이 적절하다.

서술형 따라잡기

01 (1) 개가 '짖고 있는' 것이므로 현재분사 barking이 와야 한다.
(2) 여자아이가 인형을 '가지고 놀고 있는' 것이므로 현재분사 playing이 알맞다.
(3) 화분이 테이블 위에 '놓여 있는' 것이므로, 수동의 의미를 나타내는 과거분사 placed가 적절하다.

02 (1) 접속사(When)와 주어(I)를 생략하고 동사 entered를 Entering으로 바꾼다.
(2) 접속사(As)와 주어(I)를 생략하고 동사구 was interested in을 being interested in으로 바꾼다. 분사구문의 부정은 분사 앞에 not을 쓰고, being은 생략할 수 있다.

03 문맥상 '바쁘기 때문에'의 의미로 이유를 나타내는 분사구문 Being busy가 되어야 한다. 음식이 식탁에 '남겨진' 것이므로 all the food를 수식하는 분사로는 수동의 의미를 나타내는 과거분사 left가 와야 한다.

04 (1) the picture를 수식하는 분사로, 그림은 '그에 의해 그려지는' 것이므로 the picture 뒤에 수동의 의미를 나타내는 과거분사구 drawn by him이 오도록 배열한다.
(2) 이유를 나타내는 분사구문 living in this town의 부정형은 분사 앞에 not을 붙여 나타낸다.

05 • '아파서 집에 있었다'라는 내용이 되어야 하므로 분사구문 Being sick의 형태로 쓴다.
• '코트를 입지 않아서'의 의미가 되어야 하므로 부정의 의미를 나타내는 분사구문 Not wearing을 쓴다.

• 맛있는 후식을 '즐기면서'라는 의미가 되어야 하므로 분사구문 enjoying을 쓴다.

06 (1) '금요일에 시험이 있기 때문에'라는 의미가 되어야 하므로 분사구문 Having an exam on Friday가 와야 한다.
(2) '라디오를 들으면서'의 의미가 되어야 하므로 분사구문 Listening to the radio가 와야 한다.
(3) '한가하면'의 의미가 되어야 하므로 분사구문 Being free가 와야 한다.

SELF NOTE
p.160

A 핵심 포인트 정리하기
① 동사원형, -ing ② 수동·완료 ③ 동사원형, -ed
④ 동시동작 ⑤ ~하면
B 문제로 개념 다지기
1 playing 2 broken 3 surprising news
4 Crossing 5 smiling 6 Taking

Chapter 12 수동태

POINT 01 수동태의 의미 및 만드는 법
p.162

A 1 is sold   2 by   3 resemble
    4 smells   5 is trusted

B 1 is read by that woman
   2 is visited by thousands of people
   3 was followed by teenage girls
   4 were designed by my uncle
   5 This story was written by the director.
   6 The best actor of the year is chosen by viewers.

POINT 02 과거시제의 수동태
p.163

A 1 was made by Polly   2 was stolen by a thief
   3 was baked by my mom
   4 was built by my grandfather

5 was written by Beethoven

6 was developed by a university student

B 1 were introduced by

2 were taken by

3 was painted by

4 were canceled[cancelled]

5 This dress was worn by

6 The documentary was produced by

POINT 03 미래시제의 수동태   p.164

A 1 will be explained by Peter

2 will be made by my father

3 will be guided to the room

4 will be driven to the birthday party

5 will be checked around 9 a.m.

6 will be produced by the teddy bear company

7 The final match will be watched by a lot of people

B 1 Your call will be answered automatically.
   [Your call will be automatically answered.]

2 My last exam will be finished in two hours.

3 A new theater will be built in my town.

4 Jason will be paid 100 dollars for the work.

POINT 04 수동태의 부정문·의문문/조동사의 수동태   p.165

A 1 was not taken   2 was, delayed

3 was not invited   4 was, made

5 Was, attacked

B 1 was not delivered   2 will be remembered

3 can be paid   4 may be known

5 should be completed   6 is going to be moved

POINT 05 4형식 문장의 수동태   p.166

A 1 were made for us by my mom

2 were sent to me by somebody

3 was shown to the manager by Kelvin

4 was told the rumor about Kelly and me by Laurie

5 are taught computer coding by my father

B 1 was told a funny story by

2 were given to them

3 A nice suit was bought for me by

POINT 06 5형식 문장의 수동태   p.167

A 1 The library is kept very clean by students.

2 I was taught not to lie by my parents.

3 Jenny was told to go to the ice rink by Steve.

4 He was elected president by them.

5 The tourists were asked to wait in line by a tour guide.

B 1 is called a genius by her friends

2 was expected to arrive here by ten

3 was warned not to open

4 were advised not to swim

POINT 07 지각동사·사역동사의 수동태   p.168

A 1 to play   2 to feel   3 to wait   4 to go

5 driving   6 to water

B 1 will be made to apologize by Joseph

2 was seen to come out of the classroom (by us)

3 was made to wash the dishes by my mother

4 was made to stop by the police officer

5 were heard running upstairs by Ann

6 was made to tell my secret by Janet

7 was heard talking to herself (by them)

POINT 08 동사구의 수동태   p.169

A 1 was run over   2 will be looked after

3 was put off   4 was laughed at

5 was brought up

B 1 was turned down by his mother

2 was taken care of by this woman

3 was paid for by my parents

4 was looked down on by him

POINT 09 〈by+행위자〉를 생략하는 경우   p.170

A 1 is not[isn't] spoken in Cuba (by people)

2 is not[isn't] used very often (by people)

3 is made from cacao beans (by us)

4 was pushed toward the door by the woman

5 was chosen to be the class captain (by us)

6 was built in the early 1900s (by people)

7 are not[aren't] allowed to smoke in this building (by them)

B 1 was written in   2 was not given

3 are printed   4 should be spoken

POINT 10 by 이외의 전치사를 사용하는 경우   p.171

A 1 with   2 with   3 with   4 with[in]   5 at   6 of

B 1 are you interested in   2 were pleased with

3 was known to   4 is made from

5 is satisfied with   6 am tired of

7 is filled with

내신대비 TEST   p.172

01 ③   02 ⑤   03 ⑤   04 ③   05 ③   06 ④
07 ①   08 ④   09 ③   10 ③   11 ⑤   12 ⑤
13 ②   14 ②   15 ②, ④   16 ⑤   17 ①   18 ②
19 ④   20 ⑤

서술형 따라잡기   p.175

01 (1) was given to me by my grandmother

(2) I was told to exercise by the doctor.

02 (1) was designed by (2) was pleased with

03 (1) will be performed

(2) will be sold[are being sold]

(3) is located

04 (1) was hit by (2) were surprised at

05 (1) Brian was told to be quiet by Cathy.

(2) Were the questions answered by the teachers?

06 injured → was injured / rest → to rest / postponed → was postponed

01 문이 '잠겨 있다'가 되어야 하므로 수동태를 써야 한다. 수동태는 〈be동사+v-ed〉의 형태이므로 locked가 와야 한다.

02 보고서가 '완료되어야 한다'가 되어야 하므로 수동태로 써야 한다. 조동사의 수동태는 〈조동사+be+v-ed〉의 형태이므로 빈칸에 be finished가 와야 한다.

03 be interested in: ~에 관심이 있다

04 일반적으로 수동태의 행위자를 나타낼 때는 전치사 by를 쓴다. 하지만 be known to(~에게 알려지다)처럼 by 대신 다른 전치사를 쓰기도 한다.

05 지각동사의 목적격 보어로 동사원형이 쓰인 경우 수동태에서 to부정사 형태로 바뀌고, 현재분사가 쓰인 경우 그대로 둔다. 5형식 문장에서 ordered의 목적격 보어로 쓰인 to be는 수동태에서도 그대로 둔다.

06 ④ happen은 목적어가 필요 없는 동사이므로 수동태로 쓸 수 없다.

07 ① have와 같이 소유를 나타내는 동사는 수동태로 쓸 수 없다.

08 be covered with[in]: ~로 덮여 있다
be disappointed with[at / in]: ~에 실망하다

09 ③ 조동사의 수동태는 〈조동사+be+v-ed〉의 형태이므로 be praised가 되어야 한다.

10 ③ 지각동사의 목적격 보어로 동사원형이 쓰인 경우 수동태에서 to부정사 형태로 바뀌고, 현재분사가 쓰인 경우 그대로 쓰므로 to get이나 getting이 되어야 한다.

11 ① 일반적인 수동태 문장에서 행위자 앞에는 전치사 by를 쓴다.
② 지각동사의 목적격 보어로 쓰인 동사원형은 수동태에서 to부정사 형태(to dance)로 바꿔 써야 한다.
③ 사역동사 make의 목적격 보어로 쓰인 동사원형 laugh는 수동태에서 to laugh로 바꿔 써야 한다.
④ 동사구 put off는 수동태에서 동사구 전체를 묶어서 쓴다. 따라서 is going to be put은 is going to be put off가 되어야 한다.

12 ⑤ 수동태 문장에서 행위자가 일반인인 경우 〈by+행위자〉를 생략할 수 있다.

13 ②는 전치사 with(be filled with: ~로 가득 차다)를 쓰는 반면, 나머지는 모두 전치사 by를 쓴다.

14 ②는 전치사 of(be made of: ~로 만들어지다)를 쓰는 반면, ①과 ③은 전치사 to를, ④와 ⑤는 to부정사의 to를 써야 한다.

15 4형식 문장은 목적어가 두 개이므로 두 가지 형태의 수동태를 만들 수 있다. 간접목적어를 주어로 하는 수동태 문장을 만드는 경우, 〈주어(간접목적어)+be동사+v-ed+직접목적어(+by

+행위자》)의 형태로 쓴다. 직접목적어를 주어로 하는 수동태 문장을 만드는 경우, 〈주어(직접목적어)+be동사+v-ed+전치사+간접목적어(+by+행위자)〉의 형태로 쓴다. 동사가 teach이므로 간접목적어 앞에 전치사 to를 써야 한다.

16 ⑤ remain은 수동태로 쓸 수 없는 동사이다.

17 ① 주어인 A fan letter가 동사 write의 대상이므로 수동태로 써야 한다.

18 주어진 단어들을 배열하면 'I was made to carry the boxes by my mom.'으로, 네 번째에 오는 단어는 to이다.

19 ④ 사역동사 make의 목적격 보어였던 동사원형은 수동태에서 to부정사로 바뀐다.

20 (A) be tired of: ~에 싫증이 나다
(B) 지각동사의 목적격 보어로 동사원형이 쓰인 경우 수동태에서 to부정사 형태로 바뀌고, 현재분사가 쓰인 경우 그대로 쓰므로 to pass나 passing이 되어야 한다.
(C) 5형식 문장의 목적격 보어로 쓰인 to부정사는 수동태가 되어도 그 형태가 변하지 않고 〈be동사+v-ed〉 뒤에 그대로 쓴다.

01 (1) 4형식 문장에서 직접목적어를 주어로 하여 수동태 문장을 만드는 경우, 〈주어(직접목적어)+be동사+v-ed+전치사+간접목적어(+by+행위자)〉의 형태로 쓴다. 동사가 give이므로 간접목적어 앞에 전치사 to를 써야 한다.
(2) 5형식 문장에서는 능동태 문장의 목적어가 수동태의 주어가 되고, 목적격 보어는 〈be동사+v-ed〉 뒤에 그대로 쓴다.

02 (1) 과거시제의 수동태는 〈be동사의 과거형+v-ed(+by+행위자)〉의 형태로 쓴다.
(2) be pleased with: ~에 기뻐하다

03 (1) 연극은 5월 11일에 '상연될 것이다'가 되어야 하므로 미래시제의 수동태로 쓴다.
(2) 표는 70달러에 '판매될 것이다' 혹은 '판매되고 있다'가 되어야 하므로 미래시제의 수동태 〈will+be+v-ed〉나 진행형의 수동태 〈be동사+being+v-ed〉로 쓴다.
(3) 서울 아트센터는 서초구에 '위치해 있다'가 되어야 하므로 수동태로 쓴다.

04 (1) 소년이 차에 '치었다'라는 의미가 되어야 하므로, was hit by를 쓴다.
(2) be surprised at: ~에 놀라다

05 (1) '듣다'는 수동태인 'be told'로 표현한다. 능동태에서 tell

의 목적격 보어로 쓰였던 to부정사는 수동태가 되어도 그 형태가 변하지 않고 〈be동사+v-ed〉 뒤에 그대로 쓴다.
(2) 수동태의 의문문은 〈be동사+주어+v-ed(+by+행위자)?〉로 나타낸다.

06 내 다리가 '다쳤다'가 되어야 하므로 injured를 was injured로 고친다. 5형식 문장에서 동사 advise의 목적격 보어로 쓰였던 to부정사는 수동태가 되어도 그 형태가 변하지 않으므로 rest를 to rest로 써야 한다. 가족 소풍은 다음 주로 '연기되었다'라는 수동태 문장이 되어야 하므로 postponed는 was postponed로 고친다.

SELF NOTE p.176

A 핵심 포인트 정리하기
① be동사, v-ed ② be동사의 과거형, v-ed
③ will, be, v-ed ④ not ⑤ 조동사 ⑥ to부정사
⑦ to부정사 ⑧ in ⑨ of ⑩ with ⑪ with

B 문제로 개념 다지기
1 O 2 X, Will your work be done
3 X, was invented 4 X, to clean 5 O
6 X, be looked after by her parents 7 X, with

Chapter 13 가정법

POINT 01 가정법 과거   p.178

A 1 were, could live   2 were, wouldn't buy
    3 had, would read   4 spoke, wouldn't be
    5 had, would introduce   6 would, do, won
    7 focused on, would get

B 1 If I knew the answer   2 If I had a car
    3 If I were dressed up

POINT 02 가정법 과거완료   p.179

A 1 had met, have liked
    2 had watched, have enjoyed
    3 had not[hadn't] reminded, have forgotten
    4 had taken, have gotten[got]
    5 had lived, not have used

B 1 had heard, would have answered
    2 had rained, would have been
      canceled[cancelled]
    3 had gotten[got], would have bought
    4 had not been sick, would have
      traveled[travelled]
    5 had not gone to sleep, could have eaten

POINT 03 I wish+가정법 과거   p.180

A 1 it were Saturday today
    2 I attended that university
    3 I were tall like that model
    4 we were in the same class
    5 I could sing as well as you

B 1 I can't dance very well
    2 I had Julie's phone number
    3 the boy doesn't like me
    4 I were good at math
    5 I didn't have a lot of work to do

POINT 04 I wish+가정법 과거완료   p.181

A 1 had helped him   2 had not been late

    3 had met you   4 had left
    5 had not told her   6 had not happened

B 1 I didn't know about the test
    2 I hadn't had my hair cut short
    3 I had brought my camera today
    4 I had learned to play a musical instrument
    5 I didn't memorize their names
    6 I had listened to my parents

POINT 05 as if+가정법 과거   p.182

A 1 as if she were older than me
    2 as if she knew the story
    3 as if he didn't know Sally
    4 as if she were a friend of the movie star

B 1 I were dreaming
    2 as if he had a lot of money
    3 as if I were his younger sister
    4 as if he knew everything about cars
    5 as if you understood everything

POINT 06 as if+가정법 과거완료   p.183

A 1 as if she had called me
    2 as if it had never been cleaned
    3 as if he had won the prize
    4 as if it had been his last game
    5 as if I had said something shocking

B 1 as if he had been
    2 as if she hadn't heard
    3 as if, had been   4 as if he had seen

내신대비 TEST   p.184

01 ④	02 ⑤	03 ④	04 ④	05 ⑤	06 ④
07 ②	08 ③	09 ⑤	10 ⑤	11 ③	12 ②
13 ②	14 ①	15 ④	16 ⑤	17 ②	18 ④
19 ④	20 ⑤				

서술형 따라잡기 - - - - - - - - - - - - - - - - - - p.187

01 (1) were not, could call
    (2) I could go on a trip

02 (1) had not rained, have gone

  (2) had been, not have tripped

03 (1) had been slim (2) had happened

04 had heard the news, have been surprised

05 (1) I were a movie star

  (2) I could go to Europe

06 (1) If I had been interested in the paintings, I would have gone to the art exhibit.

  (2) If I had a laptop now, I would not buy one.

01 현재 사실과 반대되는 상황을 가정하는 가정법 과거의 의문문이다. 따라서 주절에는 〈의문사+조동사의 과거형(would)+주어+동사원형〉이 와야 한다.

02 과거 사실과 반대되는 상황을 가정하는 가정법 과거완료이다. 따라서 if절의 동사로 〈had v-ed〉가 와야 한다.

03 주절의 시제보다 더 앞선 때의 상황을 반대로 가정하고 있으므로 〈as if+주어+had v-ed〉가 알맞다.

04 현재 사실과 반대되는 상황을 가정하므로 if절에는 동사의 과거형이, 주절에는 〈조동사의 과거형(would)+동사원형〉이 와야 한다. if절의 be동사는 항상 were를 쓴다는 점에 유의한다.

05 첫 번째 문장은 현재 이룰 수 없는 소망을 나타내므로 빈칸에는 과거동사 could가 알맞다. 두 번째 문장은 과거 사실과 반대되는 상황을 가정하는 가정법 과거완료이다. 따라서 if절의 동사로 〈had v-ed〉가 와야 한다.

06 첫 번째 문장은 과거에 이루지 못한 소망을 나타내는 〈I wish+가정법 과거완료〉이다. 두 번째 문장은 과거 사실과 반대되는 상황을 가정하는 가정법 과거완료이다. 따라서 빈칸에는 had been이 적절하다.

07 ② 과거의 일에 대한 아쉬움을 나타내는 〈I wish+가정법 과거완료〉를 쓴다.

08 ③ 주절의 시제와 같은 때의 상황을 반대로 가정하고 있으므로 〈as if+가정법 과거〉를 쓴다.

09 과거의 일에 대해 이야기하고 있고, 문맥상 '그녀가 열심히 공부했더라면 합격했을 텐데.'가 되어야 하므로 가정법 과거완료인 ⑤가 적절하다.

10 ⑤ 과거 사실과 반대되는 상황을 나타내야 하므로 문맥상 B의 답은 Sorry. I would have called you ….가 되어야 한다.

11 현재 사실과 반대되는 상황을 가정하는 것은 가정법 과거로 〈If+주어+동사의 과거형 ~, 주어+조동사의 과거형[would/could/might]+동사원형 …〉의 형태이다. 주어진 단어들을 배열하면 'If there were no exams, I would be glad.'이므로 뒤에서 세 번째에 오는 단어는 would이다.

12 ② 과거의 일에 대한 아쉬움을 나타내므로 〈I wish+가정법 과거완료〉를 쓴다. 따라서 ate는 had eaten이 되어야 한다.

13 ② 과거 사실과 반대되는 상황을 가정하는 가정법 과거완료이므로 if절의 동사로 〈had v-ed〉의 형태인 had not이 와야 한다.

14 ① 현재 이룰 수 없는 소망을 나타내므로 〈I wish+가정법 과거〉를 쓴다. 가정법 과거에서 be동사는 항상 were로 쓰므로 were가 와야 한다.

15 ④ 과거 사실과 반대되는 상황을 가정하는 가정법 과거완료이므로 if절의 동사로 〈had v-ed〉가 와야 한다. ①은 현재 이룰 수 없는 소망을 나타내는 〈I wish+가정법 과거〉, ②, ⑤는 주절과 같은 때의 상황을 반대로 가정하는 〈as if+가정법 과거〉, ③은 현재 사실과 반대되는 상황을 가정하는 가정법 과거이므로 모두 were가 와야 한다.

16 ⑤ 과거 사실과 반대되는 상황을 가정하는 가정법 과거완료이므로 〈If+주어+had v-ed ~, 주어+조동사의 과거형[would]+have v-ed …〉의 형태로 쓴다.

17 (c) 주절의 시제보다 앞선 때의 상황을 반대로 가정하고 있으므로 〈as if+가정법 과거완료〉를 쓴다.

18 ④ 과거 사실과 반대되는 상황을 가정하는 가정법 과거완료로 if절의 동사는 〈had v-ed〉인 had taken이 되어야 한다.

19 ④ 현재 사실과 반대되는 상황을 가정하는 가정법 과거로, 주절의 동사는 〈조동사의 과거형(would)+동사원형〉인 would have가 되어야 한다.

20 ⑤ 주절의 시제보다 앞선 때의 상황을 반대로 가정하고 있으므로 〈as if+가정법 과거완료〉를 쓴다.

서술형 따라잡기 -

01 (1) 현재 사실과 반대되는 상황을 가정하는 가정법 과거는 〈If+주어+동사의 과거형 ~, 주어+조동사의 과거형[would/could/might]+동사원형 …〉으로 쓴다.

  (2) 현재 이룰 수 없는 소망을 나타내는 상황이므로 〈I wish+가정법 과거〉로 쓴다.

02 과거 사실과 반대되는 상황을 가정하는 가정법 과거완료이므

로 〈If+주어+had v-ed ~, 주어+조동사의 과거형[would/could/might]+have v-ed …〉로 쓴다.

03 (1) 날씬하지 않았던 과거의 일에 대한 아쉬움을 나타내는 〈I wish+가정법 과거완료〉를 쓴다.

(2) 주절의 시제보다 앞선 때의 상황을 반대로 가정하고 있으므로 〈as if+가정법 과거완료〉를 쓴다.

04 과거 사실과 반대되는 상황을 가정하는 가정법 과거완료이므로 if절에는 〈had v-ed〉가, 주절에는 〈조동사의 과거형(would)+have v-ed〉가 와야 한다.

05 현재 이룰 수 없는 소망은 〈I wish+가정법 과거〉로 나타낸다.

06 (1) 과거 사실과 반대되는 상황을 가정하는 가정법 과거완료로 표현한다.

(2) 현재 사실과 반대되는 상황을 가정하는 가정법 과거로 표현한다.

SELF NOTE
p.188

A 핵심 포인트 정리하기
① If ② 동사의 과거형 ③ 동사원형 ④ If ⑤ had v-ed
⑥ have v-ed ⑦ were ⑧ had v-ed

B 문제로 개념 다지기
1 X, saw 2 X, had had 3 X, had bought 4 O
5 X, were

Chapter 14 일치와 화법

POINT 01 시제 일치
p.190

A 1 wondered, loved   2 realized, was
   3 found out, had gone   4 said, had seen
   5 thought, had been   6 hoped, could win

B 1 thought, was very kind
   2 realized, had washed
   3 believed, would be happy
   4 said, had built

POINT 02 시제 일치의 예외
p.191

A 1 knew, two and two makes four
   2 learned, oil is lighter than water
   3 knew, the sun rises in the east
   4 said, William Shakespeare was born in 1564
   5 said, her school begins at eight
   6 told, her family goes[went] to church every Sunday
   7 said, light moves faster than sound
   8 realized, a friend in need is a friend indeed

B 1 moved → moves   2 talk → talked
   3 had been born → was born
   4 slept → sleep   5 had begun → began

POINT 03 평서문의 직접화법과 간접화법
p.192

A 1 says, he wants to be a tennis player
   2 told, he was hungry
   3 said, she would meet me at the park
   4 told, she had enjoyed Jane's birthday party
   5 told, she had met her teacher at the store

B 1 said, I'm[I am] doing my homework
   2 said to, I saw you at school
   3 said to, I will leave before noon
   4 said, The Korean War began in 1950
   5 said to, You have to come home early

A 1 asked, if[whether] she had been sick

2 asked, if[whether] I would join them

3 asked, if[whether] he could speak English

4 asked, if[whether] I had any plans for the vacation

5 asked, if[whether] he could use my cell phone

6 asked, if[whether] I had ever been to Busan

B 1 Can you help me?

2 Did you have lunch?

3 Do you want to get a haircut tomorrow?

4 Is it the first meeting today?

5 Did you hear the sound?

A 1 asked, what I was doing

2 asked, why he hadn't called me that day

3 asked, what she could do for me

4 who had broken the vase

5 asked, where she was going

6 asked, where I had gotten[got] my jeans

7 asked, how long I had been there

B 1 What time does your flight leave?

2 How much money do you need?

3 What are you going to do today?

4 What is happening now?

5 Where did you buy your earphones?

A 1 what your name is

2 if[whether] Carrie and her sister study at the library

3 what his father is doing

4 Why, the hockey game was canceled

5 who will arrive at the airport

B 1 which exit we should use

2 Who, can answer the question

3 how long it takes to get to the hotel

4 if the weather will be nice

01 ①   02 ①   03 ②   04 ①   05 ④   06 ③

07 ③   08 ⑤   09 ⑤   10 ②   11 ③   12 ②

13 ④   14 ④   15 ②   16 ⑤   17 ⑤   18 ②

19 ③   20 ④

서술형 따라잡기 - p.199

01 (1) who drew this picture

(2) if[whether] he is wearing a white shirt

02 (1) He asked which school her brother went to.

(2) She asked me if I had left a message.

03 (1) When will you leave for Laos?

(2) I'm going to leave tomorrow.

04 (1) if[whether] he would leave

(2) he hadn't seen

05 (1) if[whether] I exercise

(2) what my favorite food is

(3) if[whether] I have ever been in the hospital

06 has started → had started

01 주절의 동사가 과거이면 종속절의 동사는 과거나 과거완료만 올 수 있다.

02 목성(Jupiter)이 지구(Earth)보다 크다는 사실은 변하지 않는 사실이므로 현재시제로 쓴다.

03 의문사가 없는 의문문의 간접화법은 〈ask(+목적어)+if [whether]+주어+동사〉의 형태로 쓴다.

04 변하지 않는 사실은 주절의 시제와 관계없이 항상 현재시제로, 역사적 사실은 항상 과거시제로 쓴다.

05 주절의 동사가 과거이면 종속절의 동사는 과거나 과거완료만 올 수 있다.

06 현재의 사실은 현재시제로 쓰며, 주절의 동사가 과거이면 종속절의 동사는 과거나 과거완료만 쓸 수 있다.

07 ③ Lily가 말한 직접화법 문장을 간접화법으로 바꾸기 위해서 인칭대명사 I를 she로 바꾸고, 전달동사의 시제인 과거시제에 맞춰 will도 would로 바꾼다.

08 ⑤ 의문사가 있는 의문문의 간접화법은 〈ask(+목적어)+의문

사+주어+동사〉의 순으로 쓴다. 인칭대명사 you를 we로 바꾸고, 전달동사의 시제인 과거시제에 맞춰 want를 wanted로 바꾼다.

09 주절의 시제가 과거이고 종속절이 주절보다 미래에 일어날 일에 대해 이야기하고 있으므로, 종속절의 동사로는 〈would+동사원형〉의 형태가 알맞다.

10 주절의 시제가 과거더라도 현재의 습관은 현재시제로 쓸 수 있다.

11 의문사가 없는 의문문을 간접화법으로 바꿀 때는 if나 whether를 쓴다. ③은 의문사 없이는 의미 전달이 되지 않는 문장으로, if나 whether가 아닌 의문사 what이 와야 한다.

12 의문사가 있는 의문문의 간접화법은 〈ask(+목적어)+의문사+주어+동사〉의 형태로 쓴다.

13 ④ 주절이 과거시제이고 종속절이 과거완료인 간접화법 문장을 직접화법으로 바꾸면 종속절의 동사는 과거시제로 바뀌어야 한다. 따라서 Ellen said, "He was late for school."이 되어야 한다.

14 ④ 간접화법을 직접화법으로 바꾸면 종속절의 we는 화자의 입장에 맞추어 2인칭 복수 대명사인 you로 바뀌어야 한다. 따라서 Mom asked us, "Do you want to play?"가 되어야 한다.

15 ② 격언·속담 등은 주절의 시제와 관계없이 현재시제를 쓴다.

16 ⑤ 역사적 사실은 주절의 시제와 관계없이 항상 과거시제를 쓴다. 따라서 was discovered가 되어야 한다.

17 ⑤ 변하지 않는 사실은 주절의 시제와 관계없이 항상 현재시제를 쓴다. 따라서 is covered with가 되어야 한다.

18 ② 의문사가 있는 의문문의 간접화법은 〈ask(+목적어)+의문사+주어+동사〉의 순으로 쓴다. 따라서 his brother lived가 되어야 한다.

19 ③ 의문사가 있는 간접의문문은 〈의문사+주어+동사〉로 써야 하고, 주절의 동사가 think인 경우 간접의문문의 의문사가 문장의 맨 앞에 와야 하므로 Who do you think dances well?이 되어야 한다.

20 (a) 주절의 동사가 과거이면 종속절의 동사는 과거나 과거완료만 올 수 있다. 따라서 will become은 would become이 되어야 한다.
(c) 주절의 동사가 과거이면 종속절의 동사는 과거나 과거완료만 올 수 있다. at that time으로 보아 studies는 had studied가 되어야 한다.

01 (1) 의문사가 있는 간접의문문에서 의문사가 주어인 경우 〈의문사+동사〉의 형태로 쓴다.
(2) 의문사가 없는 간접의문문은 〈if[whether]+주어+동사〉의 형태로 쓴다.

02 (1) 의문사가 있는 의문문의 간접화법은 〈ask(+목적어)+의문사+주어+동사〉의 형태로 쓴다.
(2) 의문사가 없는 의문문의 간접화법은 〈ask(+목적어)+if[whether]+주어+동사〉의 형태로 쓴다.

03 (1) 〈의문사+주어+동사〉 형태의 의문사가 있는 간접화법의 문장이므로 직접화법에 맞게 인칭대명사 he를 you로, 조동사 would를 will으로 바꾼다.
(2) 평서문의 간접화법 문장이므로 직접화법에 맞게 인칭대명사 he는 I로, was going to는 am going to로, the next day는 tomorrow로 바꾼다.

04 (1) 의문사가 없는 의문문의 간접화법은 〈ask(+목적어)+if[whether]+주어+동사〉의 순으로 쓴다. 인칭대명사 I를 he로 바꾸고, 전달동사의 시제인 과거시제에 맞춰 will을 would로 바꾼다.
(2) Ian이 말한 직접화법 문장을 간접화법으로 바꾸기 위해 인칭대명사 I를 he로 바꾸고, 전달동사의 시제인 과거시제에 맞춰 haven't seen도 hadn't seen으로 바꾼다.

05 의문사가 없는 의문문의 간접화법은 〈ask(+목적어)+if[whether]+주어+동사〉의 형태로, 의문사가 있는 의문문의 간접화법은 〈ask(+목적어)+의문사+주어+동사〉의 형태로 쓴다.

06 주절의 시제가 과거이고, 주절의 시점보다 더 이전의 일을 이야기하고 있으므로 has started를 had started로 고친다.

SELF NOTE   p.200

A 핵심 포인트 정리하기
① 과거시제 ② 과거완료 ③ 현재 ④ 과거 ⑤ tell
⑥ ask, if[whether] ⑦ 의문사, 주어, 동사
⑧ if[whether]

B 문제로 개념 다지기
1 O 2 X, started 3 O 4 X, whether they are

01 ④ 02 ⑤ 03 ① 04 ③ 05 ③

06 Feeling sleepy 07 ⑤ 08 Unless you leave 09 ② 10 ③ 11 would[Would]

12 ④ 13 ⑤ 14 ④ 15 other → the other

16 used to be 17 ③ 18 too difficult for me to finish 19 Why do you think she was

20 ⑤ 21 The opening ceremony of the Olympics was watched by people around the world. 22 I talked with a girl whose eyes were bright blue. 23 ④, ⑤ 24 (1) if[whether] he could take a picture with her (2) when her next novel would be published

01 to 이하는 선행사 the girl을 수식하는 관계대명사절로, 선행사가 사람이고 전치사 to의 목적어 역할을 하는 목적격 관계대명사 whom이 와야 한다.

02 주절의 동사가 〈would+have v-ed〉의 형태인 것으로 보아 가정법 과거완료 문장이므로, If절의 동사는 〈had v-ed〉 형태인 hadn't taken이 와야 한다.

03 결과를 나타내는 '매우[너무] ~해서 …하다'라는 뜻의 〈so ~ that …〉 구문이므로 that이 와야 한다.

04 의문사가 없는 의문문의 간접화법 문장에서는 '~인지 (아닌지)'의 뜻으로 whether나 if를 쓴다.

05 ③은 〈주어+동사+보어〉의 2형식 문장이고, 나머지는 모두 1형식 문장이다.

06 접속사를 없애고, 주절과 부사절의 주어가 같으므로 부사절의 주어(he)를 없앤 뒤, 동사를 〈동사원형+ing〉 형태로 바꾸어 분사구문을 만든다.

07 〈보기〉와 ⑤는 경험을 나타내는 현재완료이다. ①과 ③은 완료, ②는 계속, ④는 결과를 나타내는 현재완료이다.

08 '~하지 않으면'이라는 뜻의 조건을 나타내는 접속사 Unless를 이용한다.

09 첫 번째 빈칸에는 '~만큼 …하지 않은[않게]'의 뜻이 되도록 〈not+as[so]+형용사/부사의 원급+as〉의 원급 hard가 와야 하며, 두 번째 빈칸에는 '내 인생에서 최악의 날이었다.'라는 최상급의 의미가 되도록 bad의 최상급 worst가 와야 한다.

10 첫 번째 빈칸에는 '또 하나 다른 것[포크]'의 의미가 되도록 부

정대명사 another가 와야 하며, 두 번째 빈칸에는 '또 다른 기회'라는 의미가 되도록 another가 와야 한다.

11 첫 번째 빈칸에는 가정법 과거의 주절에 쓰이는 〈would+동사원형〉의 조동사 would가 와야 하고, 두 번째 빈칸에는 '~하고 싶다'를 나타내는 would like to의 Would가 와야 한다.

12 문장의 주어는 The truth이고, 동사는 미래시제의 수동태 will be known이 되어야 한다. '~에게 알려지다'는 be known to를 쓰므로 ④가 알맞다.

13 '~(하면) 할수록 더 …하다'는 〈the+비교급, the+비교급〉으로 나타낸다.

14 선행사를 포함한 관계대명사 What이 와야 한다.

15 두 개 중에서 '(둘 중의) 하나는 ~ 나머지 하나는 …'을 나타낼 때는 one ~ the other …를 쓰므로 other는 the other가 되어야 한다.

16 '(전에는) ~이었다'라는 의미로 과거의 상태를 나타내는 조동사 used to를 쓴다.

17 ③은 '나는 우리 팀의 다른 모든 주자들만큼 빠르지 않다.'라는 의미이고, 나머지는 모두 '나는 우리 팀에서 가장 빠른 주자이다.'라는 최상급의 의미이다.

18 '…하기에는 너무 ~하다'는 〈too+형용사/부사+for+목적격+to부정사〉의 어순으로 쓴다.

19 주절의 동사가 think일 때, 간접의문문의 의문사는 문장의 맨 앞에 온다.

20 ⑤ resemble은 상태를 나타내는 동사로 수동태로 쓸 수 없으므로, Henry resembles his father.가 되어야 한다.

21 능동태 문장의 목적어 the opening ceremony of the Olympics를 수동태 문장의 주어로 쓰고, 능동태 문장의 동사 watched는 과거형 수동태 was watched로 쓴다. 능동태 문장의 주어 people ~ world는 수동태 문장에서 〈by+행위자〉로 쓴다.

22 두 번째 문장의 소유격 Her를 소유격 관계대명사 whose로 바꾸어 두 문장을 연결한다.

23 ① 전치사 바로 뒤에는 who나 that이 올 수 없으므로 관계대명사 whom을 쓴다.
② 〈bring+간접목적어(us)+직접목적어(some water and blankets)〉 혹은 〈bring+직접목적어(some water and blankets)+전치사(to)+간접목적어(us)〉가 되어야 한다.
③ 조건을 나타내는 부사절에서는 미래의 일을 현재시제로 나타내므로 apologize가 되어야 한다.

24 (1) 의문사가 없는 의문문의 간접화법은 〈if[whether]+주어+동사〉의 어순으로 쓴다. 인칭대명사와 동사의 시제는 주절에 맞게 바꾸어 쓴다.

(2) 의문사가 있는 의문문의 간접화법은 〈의문사+주어+동사〉의 어순으로 쓴다. 인칭대명사와 동사의 시제는 주절에 맞게 바꾸어 쓴다.

총괄평가 2회

01 ⑤ 02 ④ 03 ③ 04 ⑤ 05 have been to
06 ③ 07 ① 08 ③ 09 My way of walking
was laughed at by my classmates. 10 ③
11 is worth watching 12 ② 13 ② 14 ③
15 the successful → the most successful
16 ⑤ 17 ④ 18 ③ 19 She asked me
where I had found her shoes. 20 ③ 21 ②
22 ③ 23 (1) where we will go (2) when we
will go (3) how we will go

01 'A도 B도 아닌'은 〈neither A nor B〉로 나타내므로 nor가 와야 한다.

02 '마치 복권에 당첨되었던 것처럼'이라는 뜻으로 〈as if+가정법 과거완료〉를 써야 하므로 had won이 적절하다.

03 '~하는 게 좋겠다'는 〈had better+동사원형〉으로 나타내므로 had better go가 와야 한다.

04 '다음 달에 지어질 것이다'라는 미래시제의 수동태 문장이 되어야 하므로 〈will+be+v-ed〉의 형태인 will be built가 와야 한다.

05 '나는 인도네시아에 두 번 가 본 적이 있다.'라는 뜻이 되어야 하므로 '~에 가 본 적이 있다'라는 경험을 나타내는 현재완료 have been to를 쓴다.

06 현재 사실을 반대로 가정하는 가정법 과거 〈If+주어+동사의 과거형 ~, 주어+조동사의 과거형[would/could/might]+동사원형 …〉을 쓴다. If절에 be동사가 있을 경우에는 were로 쓴다.

07 첫 번째 빈칸에는 금지를 나타내는 must not의 must가 와야 하고, 두 번째 빈칸에는 '~임이 틀림없다'라는 강한 추측을 나타내는 must가 와야 한다.

08 첫 번째 빈칸에는 선행사에 the only가 있으므로 주격 관계대명사 that이 와야 하고, 두 번째 빈칸에는 보어로 쓰인 명사절을 이끄는 접속사 that이 와야 하므로, 빈칸에 공통으로 들어갈 말은 that이다.

09 능동태 문장의 목적어 my way of walking을 수동태 문장의 주어로 하고, 능동태 문장의 동사구 laughed at은 과거형 수동태 was laughed at으로 쓴다. 능동태 문장의 주어 My classmates는 수동태 문장에서 by 뒤에 목적격으로 쓴다.

10 〈보기〉와 ③의 밑줄 친 to부정사는 각각 주어와 목적어로 쓰인 명사적 용법의 to부정사이다. ①은 조건을 나타내는 부사적 용법, ②는 판단의 근거를 나타내는 부사적 용법, ④는 목적을 나타내는 부사적 용법, ⑤는 명사 time을 수식하는 형용사적 용법의 to부정사이다.

11 '~할 가치가 있다'는 〈be worth v-ing〉로 나타낸다.

12 to부정사의 의미상의 주어를 of him으로 나타내고 있으므로 앞에는 사람에 대한 주관적인 평가를 나타내는 형용사 wise, foolish, clever, silly가 올 수 있다. happy 뒤에는 to부정사의 의미상의 주어로 〈for+목적격〉을 쓴다.

13 과거를 나타내는 last Friday가 있으므로 첫 번째 빈칸에는 과거형 동사 borrowed가 와야 하고, 두 번째 빈칸에는 since then이 있으므로 과거부터 지금까지 동작이 계속되고 있음을 나타내는 현재완료가 와야 한다. 주어가 3인칭 단수(he)이므로 has read가 알맞다.

14 부사절을 분사구문으로 바꿀 때는 접속사를 없애고, 주절과 같은 부사절의 주어를 없앤 후, 동사를 〈동사원형+ing〉 형태로 바꾼다. 따라서 Being too young이 알맞다.

15 '가장 ~한 것[사람]들 중 하나'는 〈one of the+최상급+복수명사〉로 나타내므로 the successful은 the most successful이 되어야 한다.

16 ⑤의 that은 '저 ~'라는 뜻의 지시형용사로 생략할 수 없다. ①, ②, ④는 목적격 관계대명사, ③은 목적어로 쓰인 명사절을 이끄는 접속사 that이므로 생략할 수 있다.

17 '~의 몇 배 …한'은 〈배수사+as+원급+as〉 또는 〈배수사+비교급+than〉으로 나타내므로 three times as tall as 또는 three times taller than이 와야 한다.

18 '~해도 소용없다'는 〈It is no use v-ing〉로 나타낸다.

19 의문사가 있는 직접화법을 간접화법으로 전환할 때는 전달동사는 ask로 바꾸고 〈의문사+주어+동사〉의 어순으로 쓴다. 인칭대명사와 동사의 시제는 주절에 맞추어 쓴다.

20 (a) 〈either A or B〉는 B에 동사의 수를 일치시키므로 don't가 되어야 한다.

(e) 〈주어+동사〉를 포함한 절이 오고 있으므로 because가 되어야 한다. because of 뒤에는 (동)명사(구)가 온다.

21 ② 그들이 '실망한' 것이므로 disappointing은 과거분사 disappointed가 되어야 한다.

22 ③ '마치 전에 많은 돈을 벌었던 것처럼'이라는 주절의 시제보다 앞선 때의 상황을 반대로 가정하는 가정법 과거완료 문장이 되어야 하므로, made는 had made가 되어야 한다.

23 (1) 선행사가 the place로 장소를 나타내므로 관계부사 where를 사용한다.

(2) 선행사가 the day로 시간을 나타내므로 관계부사 when을 사용한다.

(3) 박물관에 '어떻게' 가는지가 결정되지 않은 것이므로, 관계부사 how를 사용한다. 관계부사 how는 선행사 the way와 함께 쓸 수 없고 반드시 둘 중 하나를 생략한다.

총괄평가 3회

01 ④ 02 ⑤ 03 ⑤ 04 ④ 05 ④ 06 One, another, the other 07 ② 08 hadn't made
09 The more, the poorer 10 ② 11 it → one
12 were → was 13 ④ 14 ③ 15 ⑤
16 couldn't believe what I saw on TV
17 is the girl whose brother goes to Harvard
18 is the town where my father first met my mother 19 ⑤ 20 Her skirt is twice as long as mine. 21 ③ 22 ④ 23 ③ 24 ③
25 (1) Both, get up (2) Neither, nor

01 '~하지 않을 수 없다'는 〈cannot help v-ing〉로 나타내므로 smiling이 와야 한다.

02 과거의 습관을 나타내는 문장이므로 조동사 would가 와야 한다.

03 Mike에 의해 '깨진'이라는 의미로 The window를 뒤에서 수식하는 분사구가 와야 하므로, 수동의 의미를 나타내는 과거분사 broken이 적절하다.

04 〈보기〉와 ④의 밑줄 친 to부정사는 예정을 나타내는 be to용법으로 쓰인 to부정사이다. ①은 가능, ②는 의무, ③은 운명, ⑤는 의도의 의미이다.

05 ④ 의문사가 있는 의문문의 간접화법은 〈의문사+주어+동사〉의 어순으로 쓰므로, where his report was가 되어야 한다.

06 '(셋 중의) 하나는 ~ 또 다른 하나는 …, 나머지 하나는 ~'을 나타낼 경우, 첫 번째는 one, 두 번째는 another, 세 번째는 the other를 쓴다.

07 ② -thing으로 끝나는 대명사를 형용사와 to부정사가 함께 수식할 때는 〈대명사(something)+형용사(important)+to부정사(to tell you)〉의 어순으로 쓴다.

08 '~했다면 좋을 텐데'라는 뜻으로 과거에 이루지 못한 소망을 나타내야 하므로 〈I wish+가정법 과거완료〉가 와야 한다.

09 '~(하면) 할수록 더 …하다'는 〈the+비교급, the+비교급〉으로 나타낸다.

10 want는 목적격 보어로 to부정사를 취하므로 첫 번째 빈칸에는 to lend가 와야 하고, 사역동사 let은 목적격 보어로 동사원형을 취하므로 두 번째 빈칸에는 borrow가 와야 한다.

11 앞에서 언급된 a shoe store와 같은 종류의 것을 가리키는 부정대명사 one이 와야 하므로, it을 one으로 고친다.

12 〈all+명사〉인 경우 뒤에 오는 명사의 수에 동사를 일치시키는데, milk는 셀 수 없는 명사이므로 were는 단수형 동사 was가 되어야 한다.

13 ④ agree는 to부정사를 목적어로 취하는 동사이고, 나머지는 모두 동명사를 목적어로 취하는 동사이다.

14 ③ boiling water는 '끓고 있는 물'이라는 뜻으로, boiling은 현재분사이다. 나머지는 모두 뒤에 오는 명사의 용도나 목적을 나타내는 동명사이다.

15 '게임을 지금까지 두 번 해 본' 것이므로 경험을 나타내는 현재완료 have played가 와야 한다.

16 '내가 TV에서 본 것'이라는 의미가 되어야 하므로 선행사를 포함하는 관계대명사 what을 이용한다.

17 '오빠가 하버드 대학교에 다니는 소녀'라는 의미가 되도록 소유격 Her를 대신하는 소유격 관계대명사 whose를 써서 두 문장을 연결한다.

18 '우리 아버지가 어머니를 처음 만난 동네'라는 의미가 되도록 관계부사 where를 써서 두 문장을 연결한다.

19 '만약 ~했다면[였더라면] …했을 텐데'라는 의미로 과거 사실

과 반대되는 상황을 가정하고 있으므로 가정법 과거완료인 〈If+주어+had v-ed ~, 주어+조동사의 과거형[would/could/might]+have v-ed …〉가 되어야 한다. 따라서 if절에는 had gone, 주절에는 could have seen이 와야 한다.

20 '~의 몇 배 …한[하게]'은 〈배수사+as+원급+as〉의 어순으로 쓴다.

21 첫 번째 빈칸에는 'A가 아니라 B'를 나타내는 〈not A but B〉의 but이 와야 하고, 두 번째 빈칸에는 'A뿐만 아니라 B도'를 나타내는 〈not only A but also B〉의 but이 와야 한다.

22 ④ '~하지 않는 게 좋겠다'는 〈had better not+동사원형〉이므로 had better not waste가 되어야 한다.

23 ③ to부정사의 형용사적 용법에 사용된 동사가 자동사(sit)일 경우 전치사가 필요하므로 to sit in[on]이 되어야 한다.

24 (b) 4형식 문장에서 직접목적어를 주어로 하여 수동태 문장을 만드는 경우, 〈주어(직접목적어)+be동사+v-ed+전치사++간접목적어(+by+행위자)〉의 형태로 쓴다. 동사가 make이므로 간접목적어 앞에 전치사 for를 써야 한다.
(e) remember to-v: ~할 것을 기억하다
remember v-ing: ~한 것을 기억하다

25 (1) Amy와 Harry 둘 다 7시 이전에 일어나므로, 'A와 B 둘 다'라는 의미의 〈both A and B〉를 써서 나타낸다. 〈both A and B〉는 복수 취급한다.
(2) Amy와 Harry 둘 다 아침을 먹지 않으므로, 'A도 B도 아닌'이라는 의미의 〈neither A nor B〉를 쓴다.

MEMO

MEMO

MEMO

MEMO

MEMO

MEMO

MEMO

문제로
마스터하는
중학영문법

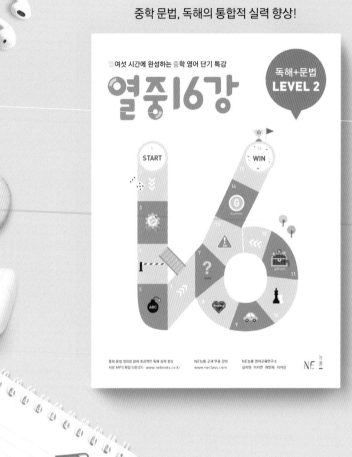